INTEGRAL PUBLISHING HOUSE

COHERING THE INTEGRAL WE-SPACE

Engaging Collective Emergence, Widsom and Healing in Groups

Edited by
Olen Gunnlaugson, Ph.D.
Michael Brabant, Ph.D.

Integral Publishing House

Cohering the Integral We Space
Engaging Collective Emergence, Wisdom and Healing in Groups
Copyright © 2016

Edited by Olen Gunnlaugson, Ph.D. & Michael Brabant, Ph.D.

Published by Integral Publishing House

First Edition

Book Design and Typesetting by Being Design Inc.
www.being.design

BrightAlliance.org

ISBN 978-0-9872826-3-7

Printed and Bound in the United States

May the emerging wisdom you discover between these pages serve your collective work and practice and benefit others for generations to come.

About the Editors

Olen Gunnlaugson, Ph.D. is an Associate Professor in Leadership & Organizational Development within the Department of Management in the Business School at Université Laval, in Quebec City, Canada. He brings an increasingly inter-disciplinary approach to his current research in conversational leadership, dynamic presencing, we-space practice and facilitation, as well as contemplative management skills and coaching. His research has been published in several books as well as numerous international academic journals and presentations at leading conferences. Project-wise, he is currently collaborating with colleagues on a number of books and articles. More recently, he was the chief co-editor of the management book, *Perspectives on Theory U: Insights from the Field*, a recently published anthology featuring applied research on Theory U by 30 faculty members and associates from North America and Europe.

Michael Brabant, Ph.D. has been trained in both the academic and clinical settings as well as studied with shamans, mystics, and intuitive healers. By synthesizing the most potent inner technologies and the nuanced conceptual understanding related to true transformation, he offers a body teaching and practice called Divine Humanity to help us build the energetic, relational and emotional infrastructure to live our lives as if every moment and everything contained within it, is both sacred and deeply intelligent. You can learn more about his work at livingdivinehumanity.com

Table of Contents

Introduction

Background of We-Space Practice in the Integral Community

Over the last decade, but especially in the past couple years, interest in the we-space has generated a strong collective response and interest internationally within the integral world. We are excited about the generative, relational, community and healing possibilities in what has emerged to date around this work. From the beginning, we have passionately held the vision for this book to serve the greater global integral community as a catalyst for broadening and clarifying existing conversations, bringing forth new perspectives, as well as new lines of critical discernment.

Process-wise, the book has become an occasion for each practitioner to reflect more deeply on their particular approach to the we-space. The book has also provided everyone involved with an opportunity to reflexively engage with and further legitimate what for many is a growing integral community of practice and inspiration that has played a formative role within each of our lives personally, community-wise and professionally.

Central to this vision, initially in putting the call out for this book, we invited the authors to clarify and frame their existing approaches in a way that elaborated upon both the theory and practice in order to better serve as a foundation from which we can each contribute to advancing the greater conversation on we-space practice within the global integral community. Part of this intention was to encourage authors to frame the chapters in a way where the chapters held immediate practice utility for the reader to begin implementing ideas that felt complimentary to their own existing we-space approach/ practice.

Looking back, we are pleased with how the authors not only generously met our inquiries and editorial feedback, but also brought to bare new insight, thinking and in some cases, new revisions and adaptations to their practice from their chapter submissions. Each author's commitment to writing and researching their chapters united everyone with the book's overall mission to serve a role in maturing and growing this exciting and ever-emerging field.

Our initial call for chapter submissions focused on well-known and emerging practitioners within the current global integral community whom are engaging the we-space as facilitators, teachers, philosophers and practitioners from different individual, cultural and consciousness vantage points. In the context of this book we have used the term "integral" to be inclusive of Wilberian Integral Theory but also to not be limited to or by it. Some authors have worked with integral distinctions more explicitly, though many have drawn implicitly on integral as way of approaching and framing their thinking on the we-space. As you will see, this initial sampling of authors brought together a rich combination of diverse yet complementary perspectives on the we-space. As such, the range of interpretations as well as contexts make this work more accessible to those with a passionate interest in the we-space.

Broad Brush Strokes: We-Practice Methods

Intersubjective or shared processes of meeting, being, and relating encompass a broad cross-section of traditions of communication, inquiry and consciousness-based methods that extend across the humanities, psychology, philosophy, sociology, education, business and many other fields. We recognized this challenge going into the project and so in the face of the vast diversity of encompassing views, traditions and approaches, made the decision to narrow our specific inquiry to the integral community and its growing interest in collective practice around this phenomena of the we-space.

The term we-space, we-field, we-practice, higher or deeper intersubjectivity and other we-signifiers (apart of a growing plethora of we-jargon, each spelled in particular and often quirky ways) denoted this growing recognition of the shared inner dimensions of our field of relating from an intersubjective position. Strictly speaking, this position is represented spatially as between us (2nd person position), in contrast to inside us (subjective or 1st person position) or outside us (objective or 3rd person position).

In the language of Wilber's Integral Methodological Pluralism, this is the inside view of the lower left quadrant or zone three. Another way of thinking about the we-space is in the context of collective stage development—that is the movement from pre-conventional through to post-conventional levels of complexity or respective capacity. Or in terms of states—of there being a predominant shared state of consciousness that collectives (with collective being defined as two or more individuals) experience when sufficient resonance and synergy is established. While the AQAL map has served some of the practitioners in this book more explicitly and many implicitly, the importance of the we-space work more broadly has been to make inroads into this rich realm of collective consciousness work. Given that the we-space generally pushes into horizons of our lived experience that are not explained well by the AQAL map or at least not in a satisfying way, we have maintained an open stance with this framework in regards to the individual chapter submissions.

Practice-Wise: What's Emerging?

Though this is by no means an exhaustive list of contributions that we-space work has offered to individuals, groups and communities. It serves to clarify and bring together a taste of the rich promise of this work as a field of inquiry, practice and collective realization and community.

In no particular order, we-space work:

- offers individuals and groups an experiential reference point to move beyond the limited horizons of the separate, conditioned self or egoic consciousness. We-space work helps groups establish a group container for collective transformation.
- helps groups explore and access multiple perspectives with less attachment
- introduces a new basis of spiritual authority in groups that is post-personal and not identified with a specific teacher or person as facilitator
- provides a phenomenological grounds for discovering authentic and generative ways of thinking, learning, and being together
- provides a social basis for shared depth and real meeting and community
- provides a practice that unites individuals with the collective, introducing a reference point of the self that extends beyond the self-boundaries into a participatory and shared journey

- provides a basis for people to have experiences of the collective intelligence of group fields of inquiry and consciousness
- offers ways of accessing a deeper grounds of relatedness collectively—arguably a new basis for engaging and co-creating culture
- introduces a novel set of possibilities for collective creativity
- introduces we-practice as a relational competency, as a cultural ability for being more fully human and receive information from groups of people and learn how to presently and skillfully engage with them
- gives an expanded inclusive sense of selfhood that depends on others, the collective and community to come into full expression
- nurtures an ethos that is relationally oriented and aware and capable of deepened experiences of being-together, relational communion and love
- recognizes the deeper generative potentials of the we-space in potentially catalyzing intelligence, new knowledge and new ways of being as a culture
- evolves a sense of nexus-agency of the we (not the dominant monad, but the collective sense of being that arises, for some referred to as the we-being, for others, collective awakened awareness, group flow or other shared non-ordinary experiences)
- brings forth a shared experience of an intimacy and experiential sense of being a unity amidst an emerging diversity (a sense of being apart of a we and a fuller individualism)
- makes a place in our lives where we can experience Eros more profoundly as well as experience and discern what evolution feels like from the inside out
- introduces a site where groups can experience collective consciousness as a catalyst for awakening, healing, learning, creativity, discovery, shadow-work, thinking together among other aspirations
- introduces a new basis for thinking about development collectively, with an interest in how this plays out across different groups and individuals
- and much more!

Within the global integral community, interest in engaging this collective experience and phenomena has given rise to a growing variation of we-space offerings as this manuscript highlights throughout. To date, the focus of these evolutionary group processes has been primarily directed toward developing a means of evolving consciousness interiorly and collectively through shared transformative experiences of collective mind and embodiment as the above points addressed.

Accompanying the growing promise of these post-personal, evolutionary groups is the need to further clarify core practices to effectively engage and enact collective intelligence and wisdom capacities, as well as improve upon the effectiveness of existing communication process methodologies so that this work can be in service both within and beyond the scope of this emerging field of practice.

Why an Anthology on We-space Work?

There has yet to be a peer-reviewed book of practitioners account of we-space practice until now. This book emerged in part as a collective response to a growing need to catalyze this work in more communities around the world. We have hopeful aims for this book and the emerging culture it represents. In raising further awareness of we practice communities to our respective colleagues as well as national and international communities, our conviction has been to advocate for the continued growth and maturing of we-space awareness, thought, practice and culture.

This book offers what we feel is a rich assemblage of current practitioner voices and perspectives on the we-space, through the featured writings of their experiences, challenges, and the growing great promise of this work. The organization, formatting and general structure was envisioned with the intention to co-create a cohesive field where there is a consistent clarity, utility and humility imbued within each chapter that reflects an overall alignment with the chapters, the book and the field as a whole.

We anticipate the primary readership of this book will be we-space practitioners, professionals, consultants, coaches and other members of the international integral community currently interested and working within the we. Our vision again is to have the book act as a resource that will serve the integral community by advancing perspectives, practices and deeper insight into where things have been, where they are at currently and where they are going. By distilling the essence of what each lineage is representing and how it contributes and connects to the emerging field of praxis/theory, our intention has been that this book will play an important role as a catalyst for new we-space developments in the greater integral community and beyond in the years to come.

A Word About Our Process as Editors

Given how important this subject is to us both, holding the space for this anthology to grow was something we both kept a high degree of commitment to. Years ago we came together via an introduction by a mutual friend and over the conversations that followed over the course of a year and half, it became evident that one of our contributions was through the stewardship of this book. Given our interest and respective areas of expertise and passion, we decided to put the call out for this anthology, which invited authors into a process of showcasing their work in a way that would be supported yet also challenged in different ways. Though the book was intended to be a practitioner anthology, our academic backgrounds led to an editorial conversation that invited authors to convey their reflections and insights in a way that embodied sufficient intellectual rigor yet was also sensitive to the distinct transmissions of each author's voice and work. At times a fine balance to strike! On the whole, we were grateful for each author's willingness to engage us at this level. As we reflect now on the path we travelled together with this book specifically over these past two years, its clear that we accomplished a core aspect of this vision, which was to convey the heart of this work in a way that gives it credibility and accessibility across different communities of practice and academic traditions.

A Word About Us as Editors

Olen's passion for collective inquiry ignited nearly twenty years ago at a secluded resort in the south of Thailand. Over a month long period, in conversation with artists, travelers and social visionaries, here began his early passionate explorations into dialogue and inquiry as a vehicle for the collective transformation of consciousness. Following travels in the Caribbean, Asia and Europe where he worked as a freelance fine art photographer and adult educator in his twenties, Olen returned to graduate studies at the University of British Columbia, Vancouver Canada to pursue research in presencing and collective contemplative approaches to consciousness-based inquiry and leadership. Currently, as an Associate professor in Leadership and Organizational Development at Université Laval, Québec, Canada, Olen's research in Dynamic Presencing explores an embodied, consciousness-based approach to Presencing for engaging leaders, coaches, teams and collectives working with Theory U. His research background and practice in Dynamic Presencing draws from his teaching and facilitation in several MBA courses offered in the US and Canada, as well as ongoing inquiry with a number of we-practice communities and global communities of practice. Further information about related research and publications on these subjects can be viewed in the footnotes of his chapter in this anthology.

Michael's interest in the we-space began as many did, through informal conversations at varying degrees of depth and intimacy in the bay area. Thomas Hübl first came to Berkeley, Michael engaged in all the retreats, open evenings and longer programs he offered for the next four years. Shortly after meeting Thomas, Michael joined We Practice, the Bay Area collective spiritual practice group, at the time led by Dustin DiPerna and Christina Vickory and then later co-facilitated the group. Alongside this work in collective practice, the teaching he is offering at this time is specifically focused on embodiment and is called "Divine Humanity" which offers a worldview that Realty is both sacred and intelligent and the practices to support living in and as the recognition of this view. He is interested in continuing to catalyze potent collective and alive we-space-informed learning containers utilizing various forms of somatic mediation, relational practice and movement. From an academic perspective, he has a BA in Psychology, completed 5.5 years of a clinical doctoral program before transferring to a non-clinical program where he received his PhD in Psychology and Interdisciplinary Inquiry. His dissertation focused upon an integrally informed approach to transformative learning within a we-space learning community via a class on leadership in a University setting and whether this curriculum qualitatively expanded the student's worldview.

Closing Reflections

As we have shared, a core intent of this book is to further cohere existing conversations on the we-space. By bringing these conversations together, our intent is this project will form a more accessible community and help each of us have a richer view of the different current offerings by other practitioners in the field. This reciprocal exploration and dialogue is designed to enable cross-pollination across approaches that support one another in the evolution of each author's offering as well as the energetic coherence of the field as a whole.

This anthology also aims to create more visibility for we-space work and to help bring some initial helpful form to an amorphous field. Through the process of supporting authors in clarifying their contributions, this book plays a role in supporting an emerging discourse that is no longer tied to each author's tradition and lineage, but apart of a larger meta-paradigmatical conversation. By making our work more visible to each other, as a reader, we invite you into the process we have held as editors, of holding a larger meta-view of the current conversations with an interest in how each approach emphasizes or develops a key dimension of this work. In a way this is basic integral theorizing, yet in another way its an invitation to engage this conversation with one another across the different communities and to help the we-space discourse evolve beyond its sphere of integral influence—something most of us would agree is needed to evolve this work.

As a reader, you will notice as you work through the book, the authors each bring their way of making meaning and sense to this phenomena of the we-space. There's a considerable amount of diversity in our ways of approaching and interpreting what the we-space is and its function and role in groups. Coming to appreciate how authors work with their own ways of communicating both inside and across differences in intention, approach and their assumptions about the we-space, consciousness and how this all makes sense in practice can be a fun adventure. It is our hope that this journey you each will take as a reader will inspire further insight, novel ideas and realizations that will be brought back to these respective communities and contributors and for this work to inspire also new contributors and approaches.

This initial volume is designed to expand the call to existing we-space practitioners around the globe and to invite more people into the conversation to enrich and enliven the current practices that are more commonly known. As the field becomes more thoroughly established and our offerings more interconnected and in touch with one another, it is our hope that this field will begin to as it grows, support and be supported by all the practitioners within it.

We are grateful to be a part of this ongoing and evolving conversation and in service to its expansion, coherence, and evolution. May we each continue in our way to be receptive to what is wanting to emerge through our experiences in we-practice contexts, our respective work as leaders in this emerging field and in Life as a whole.

CHAPTER 1

Initial Mapping and the Eternal Mystery of We-Space:

Cartography, Capacities, and Consciousness in the Inter-Subjective Field

Michael Brabant, Ph.D. & Dustin DiPerna

Introduction

In 2010, a small team (including Christina Sophie, Bill McCart, and Dustin DiPerna) co-founded WEpractice with the intention to "explore the awakened inter-subjective field." Over the past five years, the community has grown to include groups in New York, Minnesota, Washington DC, and Germany. Since its inception, over 400 people have participated in a WEpractice cohort. The insights gained as both a community of practice and facilitation team have been immense. And one of the best aspects of the whole experiment is that it is entirely open source. The practices, theory, and learning that we cultivate are freely shared and distributed. Our sense, from the beginning, was that with more practice groups engaging, co-developing, and then sharing the material with each other, the more the entire WE space ecosystem could learn and thrive.

Michael Brabant joined the WEpractice facilitation team in 2013 after having engaged as a participant since its inception. In late 2014, Dustin and Michael co-facilitated an on-going practice group for a full cycle of four months (8 sessions). The insights of this paper come from our own direct experience over the past five years and from what we both witnessed in facilitating WEpractice together.

Further, our offering here is descriptive rather than prescriptive. That means that rather than articulating the way things ought to be, we do our best to describe the patterns and events that we saw in real time and in real practice. We hope this approach can be of benefit to others also working in the field, exploring this incredible dimension of human experience.

The We-Line of Development

Most of the readers of this book are likely familiar with the notion of multiple lines of intelligence. The theory, first posited by Howard Gardner in the 1980s, has become a widely accepted idea in developmental psychology and serves as a corner stone for integral theory and practice. The general concept is both simple and intuitive: individuals develop across multiple lines of growth; each line is somewhat independent from others as it develops.

We can bring the theory closer to home by using a few examples relevant to facilitating WE-Spaces. We all likely have known someone in our lives who is extraordinarily brilliant yet lacks a certain capacity for social and interpersonal competency.[1] In the context of multiple lines of intelligence, we might say that the person has a high level of cognitive development but a low level of interpersonal and emotional development. Clearly, cognitive brilliance without interpersonal skills does not lend itself well to skillful group leadership. In a situation where this asymmetrical development is present, a leader might be able to talk *about* what is unfolding in a group in some sort of abstract way, but he or she might not be able to track and understand the varying

---

1. It is important to note here that the following analysis uses a specifically Wilberian/AQAL approach to describe "We" emergence. There are advantages and disadvantages to this approach. One could perceive that taking an AQAL approach perpetuates a form of thinking that "starts inside the model" rather than an "effort to understand the particular phenomena in question" from the perspective of "the person or group." This approach could give rise to seeing and engaging the person through the theory of AQAL wherein there is a perceived lack of understanding the other person's experience on their terms (not our AQAL theoretical assessment). Although we are sensitive to this type of critique, it is valuable to note that the WEpractice groups were themselves integrally informed through an AQAL model. Our main orientation as both facilitators and cognitive weavers of the space specifically utilized AQAL as its point of departure. For these reasons, along with a host of others, we feel confident that continuing the analysis with an AQAL frame not only serves the clarity of the chapter but deeply honors and remains in fidelity with the 1st person perspectives involved in the original research gathered to from the WEpractice groups themselves.

dynamics unfolding between individuals on an emotional level. The major point is that we all have different strengths and capacities that we've developed across certain lines of development and we all have areas of growth and intelligence that are less developed and that could use our attention. The point isn't to become as highly developed across as many lines of development as possible but rather to have a clear assessment of ourselves and to have a simple model to help each of us better understand varying capacities and developmental competencies in others. In our experience, the most successful WEpractice leaders often have a blend of highly developed cognitive, emotional, and interpersonal capacities.

Over time, we also began to notice that there were some other factors that made certain WEpractice facilitators and certain members of the community stand out. There was some skill related to how the individual was perceiving and interacting with the We as a whole. Building on the notion of multiple lines of development, Dustin referred to this specific sensitivity as *We-Intelligence* in his book *Streams of Wisdom* (2014). There, Dustin posited that just as we can train in other lines of intelligence so as to increase our skills and capacities, the same is true with the "We" line of development. The basic notion is simple: all of us have the native capacity to develop sensitivity to collective fields and, with practice, we can all learn to cultivate an increased level of awareness to that which is emerging within groups of people.

If we consider the basic stages of growth through which most other lines travel, we find that the "We" line of development follows a similar pattern. Although the following is somewhat speculative (in the sense that it hasn't been tested with empirical research), the patterns themselves that are listed are descriptive of what we have witnessed over the past five years in regular practice groups.

When We-Intelligence first emerges it is caught in its own web of narcissism. Often experiences in intersubjective fields trigger a painful sense of self-consciousness or in extreme cases paranoia. Rather than allowing one's own energy and perspective to flow out and mix with the group, We-Intelligence at this stage turns in on itself and creates a feedback loop of heightened self-consciousness. When group participation is engaged it is often done so in a way that is out of sync or disconnected from the group field. This first stage of We-Intelligence can be called *Narcissistic Amplification*. (In an Integral psychograph, using Wilber's spectrum, we can associate this stage of development with the red altitude).[2]

---

2. Its important to note that although someone new to We-Intelligence and We space might be operating at this or adjacent developmental expression, because the We-Intelligence line weaves so many other developmental capacities applied to a specific

As We-Intelligence deepens, there is a broadening of awareness that increasingly takes into consideration the perspectives of others. However, at this stage, because the gravitational pull of self-consciousness has not yet been reached, the perspectives of others become highly influential social queues for one's own behavior. This leads to an orientation that seeks conformity to social norms in the group field. Participation at this stage is simple, reflective, and safe. It neither adds nor significantly challenges the current state of the group. In more precise terms, engagement of this level often affirms the perspective of another or simply acknowledges something obvious and tangible in the collective field. We can call this stage, *Social Conformity* (amber altitude).

As growth along the We-Intelligence line unfolds, the individual continues to reflect the signals and perspectives received from the surrounding environment while also gaining the capacity to discern his or her own sense of perception from the self-conscious needs of the ego. As this occurs, the individual can stay connected to the flow of conversation and in resonance with a group field, while simultaneously offering his or her own unique perspective. We can call this stage of We-Intelligence *Social Agency* (orange altitude).

Deeper stages of We-Intelligence begin to show even greater capacity for perspective taking. As individual agency and collective sensitivity remain in place, We-Intelligence allows the individual to gain the capacity to hold a larger context outside of the immediate circumstances of the group. There is a deepening awareness and sensitivity to time, place and culture. One can maintain contact with the local "We," while simultaneously expanding the horizon of awareness to larger and larger fields (e.g., practitioners exhibiting this stage of WE-intelligence gain the capacity to feel into the way that larger social issues such as race, gender identity, sexual orientation, and religious affiliation are influencing and shaping both individual perspectives as well as the overall group field itself). As context broadens, contact with the members of the local "We" deepens. There is a sense of feeling, seeing and knowing the shared context that gives birth to the current local experience. At this stage there is a heightened sensitivity to the specifics of the others in the group. Having the capacity to feel larger contextual influences brings a universal quality to the experience that deepens empathy, intimacy and care for each member of the collective.[3] We can call this stage *Context/Contact Sensitivity* (green altitude).

---

context, we have found many people can move quite quickly through the developmental expressions we are positing.

3. This level is also often accompanied by some degree of access to the subtle layers of reality, as discussed below.

As development continues along the spectrum of growth, We-Intelligence begins to show signs of a more comprehensive orientation that transcends and includes the reference points of self, other, and context. This means that the capacity to hold both deeper context and contact that unfolded in the previous stage remain, while the individual also develops a heightened meta-cognition that is able to sense into the collective experience as a whole.[4] This level of holistic sensitivity can see, sense and feel the inter-subjective field almost as if it is a single entity and in a way that is not so caught up in content based on self and other. Leaving all ontological claims (or any arguments about dominant monads) aside from both an energetic perspective and a phenomenological perspective, there is a singular shared experience emerging. At this stage the We-Itself enters the foreground of experience while the other aspects of experience enter the background. We can call this stage, *holistic sensitivity* (teal altitude).

The simple graphic on the next page, places each of these stages of We-Intelligence on a spectrum of development.[5]

---

4. Meta-cognition is the ability to more readily reflect upon what we think, feel, perceive, and experience in any given moment.

5. There is an important distinction to be made between We-Intelligence and We-Emergence. The specific level of We-Intelligence in the given individuals present gives way to particular stages of We-Emergence. We intelligence relates to the line of development activated in the individual, where as We-Emergence relates to the specific shared experience between a group of individuals. In a similar way, the various types of We-States are examples of We-Emergence (not We-Intelligence).

The "We" Line of Development

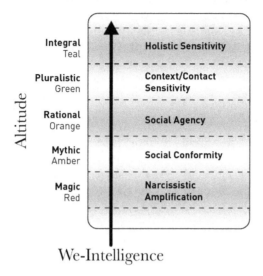

Figure 1: The "We" Line of Development

Without doubt there are further stages of We-Intelligence emerging (some of which Dustin explicated in his book *Streams of Wisdom*). For now, this list will suffice for our purposes here.

There is a second aspect of We-Intelligence which, if left out, any understanding of We-Space would be deeply partial. In addition to a basic developmental progression through the various stages of growth described above, We-Intelligence also develops along a vector relating to one's capacity to access various states and realms. Just as with any other developmental path through states, We-Intelligence progressively gains access along a pathway that moves from gross, to subtle, to causal dimensions of reality. This means that as We-Intelligence increases, one begins to feel/sense/know inter-subjective fields beyond their mere gross realm appearance of physical matter and form.[6]

As We-Intelligence develops, one gains deeper competency to sense into the subtle energies of collective fields. Many of our own early experiences in *WEpractice* involved experimentations with the

---

6. It is worth noting here that there is an intimate relationship between We-Intelligence and inter-subjective intelligence, but the two are not the same. Inter-subjective intelligence tends to focus on the capacity to read patterns and emotions between individuals. We-Intelligence, on the other hand, has a bias toward a holistic quality that takes in the group field as a whole, all at once.

collective experience of subtle energy. We would intentionally build subtle energetic structures through collective intention to catalyze deeper communion and to catalyze latent potential in our shared field. For instance, after attuning to our individual subtle bodies, we would collectively link heart, mind, and hara (belly) in a process we called WEaving. WEaving created a tangible field between us that the group could learn to influence collectively. As the process evolved, we often found ourselves as a We bathing in and surrounded by a toroidal energy vortex.[7]

Eventually, as capacity deepens, one can sense into an even subtler layer of the lived inter-subjective experience. The Tibetan traditions call this the "very subtle" layer of reality. The Hindu's call it the "causal" layer of reality. As this capacity comes online, there is a clearer sense of being aware of karmic imprints, shared meanings, and synchronicities as events arise in the field. There is a heightened awareness of every single event arising. As a group, we would access a finely attuned attention of the seemingly insignificant experiences in the space. A sneeze, a cough, and itch, all became very subtle forms of intersubjective communication with a karmic significance linked to each action. With a beautiful dance between silence and sharing, it is at this level of emergence where participants report a deeper felt sense of sacredness.

The graphic on the next page shows the basic progress of We-Intelligence as it arises in the individual and gains deeper access to gross, subtle, and causal aspects of inter-subjective fields.

---

7. In our experience, the group would begin feeling a pillar of energy in the center of the room. This pillar of energy would begin to spill overtop of and behind all of our bodies as we sat in a circle together. As the energy flowed behind us it would enter in to the ground, loop under our chairs, and enter back into the base of the pillar. It was as if we were all surrounded by a "donut" shape of flowing energy consciously contributed to by each individuals participation.

We-Intelligence as it gains Deeper Access to States/Realms

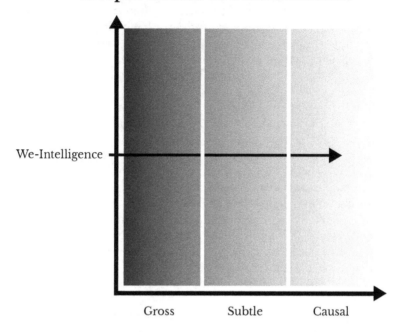

Figure 2: "We" intelligence development across states of consciousness

If We-Intelligence is allowed to flourish in both stages as well its penetration into states/realms, the possibilities are incredible to imagine.

A Cartography of We-Space

As we've seen, We-Intelligence emerges in individuals and can grow through various stages of development (red, amber, orange, green, teal, and beyond). We also noted that as We-Intelligence comes more fully online, it grows in its capacity to feel/sense/know various states of reality penetrating into gross, to subtle, to causal realms. Because We-Spaces are made up of individuals (all of whom are abiding at varying stages of We-Intelligence)[8] We-Spaces themselves can span across a broad spectrum. For example, there can be We-Spaces at every line of development. This means that there are red We-Spaces, amber We-Spaces, orange We-Spaces, green We-Spaces, teal We-Spaces, and beyond. And at any one of those stages, We-Spaces can move beyond gross realm access and open to the direct experience of subtle and casual layers of reality. The graphic below offers a pictorial representation of the types of We-spaces discussed thus far.

A Cartography of We-Space

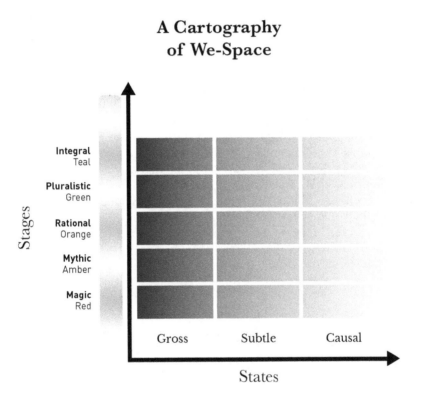

Figure 3: Vertical and Horizontal Expressions of a We-space cartography

8. Stages of We-Intelligence, like all developmental stages, are best thought of as "centers-of-gravity" or ranges across a developmental spectrum. People are not at one particular level at all times, but rather are fluid within a developmental range according to context and content.

In simple terms, this means we've now laid the foundation for more than 15 different types of We-Spaces (5 stages x 3 states/realms). And to be sure, there are many, many more.[9] Elsewhere, Dustin (2014) has articulated the elements of an Awakened We and Evolutionary We, each of which bring participants into an ever-present Nondual vantage point.[10] In addition, it is important to note that We-Spaces can fluctuate depending on the specifics of the content being enacted and the degree of shadow activation present (both individually and collectively.) This is all to say, as we shall see in a moment, that We-Spaces are seldom clean and homogenous throughout an entire interaction, but are rather constantly in flux and at times, rather messy.

A basic understanding of various stages and states that arise in We-Spaces is vital for several reasons. Firstly, the ecosystem of inter-subjective practices currently rampant in the spiritual marketplace fails to discern even the most simple stages and states of We-Space. As a result, the term We-Space is used to refer to quite a broad spectrum of diverse inter-subjective experiences. Some people call any gathering a We-Space. Some call a spiritual Sangha a We-Space. Some call the process of Circling a We-Space. People also speak of a "New We" and a "Higher We." In almost all of these circumstances, communities and facilitators don't have a clear map of what is what. The point being that, not all We-Spaces are equal. Some We-Spaces are higher and deeper than others. Secondly, a better understanding of the cartography of We-Spaces will enable each group to navigate the territory of inter-subjective reality with greater skill. A better map will help groups know where they are, where they have been, and where they might want to go together. And this is true whether the We-Space enactment is neat or messy.

Messy Enactment of We-Space

The cartography above creates a useful theoretical map for individuals coming together in collective practice space. The direct and lived experience of We space, however, weaves the levels of development expressed above in each session and over the course of

---

9. In our experience, the most common We-Space we encountered was likely one that arose from a teal altitude and a subtle state.

10. A "non-dual vantage point" is a technical term used by DiPerna and Wilber to signify the recognition of level awareness no longer confined by individual conscious-ness. This vantage point is the foundation of higher forms of We-Emergence (Awak-ened WE and Evolutionary WE) described in DiPerna's book Streams of Wisdom.

committted practice in nuanced ways. Similarly within a map of levels of individual development: shadow, state experiences that give access to more clarity in the moment, and other contextual factors all color how the individual shows up. The same can be said for We spaces with the added complexity factor of multiple individuals interacting with all of their complexity together. The flow of one session of practice could potentiate a powerful energetic sense of cohesion, collective creativity, and individual experiences of healing. This is often followed by more intense moments of surface incoherence, egoic outbursts, and a myriad of other "messy" expressions within the We. This dynamic and inconsistent expression is an inherent part of group practice. The map of collective levels of development can act as a reflective tool to see if this intellectual categorization has utility to deepen the experience of practice or needs to be augmented to more readily capture the dynamism within the field of practice. The enactment of the cartography in real time also informs the continued development of the cartography. It may be revealed that collective development, due to its complexity and dynamism, simply cannot be adequately mapped or at least not mapped in similar ways that we have mapped individual development.

As we saw through the We-line of development, this ability to rest in the unknown and be open to the perspectives of others in a nonjudgmental way is highly dependent upon what perspective someone is residing in as they relate to the We space. Often we have seen expressions of what was referred to above as an amber *social conformity* where people are inhibited to even speak into the field out of fear of being judged, nervousness, etc. We have also seen that when intensely triggered, individuals can temporarily express behaviors seeming to arise from earlier levels of development that don't normally express themselves when the space is relatively calm. In many cases, a regressive expression from an individual speaks to the potency of the space that both triggers that deeper wound and (ideally) allows for it to unwind within the agenda-less relational holding of the collective space.

As is commonly referenced, many people often fear public speaking more than death. There is a cultural conditioned sense that many people have difficulty feeling fully comfortable in expressing themselves without feeling self-conscious, unsure of themselves, etc. Anyone who has been in an introductory or even advanced We-space group has seen and most likely experienced within themselves or others a nervousness or lack of confidence about the value of their contribution when speaking up in the group. By understanding a general orientation of how people could express within a group, facilitators of We space can both have compassion for these expressions within people and continue to name potential experiences that they perceive people expressing and then "poll the We" to see who might be feeling those qualities. Often, such an intervention is not engaged unless there is a pervasive energetic feeling that the facilitator perceives intuitively coupled with clear information from several members (consisting of facial expressions, body language, and other intuitive markers) of the group so as not to potentially single one person out in an isolating manner. If such an intervention is utilized, often framing the question as "who has ever felt this way in groups?" elicits a more universal recognition that this is an experience most people go through. The beauty of the We is that we can express our "individual" neuroses and have immediate confirmation that what we thought was individual is most certainly a shared experience amongst many members of the group.

In many contexts, as mentioned above, We-spaces have been focused on solely higher consciousness (Cohen, 2011) and often, these orientations have a connotation of a consciousness that somehow supersedes the individual. While the intention for these groups is often to not get stuck in an individual's ego needs that can inhibit a greater emergence, there are ways to both not get stuck within the egoic conversation *and* not bypass the individual. The intention for why individuals come together and the context for the engagement, deeply shape what is inherently welcomed to arise within the space and how the individual can be honored and not limit a more collective emergence to occur.

The Intention of the We

A major influence on both the initial texture of the group as well as the potential for true emergence is the intention behind the gathering. The intention informs the implicit level of commitment to showing up as radically, authentically, and transparently within such a space. If the intention is simply to look for collective creativity, that might stifle the attunement towards aspects of individual and collective shadow that get invited through the intensity of collective presence. If creativity is made the primary area of focus, there is an implied message that what seem like "non-creative" or insecure aspects within individuals need to be liberated or compartmentalized before they can fully participate in a creative emergent space. Another perspective would suggest that whatever intention people have to come together, everything that arrives within the collective, moment to moment *is* emergent creativity. When we expand the definition of what creativity looks/feels like, it can encompass the feeling of a group flow state, disgruntled participants arguing without attuning to the impact it has on the group, people sobbing or displaying even more intense expressions of affect and behavior. Simply put, whatever is arising in the moment *is* the creativity of Life and it is our task to surrender to what is arising and open to how and what it is here to teach us.

Over the past five years of WEpractice, we found that setting the shared intention for awakening has the greatest potentiating effect. To be sure, the word "awakening" can mean many things. And because each group is free to interpret and use the phrase in a way most meaningful to them, all uses of the word can be useful. For now, we'll discuss two different types of awakening: Awakening with a capital "A" and awakening with a lower case "a."

Awakening might have a spiritual connotation, relating to the capacity to come to know the nature of Ultimate Reality. In that case we refer to "Awakening" with a capital "A".[11] Awakening with a capital "A" relates to our intention to sustain a sense of nondual freedom in relationship to all experience. This allows us to engage with things *as they are* and in a way that allows us to remain available as a vessel for creativity. This orientation, if engaged comprehensively, enables us to show up quite radically within the We-space. We learn to authentically engage spontaneously in service to the whole. Outwardly, the actions themselves may not appear radical, but culturally and socially, the freedom of Awakening can allow the individual to transgress social norms. In many cases this means speaking honestly about what is arising in the moment despite it potentially hurting someone's feelings or making the group feel temporarily uncomfortable. The counterbalance to this honesty is also being aware of the impact that honesty is having on others in the group and the group as a whole. There is a constant dance of what is an authentic share and attuning to its service to the group. When the offering from Awakening is authentic, the group usually finds itself at a deeper and more coherent space than it was before, even despite the potential discomfort. If Awakening with an upper case "A" is the underlying intention of a space, an individual

---

11. When we refer to Awakening, we are referring to an embodied approach to awakening informed by wisdom streams, psychological perspectives and tools, relational competency, and the recognition that within our humanity is our divinity. From this perspective, we are no longer looking to transcend anything. When there is not an explicit orientation towards this non-dual embodied approach of recognizing the gifts within shadow, divinity within humanity, or We within a group of individuals, there can exist a spiritualized agenda that prefers a certain quality of experience of emergence over another. We cannot fully be vessels of the unknown when we have a subtle agenda to how we want the unknown showing up. It is essential that we acknowledge, witness, and embrace our individual and collective shadows that are obscuring our view of clear reality.

is able to come from a space of non-separation, take interpersonal risks of speaking their truth, daring to be totally honest in response to how they feel about someone or the situation at hand, and is willing to let go of the known, security, and ego satisfaction to the degree they can see it, in service of what wants to emerge from Life itself.[12]

Concerning "awakening" with a lower case "a," this form does not necessarily require a spiritual orientation towards your life and reality. Within this approach is a deep curiosity and thirst to understand life, one's own, other's and the collective psyche, and is more interested in where things come from than the surface manifestations of reality. We are seeing this arise more and more in the mainstream marketplace with the introduction of mindfulness within organizations, conferences such as Wisdom 2.0 and approaches towards business such as The Lean Start Up (Ries, 2011) whose principles have been applied in various high powered tech companies such as Google. People are interested in both secularizing esoteric practices in service of productivity and efficiency (as in the growth of mindfulness in business and Wisdom 2.0 conferences) as well as being interested in utilizing real time feedback to evolve one's approach to their business in service of greater success by letting go of reliance on outdated, non-emergent models of business. One could say these cultural manifestations are more holistic, evolution oriented and are indicative of the awakening approach to We space that is being outlined here. As a group culture expresses these qualities of curiosity and a willingness to receive Life's agenda as opposed to imposing individual or group opinions onto reality, the next move into an Awakening-informed orientation to collective practice is potentiated. Naturally, these two levels of engagement, a more spiritual *Awakening* orientation and a more secular *awakening* orientation, can manifest very similarly within the space of practice. Both are interested in emergent potentials and have a curiosity to explore and experiment and touch into human potential not normally seen expressed in public spaces. Where you really see the differentiation is when an egoic pattern or trauma is touched by the intensity of the collective inquiry/presence and the group does not have a belief system, track record, guide, or context to hold this messy emotional and relational experience. Over time with experience, the group could learn ways to adapt their response to a person's emotional trigger and contextualize it within a larger framework of emergence.

---

12. Of importance to note is that just because an individual has access to nondual states in meditation, does not imply they will be able to sustain them within intersubjective contact. This stabilization must be cultivated and tested, often over a sustained period of practice and is constantly being refined.

The core of curiosity within the intention of awakening will support the evolution of how the group is held and operates.

Due to the curious and ever-evolving nature of an awakening approach to We space, We space groups with this intention will eventually begin to mirror Awakening We space groups having moved into further and further refined and transparent expressions of themselves. From our perspective, a spiritual orientation with the qualities of Awakening is moving towards the clearest conditions that enables repeatable engagement with more profound and clear expressions of collective creativity. What is important to note is that an explicit orientation to Awakening might not serve the development of a group at a given time. Therefore, it is important that a facilitator of a group does not superimpose what they feel is the most radical approach to collective practice on a group that is not ready for it. Leadership that is in service of true emergence is able to read how and where the field is moving at any given time and make suggestions to serve its organic emergence. It is essential that secular approaches to We space are engaged and we are full advocates of these spaces flourishing. These sections support catalyzing new or deepening existing we spaces that are not specifically "spiritual" yet also tap into increasing emergent and creative possibilities as more and more people are coming together in this way. If the We practice space is stewarded in a minimally skillful way, the space can become more self-aware and grow in ways that are more spiritual.[13]

It is challenging to truly delineate what creativity could look like from an Awakening perspective vs. an awakening perspective. In many ways, novel insights, deeply present interactions between participants, and state-experiences, to name a few, can be forms of creativity that arise in both spaces. The important distinction is that in Awakening oriented spaces, participants might have more experience navigating state-experiences through their previous spiritual practice and do not become seduced by a spiritual state of consciousness and remain focused on what continues to emerge beyond the state. Another distinction is that Awakening oriented spaces might have more comfort in framing experiences in consciousness terms that more congruently describe the energy and experiences that are occurring rather than trying to "translate down" spiritual experiences in more secular terms that do not do them adequate justice. Even what seems like a minute shift in languaging can impact the energetic quality and aliveness

---

13. This claim of becoming "spiritual" comes from research from Cook-Greuter (2005) describing later developmental stage individuals expressing qualities such as... We are suggesting that engaging in We space can potentiate shifts in worldview and perspective that enable vertical shifts in development.

of the space. Ultimately, it is the quality of collective presence and welcoming of what is arising that most impacts a We space, and this of course can be the case in Awakening and awakening informed We spaces.

One important expression of the messy enactment of the We space is around feeling a sense of completion. There is usually an innate desire for completion and resolution within an experience. We see this is the arch of mainstream movies where there is a hero or heroine that goes through a process of struggle that eventually comes to a place of understanding and completion where the audience can go home happy with their sense of resolution. Consciously or unconsciously, we are looking for this sense of resolution and feel incomplete or undone in some way when this is not the case. If we are really open to the mystery of the unknown when we come together, sometimes there will be a sense of mutual understanding and completion and sometimes emergence requires us to hold ambiguity about things not being tied together neatly in a bow and invite us to show up the next time with fresh eyes and curious minds to see where we are to go next from where we left off. The ability to handle this ambiguity is a quality of spiritual maturity that enables a dropping of this agenda of needing completion to truly be open to the way the We wants to move.

When a group commits to a certain number of sessions, there is usually a sense of completion at the end, yet within the middle there is often a non-linear flow of clean endings *and* messy unfinished business between people and the group. The glue that ties it all together is the willingness to not have an agenda for what happens to look any certain way and to hold the creative tension of life with patience, trust, and the understanding that when resolution is required, it will show itself.[14] The bottom line of the messy enactment of the We space is an invitation to drop ideals, preconceived notions, agendas for loving connection and dive in with open minds and hearts to the unknown.

We Agility

In order to leverage the We-Space cartography in service of what wants to happen without stifling creativity, it is essential that facilitators and practitioners exhibit *agility* within the We space. Going back to the

---

14. Of importance to note, there are plenty of exceptions to this rule when groups are not made interpersonally safe through poor leadership, and we are assuming in this example that the group is run with integrity and psychological and interpersonal skill.

previous lines of development discussion, interpersonal intelligence is a deeply supportive area of development to have competency in within the We space. We can look at what makes someone a skilled communicator on an individual basis. Qualities such as emotional attunement, tracking nuanced social cues, attending to body language, being comfortable with responding to the conversation partner in a way that builds meaning off what they were saying, being emotionally available so people feel connected to you, etc. In many ways, a deep and meaningful conversation with another person requires thinking on your feet, being willing to trust the unknown trajectory of a conversation, and being open to novel perspectives that are coming from the other person or the conversation itself, to name a few. There is a deep agility factor exhibited in these qualities that only expands when looking at its application to the We space.

Unlike a one on one conversation, the We space is a much more complex interpersonal/collective situation. There are many more "conversation partners" to attune to, there is usually a focus on the process of the experience as well as the content, and depending on the intention of the group, there is a broader emotional range that is welcomed to express than in a conversation you might have with a friend at a coffee shop. One way to deal with these increased variables would be to clamp down and try to track all of the nuanced variables in an overly rigid and mechanical way. A tendency for some practitioners in we space is to *try* to attune to all that is happening to make the most informed and supportive contribution. While there is noble intention in this approach, it is clear that a more relaxed, panoramic, and interpersonal flavor is necessary to develop increased skill in engaging with We spaces.

Trust is a big factor in engaging agilely in We spaces. By engaging in almost a hyper-vigilant way, one has difficulty trusting their innate ability to respond when a response is needed, is not trusting that whatever is happening is what is needing to happen, and more importantly, is not trusting that the We would self-correct if something spoken or enacted was really "off" in the space.[15] A balance that we find essential is likened to that of zoom of a camera. If one is zoomed too far in, their view is myopic and this can lead to a sense of not trusting what is happening, a tendency for controlling behavior and holding a limited and limiting view of the whole. Conversely, if someone is too broad or zoomed out, they cannot adequately *feel* the contours of the

---

15. If the majority of people are interested in what feels authentic within a space and are invited by the ethos of group to speak up, the collective will naturally self-correct any individual or isolated incident that was being omitted from the collective attention in service to what feels more intuitively aligned with the moment.

We space, cannot attune to subtler moment to moment movements, and often their human hearts are not "touchable." It's been a helpful inner metric to zoom in and out in a dynamic balance given the changing landscape of the We space moment to moment. When we can honor and understand the minutiae within the context of the greater whole, our study of the specifics informs emerging relational structures that support the evolution of the space as a whole.

What is beautiful about We spaces is that there is a potential to drop the sort of meta-responsibility of care-taking or managing a space and really rest into the stance that an individual is simply one set of eyes with a unique perspective on the wholeness of the group and is also deeply part of that wholeness. The We needs to hear from all the perspectives, or at least *feel* all people in order have a comprehensive view of itself; for one perspective is always going to be partial. This is of course not always practical depending on the size of the group. We have found that words are not the only form of currency of how perspectives are shared. Being deeply engaged in the group in presence and not with words is still offering an important energetic perspective that fleshes out more of the totality of what is arising. It is the attuning to the greater felt sense of alignment beyond personal agenda, and leaning into sourcing from the future potential of the We space itself that will enable people to drop their need for things to be a certain way to help them feel secure and be open to a collective agenda that transcends and includes the individual.

There is no gold standard of how one must participate in the We. This is because the heterogeneous stance and experience each participant holds is an essential ingredient to the creative dynamism that makes exploring the unknown potential of people coming together in a We space so exciting. While we are not speaking of a gold standard, we are saying that the ability to be fluid in relating to the We supports collective creativity showing itself more readily. Let's explore two more specific qualities of We agility.

One is the ability to sense into an emergent order of reality based on the future. Normally we take experience in the moment and try to fit it into a schematic of reality based on what we have known before. This is a human habit that serves a false sense of security that the future extends from the present in some linear fashion. In order to truly step into the unknown, a lack of categorization of what is happening is required. Whether we are categorizing reality into an integral map or simply what we have known reality to look like in the past, we are limiting the scope of creativity and the true shaping of our worldviews through novel data and experience that arises. In a We space, there could be a civil conversation taking place and all of a sudden someone abruptly interrupts another participant by voicing their frustration with the overly intellectual conversation and need to attune to another quality of being within the space that the previous conversation was not honoring. If one participant was attached to the flow of the conversation, they could be indignant with such an interruption, one that obviously was not connected to what was being said. Again, the We space ideally is attuned to both the process *and* the content. In this case, the individual was feeling an aspect of the process being neglected through focus on one area of content. In this moment, the facilitator(s) and participants must now support the group to integrate this emergent experience within what has already happened and be open to seeing where that intense movement catalyzes the next step in the process. Without We agility, the group could revert back to what they were saying after the outburst, ignore the outburst, or tempers could start flaring, dividing the group coherence further. If the content previously being discussed and the abrupt interruption could be seen as coherent pieces of a trajectory whose order has not yet been revealed, then people can continue to remain present now in service of what is next in this emergent trajectory of being together.

Another quality of We agility is to stay grounded and open and hold the conscious recognition that nothing is ever out of place from an ultimate perspective. Being grounded in one's body allows the truth that Life is unfolding perfectly, no matter how wacky things might seem on the surface, to an embodied realization as opposed to a more new age aphorism that is used as a way to rationalize intense circumstances that one does not know how to deal with. If we have ideas for what we need to experience to feel safe, seen, understood, etc., when life shows up in a way that is beyond our threshold, there is usually a shutting down or moving away quality that arises.[16] Robert Kegan (1982) speaks about development as a series of periods of stability and clarity and times of instability and confusion. If we are coming together to come-to-know what is not yet known, and to consistently develop together as a group, inherently there will be confusion, uncertainty, and insecurity as we tread upon this fresh emerging ground. In this collective laboratory, we have the option to relax into what feels like our threshold being crossed by what we *thought* we could handle. By doing so, we learn that we can experience and steward more intensity than previously experienced and we no longer have to contract around our sense of discomfort, fear, sadness, etc. For anyone involved in We space practice, intensity

---

16. There is so much nuance around trauma responses, emotional safety, etc. that is not adequately being addressed in this chapter. We are assuming as authors that there is a skillful facilitation in the hypothetical We spaces we are referring to as well as a group of people with enough psychological integration that they can tolerate interpersonal situations that are intense and emotionally evocative.

arises in myriad forms from interpersonal disagreement, someone naming the "elephant in the room," and moments when the collective surrenders enough that a palpable intensity of the "energy of the We" permeates the space. Staying grounded amidst this intensity allows individuals and the group at large to steward the creative energy while remaining present and attuned to the movement the group wants to make, despite aspects of our personality that are in protest in response to feeling overwhelmed by the intensity. The more we cannot become seduced or overwhelmed by intense energy, interpersonal chaos, and any thought form or judgment that arises in our awareness, the more we can perceive the emergent trajectory of the We that is sourced from the future potential of these people coming together. If what is arising is confusing or overwhelming, the task of the individual is to sit with these feelings and stay curious about how they are ever changing and how they are setting the stage for what has yet to present itself. If we extrapolate the future based on confusion we are experiencing in the moment, we limit how and when coherence and understanding can emerge in the next moment.

We agility could be described in different ways and the above description is by no means exhaustive or comprehensive. Our intention is simply to name a quality of engagement in the We space that can be cultivated from practitioner's experience in service of staying present and open to all that is occurring within a space. Engaging in collective practice like this is no small task and requires new skill sets in order to steward future potentials more skillfully over time. Wepractice is simply adding to this capacity building as a global community and we need the many perspectives from practice communities to more fully flesh out the necessary conditions and competencies that most readily potentiate us receiving and enacting collective creativity.

Conclusion

We (Michael and Dustin) as well as the larger "We" (all of us involved in We space practice) continue to be in an exciting process of learning, growing, and evolving our understanding of what is possible in the potent space between us. With this in mind, we wrote this chapter as an offering to our collective knowledge commons. It is clear that there needs to be some degree of shared meaning about what a We space is and how we can engage it diversely in order to readily exchange ideas and practices within the field of practitioners.

It was our hope that our orientation here could bring forth both a clear and evolving map of We-Intelligence and a better understanding of the various combinations of We-Space that are possible based on our own direct experience. In addition to the new cartography of understanding, we also attempted to portray the fact that no matter how clear or clean our maps might be, in reality, We-Spaces can be and often are messy affairs. And finally, we introduced We Agility as an important capacity to cultivate and engage within the We space. It has been our repeated experience that one of the best ways to flow with and be attuned to the ever-fluctuating dynamics of a WE is to show up with greater and greater degrees of openness and a willingness to adjust to whatever is being called for in the moment. The spontaneous capacity to respond to the present situation (in both our shared collective fields and in all aspects of life) is a skill that surely all of us can cultivate further.

We feel this anthology is more than a conglomeration of perspectives within a field, it is a stepping-stone to a whole new degree of coherence as a meta-We of We space practitioners. One of the visions of WEpractice was to create an open source online platform that would share theory and practices in service of skillful We space facilitation to be implemented across the globe in various domains. This book is a tangible start to that global knowledge commons that will both support the diverse nodes of We space engagement as well as continue to push the collective evolutionary edge of We space enactment across the field at large.

In addition, both authors shared the mutual intention to show up together again in a public way to offer what we've learned. We sought to write together in a way that mutually enhanced and enriched each other, expanding the final result beyond the offering that either one of us might bring alone.

We are grateful for the opportunity to share with all of you and look forward to entering into the great dance of inter-subjective Awakening with you in the future.

Author Bios

Michael Brabant, Ph.D. has been trained in both the academic and clinical settings as well as studied with shamans, mystics, and intuitive healers. By synthesizing the most potent inner technologies and the nuanced conceptual understanding related to true transformation, he offers a body teaching and practice called Divine Humanity to help us build the energetic, relational and emotional infrastructure to live our lives as if every moment and everything contained within it, is both sacred and deeply intelligent. You can learn more about his work at livingdivinehumanity.com

Dustin DiPerna is a visionary leader, entrepreneur, and recognized integral expert in world religions. He is co-founder of WEpractice, a global community dedicated to exploring the awakened inter-subjective field. In addition to serving as coach, mentor, and meditation teacher, he is author of three books – Streams of Wisdom, Evolution's Ally. And Earth is Eden – and co-editor of The Coming Waves. Dustin is also author of several articles on We-Space including Rejuvenating Religion in an Integral Age: The Emergence of the Unique Self and the Unique We. Dustin holds an undergraduate degree from Cornell University and a Masters of Liberal Arts degree in Religion from Harvard University. Learn more about Dustin and his work on his website: dustindiperna.com

References

Cohen, A. (2011). Evolutionary enlightenment: A new path to spiritual awakening. New York, NY: SelectBooks, Inc.

DiPerna, D. (2014). Streams of wisdom: An advanced guide to integral spiritual development. Occidental, CA: Integral Publishing House.

DiPerna, D. et al. (2014). The coming waves: Evolution, transformation and action in an integral age. Occidental, CA: Integral Publishing House.

DiPerna, D. (2014). Evolutions Ally: Our World's Religious Traditions as Conveyor Belts of Transformation. Occidental, CA: Integral Publishing House.

Ries, E. (2011). The lean startup: How today's entrepreneurs use continuous innovation to create radically successful businesses. New York, NY: Crown Business.

CHAPTER 2

Embodying Higher Consciousness:
Awakening Through We-Space to a Higher Frequency of Life

Stephen Busby

Embodying Higher Consciousness is a coherent set of practices that have emerged over the last three years through groups engaged in collective inquiry in various countries. The groups that I have facilitated have tended to consist of between 15-40 people, and occasionally larger, in formats ranging from intensive trainings to weekend workshops to week-long retreats. I will explore here what is cultivated through the practices, the implications for our understanding of embodiment within we-space inquiry as well as its awakening potential, and how in groups we work phenomenologically to effect systemic change at cultural levels. Through small and large group exercises, dialogue, systemic constellational process and inner work, those of us who gather in inquiry deepen our sensitivity to the subtle realms of life and explore the impact of invoking higher consciousness. We observe how healing emerges as we listen into the unknown spaces beyond where we normally relate from, responding to the invitations we find there. At the core of the practices is a deepening capacity to presence oneself, other people, and a collective we-space. Participants are encouraged to cultivate this through interpersonal attunement, witnessing practice and transparency.

Interpersonal Attunement

In interpersonal attunement exercises, in pairs or triads, we listen and learn to sense into the subtle context behind whatever overt themes we are exploring. I note here a fine line between myself as facilitator and participant within these groups, which leads to a sometimes blurred linguistic distinction in referring to myself, to participants, and to the "we" as a whole. While this leads to a difficulty in articulating all of the nuances that occur in language, the focus of stewarding the group while also deeply engaging as a member of it enables a much more tangible experience of a we-space from my experience, as opposed to a teacher or facilitator who is stewarding the we-space from outside of it, or who maintains a clear hierarchical distinction from the other members of the group.

In the exercises we attune to and offer feedback to whoever is speaking from a theme. Participants are encouraged to allow feedback to arise through the felt space of their pair or triad from beyond the content of whatever is being explored, to check for the felt resonance of the feedback, to learn to direct their awareness with intent, to hone and focus subtle perceptual and attunement abilities, and to sense the energetic vibrational qualities of we-space. Together we witness the amplifying effect of these practices: how the space of inquiry becomes intensified often through spontaneous insight and a sense of de-cluttering at the mental level. We become alert to the properties and potential of small-group space beyond where our agenda for it may take or limit us. Thus participants become progressively sensitized to the subtle aspects of the larger group of practitioners, exploring nascent sensitivities and capacities there and stretching themselves more confidently within the collective. Speaking from the background context of the subtle realms can amplify felt intensity within the localized field of an exercise. Our questions and responses can take on a more essential quality, appear to 'hit home' and strongly resonate when allowed to arise and be shared spontaneously. Through suggested phases of reciprocal feedback and mirroring we become more present to ourselves and with whatever is arising somatically through with the subtleties of the body-mind system. People are encouraged to learn to listen beyond the conditioned self, attuning to the quality of their own internal experience as well as that which appears to be outside selves. We deepen into interiority primarily through the feeling-sense, opening to physically based sensation, textures of energy, emotions and images. The felt energetic space can become clearer; whatever is shared is expressed more transparently: more essentially, economically and powerfully with intensity and insight. Participants become sensitive to and expressive of the content of the subtle realms and may experience more of the collective field 'from the inside': more attuned and aligned with its essence, its shadows, its potential for unfoldment and growth.

Feeling Capacity

Most people usually need time when invited to sense. For many of us, our feeling capacity can be hard-won territory, recovered from earlier in life when it was not validated. Kai Ehrhardt frames our dilemma:

> What sounds fairly simple at first turns out to consist of lots of unfamiliar layers, which can cause confusion. What really is a sensation, an emotion or a thought? How do I distinguish them? What are sensations that are always available even without the presence of pain, pleasure or other strong stimuli? Am I memorizing sensation... or is it happening in real time...? When people truly arrive at the level of their sensations... they realize several things [including that] sensation is an experience only possible now. It connects us to what is actually happening – instead of stories, fantasies or emotionally triggered information that stems from an older or an imagined context. [Secondly] evaluation, comparison and judgment are not possible at the level of sensation. There is no object/subject split – things just are. It is not possible to have a preference...(Ehrhardt, 2012, p.16)

In small-group exercises we inquire into the complex territory described here, reclaiming the ground of feeling capacity, noticing where it leads us. Building relationship to one's own feeling capacity can prove exhilarating, often humbling, and can begin to expose us to the extent to which we may have closed off to entire unwanted or invalidated dimensions of ourselves. As Ehrhardt infers, it may prompt awareness of how dualistic feeling and thinking arise and are sustained within us, often as a response to early wounding.

We provide containers for each other where feeling and emotion may be transparently present or allowed to emerge. In one exercise we support whoever has the focus to inquire into the quality of their inner contact with something that may have been previously experienced as (or believed to be) 'too much' to bear or be felt. In this we are sustaining 'movement towards' rather than away, foregoing our conditioned tendency to retreat or contract away from wounding. We are withdrawing our investment in the inner structures that underpin our conditioning, loosening the ground in which unhealthy autonomous ego-structures find nourishment. Cultivating inner intimate contact like this in an exercise may support someone in validating their own presencing capacity, i.e. their ability and readiness to bring into contact within themselves, through sustained awareness, whatever may habitually be excluded from that contact. Presencing would therefore also include an ability to 'catch' that exclusionary mechanism or movement. It can afford a person authentic contact with their own emotional content or with dimensions of their body experience, reawakening their somatic intelligence, perhaps for the first time. This may lead, as they learn to trust the integral perception of the body, to healing movements or to realization: "The inner experience of the body is the beginning of realizing this deep connectedness to all that there is" (Hübl 2012). Judith Blackstone writes: "Through this internal contact with our body we come alive within our skin, at the same time that we experience ourselves as open and unified with everything around us" (Blackstone 2008, p. xii). Interpersonal attunement also connects personal process – through our feeling capacity – with the larger collective field of the practitioner group, leveraging its transformative potential.

Witnessing

The core of witnessing practice consists of focused external observation and simultaneous strong inward self-attention, noticing and sharing aloud perception of whatever phenomena are concurrently arising through subtle sensation or awareness. This bi-directional attention is often experienced as a kind of interior stretching. It tends to surprise and awaken people to their potential for working at vibrational levels: learning – through the feeling-sense – to notice and track energetic shifts, and increasingly experiencing people, structures or systems from the inside. There is "a felt sense of both our internal experience and our oneness with the life around us. We can therefore experience oneness with another person while remaining attuned to our own internal being" (Blackstone, 2011, introduction, para. 13). We support each other in dwelling within feeling-sense. Through attunement and feedback we learn to witness where somebody is living within their body and where they are not – where relationship within is being withheld. We may choose – through mirroring – to be guided by a partner in allowing more intimate contact with – and navigating through – those dimensions of our somatic experience, of our inner worlds, that are as yet uncharted.

As groups of practitioners we are cultivating a dual capacity to focus narrowly with intensity upon the foreground of our experience while holding a wide focus upon the subtle background canvas of our awareness. In doing so, most people discover that they are simultaneously deepening sensitivity to a subtle informational field, sometimes referred to as the evolving Akashic or zero-point field, which carries in-formation that shapes or provides blueprints for material reality (Kinney 2014). Deepening the felt-sense is an integrative way of bringing different kinds of information together, an integrative perceptual skill. Most of us are not well educated in honoring inner information, tending to dismiss it just as we were most likely dismissed when sharing it in childhood. Learning to direct and sustain our attention bi-directionally tends not to be supported in early education or generally in occidental cultures. Yet if participants inquire here – through an exercise or through directed inner work – with a focus freed of intent, then they may experience that their sense of self – whether localized to their own internal body-space, to the small group or to the larger collective – is rendered transparent to higher intention and more easeful manifestation in life. This facilitates and furthers the deeper collective purpose of those who gather to pursue these kinds of practices. I believe there is no deeper capacity we can cultivate than to honor whatever arises in awareness, whether or not we experience that as 'our own.' In doing so we open ourselves to a quality of love and unconditionality that transcends our conditioned attempts to 'get something right.' Or, framed differently:

> When we allow ourselves to enter luminously into the embodied, subjective experience of another – without the projection of burden that they change, heal, shift, awaken, or transform – and when they feel us with them inside of the cracks and crevices of each and every cell of their heart – love takes over, the great natural perfection begins to whisper its secrets, and we turn toward home, together. (Licata, 2014, para. 2)

To cultivate inner-witnessing capacity through the we-space practices suggested here is to explore a quality of profound receptivity in ourselves. If I am learning to attune to interpersonal space while simultaneously witnessing whatever is co-arising 'inside and out' then I am becoming more identified with the powerful ways in which it is possible to be with others and with myself. Synchronizing what were previously perceived as two separate spaces enlarges consciousness. I will be less identified as an autonomous separate structure with opinions and packages of experiences, a less crystallized as ego-structure, and will be more allowing of what wants to come through me and the space of collective practice and also of what that space has the potential to become. I will have a growing sense of a larger, less personalized movement of intent and a stronger ability to surrender through inquiry to where that sense of intent may carry me. We are learning:

> To direct our awareness to our inner felt experience – to the parts of us that are naturally drawing our attention, and then connecting with them by feeling them. This involves switching from willful output mode to receptive mode... [If we direct] our mind toward the parts of our energy body seeking our attention, and we feel these parts of ourselves, we are connecting with life force and building energetic strength and a clearer navigational compass... [We are] available to notice, feel and spontaneously act upon what is wanting to happen moment-to-moment... where actions organically follow energetic impulses. As people build their ability to feel whatever comes up when they are not running the show, their capacity to follow rather than control life expands. (Emmons, 2013, para. 26)

Structures of Being

Learning to notice different energetic qualities and vibration in whatever is arising within, and to discern there a call to spontaneous action, require for most of us sustained spaces of practice, at least until noticing-capacity becomes more integrated as a natural state. We discover that there are:

> A whole host of energetic processes occurring in our bodies all the time... Beginning to feel these subtleties will allow them to manifest more and more clearly. Our awareness creates a sort of amplifying feedback loop, because the outer reflects the inner: that which we give our attention to will determine what we experience on an ongoing basis... Your physical body (and the senses that are an extension of it) tends to experience that which is in accordance with the templates that are anchored in your mental and emotional bodies. (Greendyk, 2014, para. 13)

I call these templates 'structures of being': inner scaffolding through which we unconsciously filter and determine our experience and thereby our interpretation of reality. Our work in the groups thus far indicates that such structures are only personal to the extent they are mirrored in larger cultural contexts, hence the potential through our practices to work with 'the whole' through 'the local.' Through an exercise, my partner supports me in relating to what feels inside increasingly like an inner structure. Through the quality of her relational presence I am able to explore this, and may encounter a sense of layering – structures leading to structures. Slowly she guides me in investigating and sensing their shape and contours, and some shadowy places where I tend to leave contact. She's there as I return and reconnect more fully within myself and to her. I gain a feeling-sense of how the structures show up in my life: their energetic regressive characteristics and qualities; slowly I may uncover – through further layering – what feel like roots, perhaps even a possible original defensive or protective function. Here I am presenced by my partner in some strong emotion which wells up. I've a sense of how a structure has served me, of the much younger dimension of myself who birthed it and, as we presence further, how it may be available for more inner movement. There may be some felt release. This personal work will not be without impact on those working with me, witnessing the space. 'My' structure may find resonance in them too, translated differently. We may find upon reconvening in the larger group that we have touched upon something with strong systemic resonance, and so feel guided to inquire into it more collectively. Through presencing it there we will discover more of 'its' function and how it seems to play out in different forms across the human collective and psyche.

Shadow and Transparency

Transparency nurtures my ability to both feel the ways in which I tend to separately identify from others and my capacity to witness others and myself more intimately. Interpersonal attunement in turn nurtures transparency. Transparency within and between people requires a willingness to explore and confront forms of personal or collective shadow so that their energy may, in turn, become available to inquiry. The challenges many of us encounter in this – the extent to which we are stretched – tend to enrich and deepen relational space. In small-group transparency exercises, participants may find that the energetic embrace of awareness allows something to be felt more wholly, and that there is a sense of inner movement, perhaps allowing them to re-integrate those aspects of themselves from which they have dissociated. Shadow that is explored through intensified intersubjective space is no longer 'mine' in the sense that it:

... can only exist as long as there is an outer life that collaborates with it. If you and I are not aware of the same thing it will continue. If one of us is aware of it [then] it cannot continue, because it is now becoming aware of itself. (Hübl, 2014a)

In witnessing the expression of shadow through inquiry into its symptoms – in consenting to sense and inhabit its vibration and to fill it with the light of our awareness – we are also witnessing the ways that structures of being manifest in our lives in real time. In other words, the ways in which they have formed and are expressed through the egoic framework, and how they form still: how the personality tends to nourish and update them, creating fresh ones unconsciously. There may be insight too into the ways in which we invest in each other's shadows, negotiating reciprocal agreements to restrict risk in our relationships and maintain familiar dynamics, and how we contribute to the ways in which culture – through us – does this.[1]

Relational Space and Healing

As we-space practitioners, we begin to discern through inner attention where the deeper energetic impulses of life lead us: where they support us in opening to the invitation of those crystallized aspects of ourselves that have formed as structures. It is critical here that we be presenced in interpersonal space where relationship – authentic contact with a partner – is maintained, as described above. We can then begin to witness and leverage the true evolutionary potential of relational space: how we relate through and as life, not as objects in relationship but as relational space itself. The healing to which we bear witness when we are held in and as relational space seems to unfold as movement. For those who are sensitive to the inner flow and shifting texture of energy, it is as if a structure is touched with a quality of awareness in a certain way for the first time. We are consenting to re-connect with those aspects of ourselves where subtle energy has

---

1. I note here the significant contribution of Thomas Hübl's work to the field of we-space inquiry through his Transparent Communication® practices. According to Chris Dierkes, the transparency Thomas speaks of "is a radical simultaneous addressing of all dimensions, lines, and levels of being, as well as individual and collective communication" (Dierkes 2011). Other formative influences include Judith Blackstone, Bert Hellinger, Judith Hemming, Richard Moss, James Finley, Arnold Mindell, Thomas & Gitte Trobe, and David Spangler (ref. more complete sources at www.stephenbusby.com).

crystallized, and to bring them into conscious relationship. The effect is often felt as a relief and release: something moves within our structures and emerges through us with recognition. Attention has enabled energetic transformation. Insight may accompany and accelerate the process – sometimes a spontaneous whole-view of how an inner system has held itself in integrity: how structures of being are inter-related, perpetuating themselves through compensatory behaviors and beliefs, perhaps as physical symptoms or crisis. Through trauma we creatively develop early subtle holding patterns for defensive-protective imperatives. Healing is enabled because these patterns can be met through presence and be received, held and embraced in life in a different way.

The heightened energy we are being invited to embody tends to attract to each of us those next layered issues in our life that are available for awareness. Judith Blackstone notes: "The subtle body is imprinted with memories, desires, tendencies and attachments [and that] these imprints produce life circumstances for their fulfillment or resolution" (Blackstone 2008, p. 58). She asserts that repressed or denied needs, memories and emotions embedded in the tissues are "too tense and rigid to be easily penetrated by our consciousness" (p.41) and that "as long as our body, energy and consciousness is bound up in the past, they are not available for present experience" (p.64). The practices described here, whereby one may experience a strong stream or ground of consciousness through we-space, mean that relationally we are enabled to connect with those split-off parts in ourselves and, through witnessing and healing movements, to become less fragmented. Since our inner structures are layered within us, and include karmic dimensions, the work opens us to that next part of ourselves ripe for potential re-integration. Through small-group exercises, participants inquire into whatever life-theme or issue is alive, moving or stuck in their life, attuning to its outer symptoms – to the play of symbols or circumstances that attract their attention. In a small group my co-inquirers will reflect back to me in real-time to what extent I am consenting to authentically inhabit an issue and the layers beneath it – where I remain in relationship, with them and myself, and where I flee from it by resorting to evasive or compensatory strategies that energetically are rendered transparent in our space. Through honoring the role of such strategies – consciously including them – and through mirroring and feedback, I am enabled to feel and relate to dimensions of myself that may never have been held in authentic contact. Whatever is held in relationship reveals movement. By consenting to stay in contact – outside and in, I will be able to attune through my feeling-sense to densities and shifts in the energy of whatever structure is being touched or triggered. There will be movement, however subtle, as subsequent layers are exposed. Personal issues will always touch and connect in other people too, echoing within their structures and unearthing new dimensions of what begins to take shape as a more archetypal aspect of culture reflected in we-space. As small groups report back within the larger space, and notice synchronous themes arising, people may begin to sense the systemic work awaiting those collectives prepared to commit to deep work on behalf of others (which I will describe further below).

The Transformation of Self

We are learning to embody higher consciousness through presencing ourselves, each other and the space in-between, becoming more transparent vessels for a higher frequency of life. One effect of this at the level of the individual is "to release bound emotional pain from the body, energy system and causal level of consciousness" (Blackstone 2013). We are vessels for unresolved residue from the past and, because of its crystallization within us, may tend to take on a false sense of individual ownership of this. That which is being worked through us, at the causal level of Soul, is not (I believe) exclusively 'ours.' The healing movements witnessed through we-space are embedded aspects within larger fields of healing. As practitioners we are tapping into unlimited realms of potential and cannot claim that the work of 'our' we-space is separate from the wider field, nor that our wounding is just our own, just as we cannot know the whole extent of what we construe as "healing work." Healing is a side effect of a larger movement in human potential, one that at a societal level is characterized by crisis, inherited trans-generational trauma and cultural pathologies – themselves symptoms of a larger developmental and evolutionary canvas.

Witnessing practice leads people to dis-identify exclusively from immediate experience and can undermine the conditioned ways we tend to re-present the world inside us, and therefore outside ourselves too. I may, for instance, observe you arising in my sphere of reality at one level while I am interpreting this arising as something apparently separate from myself, and while – simultaneously at another level – my awareness penetrates through these conditioned mechanisms and I am confronted in the act of interpretation. Thus we are learning to disrupt our templates of reality (our received notions of what is 'real'), to leverage our awakened potential, to wake up "from the view of reality that [we] know[,] into a new way of being aware of the world" (Hübl, 2011). Such awareness feels to me generative of new worlds, as I learn to embody insight into – and take responsibility for – how I re-present life. In relational space practitioners explore boundaries between seen and seer, witnessing a heightened sense of transpersonal connection. This can seed a radical shift in their locus of awareness and prompt insight into a less referential version of the self; a version that is less bounded, discrete and autonomous and more a flexible self-process where, "our identification with the localized self diminishes and a broader and more generative sense of self begins to arise" (Senge, Scharmer, Jaworski & Flowers 2005, p. 100). Francisco Varela speaks of:

> A constant reframing of yourself into what seems to be more real in each emerging moment... the paradox of being more real means to be much more virtual and therefore less substantial and less determined... [We are] letting the virtuality or the fragility of the self manifest itself. (as cited in Senge et al. 2005, p. 100-101)

We are also healing the culturally conditioned perceptual reflex whereby we tend to perceive mutually exclusive opposites rather than complementarities or even integral wholes. Through witnessing practice we may find ourselves "connecting with a deeper reality in which all distinct or separate things are aspects of the unnamable, in relationship" (Busby 2012a, para. 3).

Intelligence and Transmission

As we change and become present to more of each other and to the inner landscapes of the we-space, we are able to embrace more depth of field, like a camera with capacity for stronger resolution. We pick up more 'pixels' or particles where before none were discernible. We tend to develop a vibrational register that sensitizes us to the contrast between someone skilled in being and speaking from or inside this field experience and someone who instead is talking about it – with less aliveness and concision. We notice immediately when language starts to be used by the unhealthy aspects of the egoic mind rather than the deeper presence of connection, and may even feel the precise instant of disconnect. When participants are encouraged to reflect this transparently then the dialogues that unfold through attunement in the exercises become vehicles for an alive form of creative intelligence that is becoming more aware of itself through the space. Such dialogues may take on their own energy and purpose and direction, independently of any one person's position. They become containers for enhanced multiple perspectives. We who are participating may experience ourselves as more conscious channels for the intelligence seeking expression through us. As we deepen inquiry through we-space we are enabled to serve this intelligence more effectively and with much less personal investment in – and identification with – whatever is being spoken or shared individually.

The premise here is that there is more inner information available to us through subtle channels than we normally allow. When we do learn to allow it by cultivating a deeper sensitivity within ourselves to the informational fields in which we participate then our access deepens. The content of this information and the process by which it is brought forth seems to be transformative in its effect. When we allow our attunement and feedback practices to become ever more informed by subtle content then there is a felt intensification of the field, and the impact on us of the information that becomes available is also perceived to increase. Its impact is sometimes referred to as evolutionary in that it awakens people to their next steps in terms of evolutionary unfoldment, facilitating the emergence of higher-level human capacities and sensitivities. For instance we learn to discern the vibration of inner information that is suggestive of innovation, sometimes framed as 'future-based': arising in us 'as if from the future.' Thomas Hübl reminds us that this is not the future that we think of as tomorrow but rather that which is available to us as the highest potential – enfolded and available within the present – as a result of the embodied presence that we cultivate:

> The future… is that which is calling to us to bring itself forth into existence. The Creative Future is a desire, an urge from the Source to give birth to creative new potentials and it requires us to tap into this urge, follow its movements, and bring it to life on Earth. It is Us and We are It. (Dierkes, 2011)

The outcomes of our we-space work often include new projects, partnerships and creative forms of collaboration, as we learn to embody the future together. We are doing much more than accessing information about what the future might be and are instead becoming living emergent expressions of this future, portals for evolutionary unfoldment. We are not 'getting visions of the future' but are becoming agents of it, now.

If, in relational space, participants allow themselves to be guided by the subtle dimensions of life then they are opening to what is more original, essential and causal, rather than speaking from concepts that arose in the past. The field from which the content of communication is arising vibrates within people as listener-receptors and its vibration is often distinct and discernible. There is more direct communication from higher dimensions of consciousness and more felt resonance with it than in habitual relational space. This resonant vibrational quality we call transmission. In small-group exercises participants can learn to listen for more sustained or higher transmission, and can then validate those qualities of relational spaces that favor it. To dialogue in relational space that optimizes the quality of transmission, and to call each other whenever we leave it (inquiring into the inner structures that prompted our departure) is to intensify inter-subjective space, to amplify access to the informational realms, and to become more permeable to higher frequencies of consciousness.[2]

Primary Knowing and Essence

As the practices described here develop, those qualities of attention that render relational space most translucent are conducive to insight, and induce healing, become more apparent. We may expect our quality of presence and of our interventions to be non-invasive, appreciative and inviting. Increasingly available to many practitioners is a deeper quality of agenda-less attention and essential presence that is (more) empty of any subtle therapeutic intent. In time, some participants are more enabled to affirm to each other "the reality of the quality of the unfolding experience" (Schmidt 2006, p.110). To the extent that most of us usually fail in this stance, we are confronted with the unconscious strategic agenda that underpin most of our social interaction. This is why in the exercises I encourage people to invite a slowing-down of attention and intervention, so that resonance with the subtle realms is heightened and the feeling-sense may be relieved of the burden of any driven restlessness and unconscious intent to change something or someone. Slowness leads to more silence, which invites more slowness and more opening, so that we are even further relieved and educated, "the more we are present and the more fully we are experiencing and being our essential presence, the more we will experience things slowing down" (Almaas 2008, p.5). Johannes Schmidt notes that: "the reciprocity of field information and its somatic, emotional, and cognitive resonance within us seems to be uncharted territory" (Schmidt 2006, p.28). To begin to navigate there slowly, through an embodied inner compass, can lead, according to Henri Bortoft, to "a sense of the generative process underlying present reality... encountering the authentic whole" (as cited in Senge et al. 2005, p.48).

An unfolding experience of 'the whole' is a feature of these practices, which I find hard to articulate. Some people gain insight

---

2. Parts of this paragraph and those preceding it in this section are derived from Busby (2012b).

through their witnessing to the conditioned nature of perception and, through more agenda-less attention, coming to know more directly and transparently. Perhaps this is 'primary knowing' which, according to Eleanor Rosch, arises through perception of:

> Interconnected wholes, rather than isolated contingent parts, and by means of timeless, direct presentation... Such knowing is open rather than determinate, and a sense of unconditional value, rather than conditional usefulness, is an inherent part of the act of knowing itself. (as cited in Senge et al. 2005, p.99)

She also speaks of allowing perception to arise from the whole field; "primary knowing is possible because mind and world are aspects of the same underlying field," and equates this with the field knowing itself (as cited in Senge et al. 2005, p.99). My understanding and experience is that this is a feature of the essential presence of higher consciousness, whereby we consent to embody more of our multidimensionality. I find the practices facilitate a more direct experience of the uniqueness of phenomena arising and a deepening capacity to tune-into what lies beyond. Experience in some of the groups so far points to some practitioners sensing and gaining insight into complex hidden layering beneath surface phenomena, discovering what it means to shift from symptom to essence, to a more essential aspect of consciousness, in ever-deepening cycles. Tasting this, it seems hard to completely accept or collude in the same separateness again; life is no longer a phenomenon of separateness. I believe we are learning to create spaces that can hold energy, hold movement and life, in dynamic ways – learning to become more essential and to embody relational space rather than holding it.

Systemic Constellational Process

In the groups, we practice slowing further through another variant of this work, seeking to explore through other channels the healing movements that higher consciousness makes available. One exercise integrates the witnessing principles and systemic phenomenological inquiry, pursuing a process-oriented refinement of Systemic Constellation work (in its family and organizational forms) that I have distilled. We use systemic principles to inquire into subtle space through heightened somatic awareness.

Participants may each explore a personal topic, question or issue where, taking turns as issue-holder, they do not disclose the content or theme of their inquiry to other small-group members. The theme should have the quality of an 'underlying thread' running through their life – something which to the issue-holder seems to be of evolutionary intent, manifesting through symptoms, behaviors, attitudes or persistent surface issues as if wanting her or his attention. The hypothesis here is that the thread underpins people's more overt issues or questions and is not something that could be articulated. It tends to remain in background awareness and is hard to pin down, often giving rise to movements in life that are cyclical or repeating. Given its unspecific nature, participants are asked to focus phenomenologically on the relational field between people who stand and represent different aspects of the issue-holder's inquiry (as in a Constellation) rather than on the content of his or her theme. Life-themes with heightened resonance may include, for instance, 'perceived impediments to my unfoldment', 'my experience of soul', 'the nature of personal and transpersonal intent', and so on.

As issue-holder within a field of inquiry, I will ask my two or three partners to stand for (represent) unknown aspects of my theme. I will set up the field by intuitively positioning the others while staying attuned to the theme in me. The ensuing inquiry process unfolds slowly through inner listening and mutual witnessing which, with systemic somatic principles, give rise to intuitive movements, emotion or insight within and between each representative. Whatever arises may become more acute as I intentionally refrain from any attempt at understanding, resolution or closure. Instead, restraint, heightened awareness and a refined witnessing capacity all amplify the translucent nature of the field. As is customary in Constellation work, we attend to phenomena arising through bi-directional awareness, yet here – as issue-holder – I will forgo any facilitation of my own issue. Rather I will encourage sustained attention and be as interested in the nature of my own personal unfolding intent and impulses as I am in any external movement. The exercise is a marvelous mirror for those structures in each of us that tend to speed up, manipulate or step over insights or phenomena by way of compensation for discomfort. Schmidt writes of learning to observe "the unfolding of an autonomic process" (2006, p.110), reminding us that:

> Systemic implies that we see what is not obvious, reckon with interconnections that are not explicit, and reach beyond the immediate experience of things. We learn to discern what is not being told, what is not... conspicuous at first sight, but to look at situations in terms of interconnected realities and effects rather than linear, one dimensional cause-effect chains. (Schmidt 2006, p.132)

The structures uncovered through these exercises and the healing movements that unfold may be replicated in the larger collective too, and be expressed there through large-group process that can suddenly erupt. Phenomenological systemic process-work surfaces deeper cultural and archetypal shadow structures, to which we bring the same sensitivities and practices cultivated in small-group exercises. The unknown multi-layered dimensions that lay beneath surface issues and symptoms of trauma may be more elusive here. In a group, with intensified presence, movements will arise and there may be a sense of shifting disintegration in cultural structures, release, and opening. There is much that can heal, and Thomas Hübl's invitation is stark:

> Humanity is literally crying out for new developments that enable us to work through our individual and cultural traumas. If we do not succeed in this, the traumas that have not been integrated will force us to repeat the corresponding traumatic experiences again and again. This principle applies to the further development of the world as well as to the individual journey of healing. (Hübl, 2015)

Towards Embodiment

I believe that systemic phenomenological inquiry can mirror our varying capacity to embody life and be incarnate – to allow the light of higher consciousness to permeate through those who participate in it to the degree that their somatic sense of internal depth becomes their ground in life. Through the practices described here, participants can learn to presence themselves and each other wherever someone may tend to disconnect from the stream of consciousness or from life around them. When witnessing disconnection we are inquiring into those layered structures that are next available for awareness. I will only be able to include everything within my inner reality without dissociation to the extent that my awareness and presence are integrated. Referring to 'radical inclusion,' Thomas writes that in developing higher levels of coherence within ourselves, "we are able to include everything within our inner reality, and may even experience ourselves as everything. Then we learn to participate in life as a constant creative process. We speak from within life rather than about it" (Hübl 2013).

Most of us have learned to favor and embody more fully some aspects of ourselves – of the body and of the emotional palette for instance – than we have of others. The bi-directional awareness exercises will challenge and stretch me here. I will gain insight to my tendency to see and feel:

> apparent polarities or contradiction whenever remaining on the surface of things. If I bring awareness to my dependency upon surface, to the play of symbols there and to the sense of security this affords me, then I am enabled more vulnerably to experience more wholly. (Busby, 2012a)

For those of us on a journey towards fuller embodiment, we-space relational work is becoming more available, edgier and, I believe, effective.

> How can I practice, [through relational work] creating a space that can hold the energy; to have a strong enough structure – like an anchoring in my body – an emotional structure, a mental structure, that can hold movement in a [relational space], in a dynamic way?" (Hübl 2014b)

This is a radical inquiry: its implications are far-reaching in evolutionary terms. Each iteration of it – each of the exercises to which I have referred – will reflect the incarnational heights to which many of us aspire and the terrain stretching in front of us. We keep walking, held within a more immense we-space than we can ever know. "The deeper [we] embody, the more aliveness [we] experience" (McNamara 2012).

The Emerging Potential of the Practices

What is the unfolding transformational potential of the practices? My experience leading or co-leading the groups and gatherings, and of the container for this work, is that the vibrational potential of we-space becomes ever-stronger than the pull of the personality. There is an acceleration in consciousness; more people are feeling called into the field. The work is spilling into more organizational arenas, where some people and places are beginning to enact future-based governance and leadership, and starting to stretch their innovation capacity. Many of us engaged in these practices are learning to ground and stabilize in higher dimensions of consciousness, to integrate more inner and outer awareness – to develop higher-order integrative perceptual skills. We are deepening subtle we-space capacity, "tracking and directing the energy of a group or a whole system" (Francis, 2005) and we are becoming awareness that can be bigger than a collective dynamic: an urgent evolutionary imperative. As practitioners we are learning to bring light and movement to all those dimensions of ourselves where we hold back from a fuller expression of life while, at the same time, becoming more aware of the one body – of source, of life. My experience is of awakening to higher unified levels of consciousness, consciousness that can contain more, that is more world-aware and Kosmocentric. I propose that there are shifts in the level at which life is embodied in more of the human collective, as the crises and dilemmas that humankind faces become acute.

I believe to consent to more consciousness is to choose to transform structures of being, for oneself and all others, through awareness, rather than to have to induce change through crisis and circumstance. Choosing this entails a constant clearing and polishing of our individual and collective vessels which thereby become increasingly synchronized, and through which healing movements arise. Perhaps this is less about awakening and more about responding to a call to higher collective responsibility. To listen to this call is to learn to cultivate relationship to what is consciously unknown, to allow that to move and become ever more embodied through us and our practices.

Join us in deepening our inquiry, becoming a clearer we-space for an ever-higher frequency of life.

Author Bio

Stephen Busby has a coaching, consulting and healing practice and has been serving higher human potential and purpose for over thirty years. Born in England, he is based at the Findhorn Foundation Community, where he also served as Director of Studies. He trained in systemic constellation work with the UK-based Nowhere Foundation and pursued a path of higher evolutionary potential with Thomas Hübl at the Academy of Inner Science in Germany. Stephen has distilled new applications of phenomenological systemic methodologies to whole-systems healing in collective fields, from which his distinctive we-space practices have evolved. His several careers in education and consultancy have spanned the corporate world, transnational public service institutions and not-for-profit organizations in Europe, Africa, Asia and North America. More on the background to Stephen's 'embodying higher consciousness' and we-space work is at: www. stephenbusby.com

References

Almaas, A.H. (2008). The Unfolding Now. Boston, MA: Shambhala.

Blackstone, J. (2008). The Enlightenment Process. St. Paul, MN: Paragon House.

Blackstone, J. (2011). The Intimate Self. Boulder, CO: Sounds True. Retrieved from http://realizationcenter.com/excerpt.htm

Blackstone, J. (2013). Spiritual Psychotherapy (Subtle Self Work). Retrieved from http://www.realizationcenter.com/spiritual.htm

Busby, S. (2012a). Beyond the Constellation Room: Aspects of a systemic consciousness and its potential impact on our lives at the level of self and society. The Knowing Field, 19, pps. 63-64.

Busby, S. (2012b). An Experiment in Downloading the Future: Reflections on the inner science of the Vision Lab process. In: J.C. Wehnelt & P.H. Novak (Eds.), Soul-food for the Future: Tools for the New We (pp.10-25). Retrieved from http://www.siebensinne.net/sieben-sinne/ressourcen/

Dierkes, C. (2011). The Spiritual Scope of Thomas Hübl, Section #2, paragraph 11. Retrieved from http://www.beamsandstruts.com/essays/item/399-thomas

Ehrhardt, K. (2012). Living Body Principles. The Psychotherapist, 52, pps.15-17.

Emmons, D. (2013). Feeling One's Way Forward. 4.24.13 Retrieved from http://befriendinglife.com/2013/04/24/what-to-do/

Francis, T. (2005). Working with the Field. British Gestalt Journal 14:1, 26T33, p.5, para. 5

Greendyk, R. (2014). Secrets of Developing Energetic Sensitivity, Part III. Retrieved from http://lightlabcreations.com/wisdom/spirituality/secrets-of-developing-energetic-sensitivity-avoiding-the-pitfalls-of-power-part-i

Hübl, T. (2011). Spiritual Competence: Ethical Premises for Spiritual Work, Section 9, paragraph 2. Retrieved from http://www.thomashuebl.com/en/approach-methods/spiritual-competence.html

Hübl, T. (2013). A Course in Mystical Principles (Published online description). Retrieved 12.20.13 from http://online.thomashuebl.com/

Hübl, T. (2014a). Posting on Thomas Hübl's page, Facebook. 7.6.14.

Hübl, T. (2014b). There is no Relationship. Celebrate Life Festival. 8.2.2014. Retrieved from https://www.youtube.com/watch?v=ejXxjhtA8Pc&feature=youtu.be

Hübl, T. (2015). Newsletter, February 2015, Section 1. Retrieved from http://www.thomashuebl.com/en/news/579.html

Kinney, D. (2014). Frontiers of Knowledge: Scientific and Spiritual Sources for a New Era. Bloomington, IN: AuthorHouse.

Licata, M. (2014). The Playground of Love. 7.29.14. Retrieved from http://alovinghealingspace.blogspot.co.uk

McNamara, R. (2012) The Three Facets of Embodiment, Integral Post. 7.23.12. Retrieved from https://www.integrallife.com/integral-post/three-facets-embodiment

Schmidt, J. (2006). Inner Navigation: Trauma Healing and Constellational Process Work. Hamburg, Germany: Hamburg Aptitude Academy.

Senge, P., Scharmer, C.O., Jaworski, J., Flowers, B.S. (2005). Presence: Exploring Profound Change in People, Organizations and Society. London, UK: Nicholas Brealey Publishing.

CHAPTER 3

A We-Space Process Ecology:

Navigating the Paradox of Injunction and
Method-Free Process Facilitation – a Praxis
Report.

Anne Caspari & Mushin Schilling

"One must still have chaos in oneself to be able to give birth to a dancing star."
– Friedrich Nietzsche, Thus Spoke Zarathustra.

Prelude

Due to the controversial material and interpretation we give here
we, the authors of this chapter, want to state clearly and up front that
everything we say comes from our own action, research and numerous
in depth conversations with people experimenting in this field. We
would even go so far as to say that the nature of what we were and
are experimenting with does not lend itself to objectivity without
losing what we found to be the most valuable insights our material and
interpretation offers: to participate in the birth of dancing stars out
of the chaos that lives inside us. Our intuition is that what we offer is
synchronous with and may help some of us to psychologically process
the environmental and societal chaos that besieges humanity.

Imagine...

You find yourself in an ancient forest with islands of ancient
trees and patches of younger ones, with clearings and marshes, and
everything else that lives in a natural environment untouched by
human social life. All beings participate according to their inborn
nature. There is elegant complexity, evolved over a long period of

time and through adaptive self-organization. There is a thriving diversification with the emergence of new forms, agents and processes.

Now imagine yourself in a circle of people, say 10 or 15, intending to bring forth something similar, inspired by nature and future possibilities. They came to discover what the real nature of participation is and what new types of ideas would emerge naturally among them. Now how would they go about designing the process? Can it be designed at all? How would they go about creating a supportive process structure that could orchestrate a coherence with multiple flows of understanding in a group of diverse people, substituting for the role of time that makes a grown forest so awe inspiring and generative?

Properties such as self-organization, coherence and structural elegance, as it is often found in nature, are at the root of *emergence*[1] and cannot be designed in our view. They evolve over time with the participation of all elements. An ancient jungle can well be described as being in an *authentically chaordic*[2] process in a continually emergent, dynamic whole: everything adds to its life and nothing is wasted. If, following our guiding metaphor, we look at group inquiries in this context then this would mean that some form of "chaos" has to be a necessary and intrinsic part of the process in order to arrive at such a natural and generative way of being.

For reasons that will become clear in the course of this chapter, it seems that in the field of researchers of this process there is little awareness of "chaos" being an intrinsic requirement of a process that aims to reach a truly "natural order." Rather all facilitators we have seen so far are trying to *make it happen*, trying to maneuver group-members into a natural participation in a chaordic field. This is often painful as we will see also, with little resemblance of the elegance as it unfolds in our forest.

The problem with intrinsic chaos and how to deal with it is not new [3](Peck 1978). Also, there are quite a few tools and approaches that are designed to harvest the fruits of collective processes (Bohm 1996,

---

1. Emergence is latin for appearing "arising" or "arising out of" is the spontaneous coming into being of new characteristics or structures of a system out of the inter-play of its elements.

2. The term chaordic refers to a *system* of organization that blends characteristics of *chaos* and *order*. It was coined by *Dee Hock*, founder and former CEO of the *VISA* credit card association. We use it to describe the way nature is organized, in particular, living *organisms* and the *evolutionary* process by which they arise.

3. Scott Peck, the grandfather of this process, called this phase chaos in his writings. We have added authentic to it because the chaos only starts to appear after the participants become more authentic.

Senge et al. 2004; Brown 2005, Scharmer 2007, Baeck & Titchen Beeth 2012, etc). In the last few years there has been an increasing interest in the much vaunted 'we-space' practices[4], which could be said to generally aim for what we describe as taking place within the *authentically chaordic phase*. However, despite the many efforts around such collective processes, when it comes to actual phenomenological research into the more hidden and challenging aspects of the relational dynamics in connection with novelty and real emergence in group life, there remain many unanswered questions.

We, the authors of this chapter, have been involved in the application of meta-theories in the field of transformative collective processes and their emergent *action logics*[5] to gain new insight and to finding new types of processes and outcomes – for "prototyping." Our action research focused mostly on the basic phenomenology of such processes in individuals and groups, including phase and pattern recognition in relation to mapping adaptive pushback, resistances to change and methods for correcting it[6]. With the backdrop of this research and experience[7], we describe in this chapter the focal points in our research and reflect on this learning. The pervasive generative processes in an un-spoilt Urwald[8] intrigue us; we have been especially interested in working with group processes that involve minimal to no facilitation or priming.[9]

---

4. For instance the works of *Andrew Venezia (2013); Dustin DiPerna (2014); Thomas Hübl (2011); Terry Patten (2013)*

5. Cook-Greuter, S. (2002): A detailed description of the development of nine action logics in the leadership development framework: adapted from ego development theory. http://www.cook-greuter.com/

6. see for example: https://mindshiftintegral.wordpress.com/working-with-resistance/

7. We have also incorporated the experience that Mushin has had in his experiments between 2002 and 2005 in his Serenity Center in the Czech Republic.

8. Urwald: primeval forest. Anne's 1995 final thesis in environmental planning on natural forest ecology argued for turning German standards for nature conservation on their head by not just protecting small static bits of rare forests, but large woodlands including their natural processes. The thesis project was implemented in 1998 and is now a protected Urwald.

9. Priming: in this context explicit or implicit, conscious or unconscious directing of a process towards a desired result by words, ritual, exercise or other method.

Priming – No-Priming

As part of our action research, we also participated in three experiments at the Alderlore Insight Center (AIC) run by Bonnitta Roy in Torrington, Connecticut. While the first of these experiments at the AIC[10] was both primed and facilitated, the last two were run deliberately with neither priming nor facilitation, which was an integral part of what we have come to call *minimal elegant process design*. Both no-facilitation and no-priming are concepts that are central in our thinking about this phenomenon. Usually group processes are *directed* by specific practices and methods using specific rules geared to come to particular results. This, for us, differs from the unfolding of a complex process interaction, mediated by a process of *self-organization* (Ashby 1947, Maturana & Varela 1980, Prigogine & Stengers, 1984)

Without chaos, in our view there is no real emergence and authentic participation remains elusive. At the very best, in our view, you get domesticated participation; domesticated in the sense that it is geared towards getting *insights into the known,* whereas we are of the mindset that in authentic participation there is a high probability for an *emergence of what we do not yet know.* Thus, if someone facilitates or mediates a group process by using direct or indirect interventions based on some form of design principles, in our view the outcome is filtered by the priming and procedures used. In a way, it is "landscaped."

Consequently, it became clear to us why even integral priming coming from the developmental level called Turquoise[11], which was attempted by some participants during the second AIC experiment, interfered with authentic emergence (more on the reason for this below). We were curious what novelty and insights we would be able to come up with together, given that there was ample diversity of conviction, expertise and experience in the room. Our implicit assumption was that the absence of any given leading question, any specific facilitation method, or any approved approach to we-space practice would set us free from outcomes that then would be inevitably colored and informed by that approach or method. What came as a surprise for us is that our minimum elegant structures were not welcomed. Some participants actually demanded more structure or

---

10. One of these experiments, done in November 2013 was explicitly conducted with people who had extensive backgrounds and diverse practices of an integral nature. 16 participants took part in this 5-day exploration.

11. In Clare W. Graves' Spiral dynamics model; the equivalent in Susan Cook-Greuter's developmental model is construct-aware, and in Bill Torbert's remodeling of Jane Loevinger's developmental model, it is the level of the alchemist. In Robert Kegan's 5 stage developmental model it is the fifth stage.

even pushed for their respective favorite facilitation methods, tools and ways to get us all through the process. However, a noticeable phenomenon in the room was, that as long as these moves came from a space of; trying to fill in gaps ('healing'), avoid what was going on ('escape') or push for a certain method ('power'), they were all rejected by the other people in the room[12]. It led to people refusing to adopt anyone else's conviction, method, or priming. No matter how high the goal, all facilitation attempts simply prolonged the duration of the authentic chaos phase. This includes also other kinds of unintended implicit priming. For example, some people in the larger group had previously worked with each other in other contexts and or shared particular concepts. Simply labeling phases, states and phenomena as, for instance, "the bottom of the U" or "causal", "source", "circle being", created priming, expectations and in some cases even fallacies and traps. In hindsight we observed that it actually activated pushback and shadow and thus created *more chaos*. We found that a good way to avoid turning the naming of phases, states and arising phenomena into something negative is instead to surf the paradoxes created by this naming activity, and stay aware of the priming power of concepts while using labels.

Enter the Unknown

When we did our second experiment at the AIC, we, the core crew, did not set it up to be chaotic even though we did aim for no facilitation and no priming. As the core group, we found ourselves in the midst of it, which was unexpected to us and most participants, since all of them were highly trained individuals from different schools of thought and therapy. In the beginning of the first day, all of us participants were still quite polite. This did not last long because not having a facilitator, and in the absence of formal priming, every utterance, including strategic silences, turned into grist for the mill. When someone suggested, for instance, that we do a formal round of introductions, things became chaotic as we were already on the brink of a deeper authenticity, and formal introductions simply did not cut it. So we started the chaotic meandering through the authentic material that every participant brought to bear on the situation. Any attempt to skillfully facilitate it away failed and thus just added to the chaos. The atmosphere became more real as participants dropped polite forms of discourse and aspects

---

12. For a more comprehensive list of these type of moves see the chapter on 'Relational Dynamics in the Chaordic Phase'

of their learnt roles, moving closer to what really moved them. What we observed[13] was, the more painful the chaos felt, the more strategies were sought to get away from it, which only deepened it. Any attempt to give the process a direction was thwarted, sometimes immediately, sometimes after a few minutes of "let's try this." At that time, in that space, there appeared[14] to be no way out of the chaos at this point, so we had to stay in what was coming up and sit it out. It was *only in hindsight* that it became clear to us as core group how important this phase of authentic chaos really is, at the time it was simply difficult for us. What also dawned on us was that *any kind of priming and facilitation leads to an outcome of a different nature,* outcomes that are already on the map and possibly much desired for and helpful in particular situations but not new and unmapped, not *chaordic.*

The Presence and Absence of the Social Self

We have found that a group of human beings can gain food for mind, soul and heart, for their organizations and other social contexts in which they are embedded without any guidance, facilitation, and priming. To better understand why this is so let us introduce the way we use the concept of the "*social self*[15]" We regard the social self as that realm of our human psyche where our strategies, tactics, roles, social life and culture reside; all the patterns that we learnt symbiotically and explicitly, and which help us survive and thrive in our social contexts. In our view, it is *not* the source of, for instance, creativity, insight, care, play and love, or fear, panic and hate. Rather, it *mediates* all the original emotive material that comes from the deeper reaches of our individual

---

13. We wanted to stress the fact that the phenomena we observed in the room in real time came as a surprise for us (authors and core team). Our assumptions were almost in the opposite direction. We did not design this process to lead to chaos nor did we expect it. Nor could we call this out in the process itself: any injunction in the direction of "let's all be open to chaos, let's hold this" would have created just more pushback.

14. This is, again, clearly our interpretation of what we observed in that space and in our own phenomenology. We did also experience a direct correlation between the willingness to stay and sit it out and the amount of "skin in the game", of a real interest in both process and outcome. We are, of course, open to different interpretations.

15. We prefer this much above the more popular term "ego" with all its psychological and social baggage. However, as far as we are concerned there is much similarity to that term and what it means in a more practical sense. The more traditional use of the term was coined by George Herbert Mead in 1901; see: https://goo.gl/oU9e8u

and collective "psychosphere[16]." Thus, to our thinking, all facilitation and priming originates with the social self and its regulatory functions. Authentic chaos, then, is what you get once the social self's common politeness-filters are absent.

The social self *develops* more or less adequately in social settings by continually adapting to the sociosphere in which it lives, while the generative self *emerges* and *evolves (Roy & Trudel, 2011)*[17]. We take the generative self to be the self that naturally springs to life in a human being. The mediation by the social self of what comes from our generative self has become highly complex due to the steadily increasing complexity of most societies on earth. In the last century the rate of complexification has only been accelerating – so much so that in the near future we may actually *need* artificial intelligence to stay abreast the now exponentially rising wave (Turchin et al. (2006). The participatory process we are talking about, once it has become authentically chaordic, brings great elegance into this complexity, and allows individuals a lucid way of interaction that seems to be in touch with a "simplicity beyond complexity."

Relational Dynamics in the Chaordic Phase

We have analyzed the phenomena that happened in the three most prominent group experiments at the Alderlore Insight Center, and a few others in between. They appear to follow certain recognizable patterns indicative for the different cycles of the process. For example, participants learn to recognize their own coping and escape mechanisms, which occur and feed into the authentic chaos phase – learning not to take themselves too seriously when in that phase. Alternatively, they might distinguish between coherence and cohesion[18], which have distinctly different outcomes and learn to

---

16. Psychosphere (aka Noosphere); the sphere of human consciousness. Akin to its sister the biosphere, full of images, audible 'objects' aka thoughts, ideas, dreams, symbols, fantasies and so on. We didn't want to use the term collective (un-)consciousness because the associations with this term are psychological and the psychosphere encompasses everything touched by human views however (un-)conscious they may be.

17. Roy & Trudel (2011) give a helpful and detailed disambiguation of the different properties of generative processes, such as development, evolution, emergence and autopoiesis

18. The way we use these two words here needs some elucidation: By coherence cycles we mean people, matters, ideas, ways of thinking organically and in a self-organized fashion "stick together"; by cohesion we mean the group practices that keep people within social confines of a group where naturally there is a "with us" and a

harvest these depending on the purpose of the group process. In addition, taking a closer look at the shadow side of these patterns has revealed some potent traps even for the more experienced facilitator. For these reasons, we portray the different phases of the process in more detail.

In our experiments, and from what we learnt from earlier group processes, groups cycled through four phases and several patterns within these phases. An initial inventory is as follows:

- Politeness: Entry phase
- Authentic chaos: often starting with rebellion against the limits of politeness
  a. Rebellion
  b. Rally around my flag
  c. Organize it
  d. Philosophy
  e. Q&A games
  f. Politics
  g. Self-realization games
- Silence
- Authentic Chaord: The Clarities
- Emergence

Endothermic Process[19]: Burning out Relational Dynamics

From polite beginnings, where every difference is equalized and anything that could cause conflict is immediately down-regulated, warded off, neutered, stereotyped, or corrected, to name but a few of the tactics used to keep everyone in a civil space, the participatory process moves into chaos relatively quickly, certainly once participants in a group with diverse backgrounds start to express themselves more authentically, often at first as a kind of rebellion against polite statements.

"not part of us" or even "against us."

19. Endothermia is Greek for "inner heat"; endo- "inner" and thermia, "heat."

In the beginning of the chaos phase, resulting from un-facilitated authenticity, (hence *authentic* chaos), people often try to regain the polite status quo by; an introduction round, by making commonplace remarks by pointing out that "that is not such a big difference", by offering good advice, by trying to "heal" or "fix" things, and similar interventions. These only deepen the chaos because by now, as people are trying out more authentic views and utterances, they resist being told that this is "not a big difference" or by "I can really understand how that hurt you." Consequently, there might be a call for authority to come fix the situation, which becomes more and more uncomfortable, or alternatively by someone trying to take the lead. We have come to call this cycle, Rally around my flag! A few variants of this cycle are patterned around alliances, "let's get together" under my or your leadership, demanding the organizers of the gathering to "take the lead!" and so forth. Sometimes people try to get together to organize it. You may see a bigger circle fall apart for periods, some participants trying to find a form in which to help or coerce others to "do it our way." This breaks down when, again, it meets rebellion or other forms of refusal to let someone or a group within the group take control of the process.

Sometimes we observed debates over the right philosophy to apply to the process. Part of these exchanges may be comments and meta-comments about the process or stages of the process. They are rarely self-reflective in the sense of "what I'm trying to do here is…"; but even that, when it happens, is grist for the authentically chaotic mill because essentially all these endeavors are geared to *stop the chaos* from running its course[20]. Another pattern may appear here when two or three people keep up a Q&A game by tossing each other the communicative ball by asking questions that have obvious answers or keep the conversation between them going for longer periods of time. Sooner or later someone will try to get in a word or two, calling this little "elite" on their content or form, or use any of the numerous social politics humans have developed to "get something done" or to "arrive at something that makes sense" or to stop us all from "turning in circles" so that finally we can "get somewhere."

In groups where participants are involved in some kind of work on themselves the self-realization game may appear. Someone may say, "I'm so thankful for this group as I came to learn…" or "listening to some of you I come to realize that…" This can also take some more funny forms where people try to make fun of themselves and or

---

20. If we are allowed a socio-psychological comment here: there is a conviction in civilized humanity, it seems, that if we're really authentic than "nothing good can come of this!" It seems to belong to a deep-seated collective fear of the "wild".

others. Attempts to 'heal and fix' can also be observed in the context of this when someone offers a deep authentic hurt or pain and it is immediately placed in a spiritual, therapeutic or philosophical context.

As our readers may imagine going through authentic chaos hurts, sometimes deeply, regardless of a participant's developmental stage[21]. Within this chaos, all ways to "come to grips with the situation" and lead to a desired result surface and are unmasked as just another social strategy or tactic to down-regulate socially uncomfortable feelings (Panksepp, 2005). Eventually every such maneuver only leads the group deeper into authentic chaos. At some point all attempts at priming, facilitating or directing the process have "burnt out." It becomes obvious that one cannot make emergence happen.

We found that the minimal elegant design of this process is simply resisting all temptations to intervene in order to balance, lead, integrate or catalyze. Interventions do happen, but they are self-organized and self-organizing, arising from the process itself. Anything else can only lead to a paradox à la Watzlawick[22], "Be spontaneous! Be authentic! Come from source! Stay in the causal! Find deeper meaning!" In our process, none of the above ways and means sketched work, which becomes obvious, and finally all participants gave up trying to direct the process. One could say that a sense of "capitulation" settles upon all. Emptiness. Silence, which may at first feel gloomy and has the taste of failure. Then the surprise: tangible clarity sets in.

All Clear

We call the internal state that participants now fall into *sensory clarity*. It does not obliterate unique individuality in any sense, but the social self has certainly stepped back. Nevertheless, one's boundaries are no longer experienced as limits: we-being, we-fullness, we-space – this experience has led to a number of terms centered around "we."

The phenomenon we call sensory clarity does *not* correspond to the "causal" state of consciousness that Ken Wilber described as

---

21. The capacity of participants to handle painful situations like this, as with all aspects of this process, is dependent on the developmental stage of the individual; nevertheless, these capacities must be trained and practiced, regardless of one's level of development.

22. Paul Watzlawick: (1921-2007) Austrian-American philosopher and psychoanalyst has done extensive research into human communication, especially paradoxes. See for example: Pragmatics of Human Communication: A Study of Interactional Patterns, Pathologies and Paradoxes (2011).

awaiting us all at the bottom of the U (Scharmer 2003)[23]. We take this to be a simple confusion of state-qualities. When authentic chaos has removed all filters, masks and maneuvers, what remains is simple and feels utterly natural: sensory clarity. Erroneously labeling this to be causal consciousness arguably makes real emergence at this stage all but impossible, robbing the process of possibilities that would be *really* new, in the sense that they have never before been possible. The causal is, after all, defined as that what according to Wilber, Aurobindo et al., "has always been there," and realizing it is regarded as a great step towards the ultimate goal in that tradition, timeless and changeless non-dual consciousness. Due to all the Integral literature on gross, subtle and causal phenomena, this interpretation focuses the attention on state-qualities and their numinousity, whereas interpreting it as *sensory clarity* directs it towards what comes up first and foremost via the five or six senses without filters.

The Authentic Chaord

Our action research has revealed sensory clarity to be the first phase in a larger unfolding that we have been and continue to explore, and whose minimal elegant interpretation we are working on in an ongoing dialogue with the AIC and other pioneers of the process.

If the group or the action researchers can remain in sensory clarity and let possible contradictions, apparent paradoxes, strangeness, etc. "be whatever they are," a next phase of clarity can unfold which we call *subtle energy/emotional clarity*. This alludes to the participants' capacity or willingness to remain clear in these sometimes quite strong emotional dimensions. If, moreover, the group is diverse enough – meaning that it encompasses more than just one mindset or culture – then a *cultural/identity/intersubjective clarity* can unfold. In this clarity, finally, it is also possible for what we call *conceptual clarity* to become a shared reality. The basic content of this chapter originally emerged from the latter clarity after having sought to understand and model this process into a process view that would not prime further action research but would, rather, provide a minimal elegant structure that could foster further investigation and collaboration among the pioneers of this process (Roy 2015[24], Murray, forthcoming).

---

23. For another description of the states at the bottom of the U see: Jaworski, J. (2013): Source.

24. Roy, B. (2015): Open to Participate. http://alderloreinsightcenter.com/portfolio/cppei/ ; CPPEI collective participatory process for emergent insight

Emergence

Imagine eight people sitting on the grass of a huge garden. They have passed through all the stages of authentic chaos. They have learnt that the chaordic phase of the process is both individual as well as collective; individual in the sense that they have dropped all social self-strategies of choice, of trying to gain any control over what is going to happen next. All of them are effortlessly present, senses and emotions are *clear*. One of the eight mentions something important to him. A few minutes later, another adds something seemingly disjunctive, not fitting from the point of view of a social self, that is; but because the eight aren't responding on that level anymore, what has been said is just another audible object in participatory space, just like the "important issue" before. And as participants utter things significant enough to them it *seems*[25] like a larger intelligence is at work constellating or orchestrating the utterances which half an hour later leads to an important insight for the one that started up this particular cycle within the larger chaord. But not only to him, for now someone else has a seemingly unrelated but important enough insight for her to say, "Holy fuck!" as she's unwrapping some of the communicable part of this insight even more related and unrelated matters fall into place for some participants and a whole series of significant insights ensue. Then silence, a rich space where nobody feels a need to say anything; maybe because the insights all of a sudden create clarity where before things were obscure or because it is a joy to sit with people in the grass, simply present without social selves interfering. In the course of the further afternoon, a few more insights tumble out of the participatory space but also laughing and some larger conceptual clarifications.

The ancient forest, our guiding metaphor, is a good analogy to what happens in a participatory process in its authentically chaordic phase. Nobody is doing anything in particular other than what really moves him or her to "put an audible object in the participatory space,"

---

25. "Seems" because we are not suggesting such an intelligence as a separate entity, a somewhat independent entity as an agent that does the orchestration. Nevertheless some people relate to this intelligence as if it where an other. When Mushin was experimenting with this process calling it "Circles of the Heart", he actually related to this as the "Circle Being." We know of several people pioneering this type of work that use similar terminology, and where they are influenced by New Age like spiritual narratives this work relates to getting to a space where this Being is deified to quite an extent. This comes as no surprise as the phase we call authentically chaordic allows for almost any spiritualized interpretation to be held as "really, really true." See also Murray, T (forthcoming): Contemplative Dialogue Practices: An embodied inquiry into deep interiority, shadow work, and insight.

coming, so it seems to us, directly from the generative self. We hold that one cannot thus access the generative self without having gone through authentic chaos. It is not required to have that happen in one long process if people have enough experience with going through it; but our experience is that even then, a certain amount of authentic chaos is bound to happen as social habits are amazingly strong.

Paradoxical Territory

We have found repeatedly that any attempt to lower the 'internal heat' during the chaos phase takes transformative energy out of group processes, and constitutes a trap that seasoned facilitators frequently find themselves in. The application of theoretical frameworks, like, for example, Scharmer's U-Theory has complemented and enriched the landscape of transformational processes and added the much needed process element to some more static frameworks, such as Wilber's AQAL map. In this, the warning (Korzybski 1958) to not confuse the map with the territory has been heard. However, the next fallacy is just around the corner, taking the experience of an authentic chaos process and turning it into a recipe and program with certain stages and steps for it complete with a facilitator's manual and toolbox.

Following a specific method and set of instructions, that, like an educational trail in an ancient forest, intends to help participants to navigate through collective processes will get certain predictable results. While these might be good outcomes, they are typically reduced and filtered through the given structures. This confusion is easy to fall into, and avoiding it invites practitioners to a constant dance in paradoxical territory. If our view is correct, then to get to the magnificent phase of sensory clarity and its potential emergences, participants have to stumble through a chaordic process, a process that cannot be prescribed in an orderly program with eight neat steps to follow in order to get there. What you get if nevertheless you try are flatland versions of hitherto valid processes that are neither transformative nor authentic.

Senge, Jaworski, Scharmer and Flowers have done a wonderful job of describing such collective chaordic change processes in their own group and in other groups of different composition, size, and topical direction in their book "Presence" (2004). But when it comes to practice, the authors of this chapter have in many instances encountered processes that reduced the U-Process to a shallow *pre*scriptive set of instructions ("Step 4: feel the field; be authentic. Step 5. Find deeper meaning and purpose" etc.) which render such attempts mere caricatures of what led to the original findings as portrayed in the Presence book, leaving participants perplexed and in resistance.

We are aware that we are operating in a field where what we describe is a highly complex process experience hoping to make it possible for new explorers to repeat the experience. We explicitly want to make it a point to stay aware of the "description – prescription – fallacy." And we position ourselves as promoters, maybe even as guardians, but not as facilitators of natural chaordic generative processes. In addition, since there is no outside to this process once started, we fully participate in the dance.

Dancing with Paradox

In closing, we believe that what emerges in a participatory process of the kind we have been describing *includes* authentic chaos and cannot be predicted or foreseen. Any attempt to do so is priming or facilitating it in directions that steer it away from real emergence. Being *authentically chaordic* is experienced as wholesome. It seems that we humans are very able to recognize this way of being regardless of our level of development, just as we can recognize light or darkness however much we have further developed the intricacies of what is visible. Conversely, the *interpretation* of what emerges in the collectively experienced lucidity and how individuals use in their life, does depend on their personal and collective development. Since, in our view, the capacity to allow for authentic chaos grows with every developmental stage, it may be that in earlier stages priming and facilitation are inevitable; further action research is needed to determine if this is actually so. This leads us to venture that several other interpretations of this process have been much too quick to develop means and methods to constrain and restrict authentic chaos, even if done to reliably create a predictable and wonderful we-feeling of some spiritual depth, however beneficial this may otherwise be.

Finally, we hold the intention of supporting participatory collectives to experience the clarities described above, and find or create something really novel to move towards, as a real next step. Being aware of the paradoxical nature of this statement, we are convinced that, with enough maturity to allow this process to unfold in its entirety, this is a next evolutionary stage of self-organization in a collective, group or organization and its emergent action logics.

Author Bios

Anne Caspari is a coach and specialist in change management, for both personal and cultural development & leadership in organizations. She focuses on deep transformative processes in all contexts. With an MSc in Environmental Development from Hannover University, Germany, she draws on two decades of experience with complex systems, adaptive pushback and obstacles to self-organization. This knowledge, combined with more than 15 years of work on adult development and transformation gives her a unique view and experience. She has worked extensively with the application of Integral Theory and Theory U and has compared both maps with the territory of transformation. She has worked on change projects throughout the EU and worldwide and operates currently operates from Basel, Switzerland, working with small enterprises on conscious business. Together with Mushin Schilling, she has been exploring the phenomena regarding collective processes and we-spaces in the past 4 years. They have published articles on their experiences and observation in the German Integral Perspectives paper. www.mindshift-integral.com; Caspari and Schilling are Partners at Entz von Zerssen, Caspari & Partner Coaching & Consulting, www.ezc.partners

Mushin J. Schilling is a consultant and trainer working in the fields of organisational and systems-design, business development and the design and application of governance and management-models. Starting in the 80s with self-development seminars, in the 90s he came to be known for his dynamic seminars. He has been working in Germany, the Netherlands, Japan and led an experimental spiritual community in the Czech Republic until 2008 when he dismantled it in the service of his "participatory turn" away from all traditional, hierarchical ways to personal and social development. In the early 90s he started with a series of non-primed seminars, which later became known as "we-space" processes, that at that time he called "Circles of The Heart" and later "Hieros Gamos." With the co-author of this chapter, he participated in a series of experiments from 2013 to 2015 that turned out to function in a very similar vein as his earlier experiments.

References

Ashby, W. R. (1947). Principles of the self-organizing dynamic system. *Journal of General Psychology* 37: 125   −128.

Baeck, R. & Titchen Beeth, H. (2012). Collective Presencing: A New Human Capacity; and the Circle of Presence: Building the Capacity for Authentic Collective Wisdom. Kosmos Journal, Spring 2012 and Fall 2012.

Bohm, D. (1996). On dialog (L. Nichol, Ed.). New York: Routledge.

Brown, J. (2005): The World Café: Shaping Our Futures through Conversations that Matter, Berrett   -Koehler

Caspari, A., & Schilling, M. (2014): Beziehungsdynamiken, kollektive Transformationsprozesse, "we-space" − ein Vergleich integraler Landkarten und der dazugehörigen Territorien. Integrale Perspektiven, Ausgabe 28, Juni 2014.

Cook-Greuter, S. (2002): A Detailed Description of the Development on Nine Action Logics in the Leadership Development Framework: Adapted from Ego Development Theory. http://www.cook-greuter.com

DiPerna, D. (2014). Streams of Wisdom. Integral Publishing House.

Hock, D. W. (2000): Birth of the Chaordic Age. Berrett-Koehler Publishers; 1st Edition/ 1st Printing edition

Hübl, T. (2011). Transparence: Practice Groups − an adventure in seeing yourself and others more clearly. Germany: Sharing the Presence.

Jaworski, J. (2012). Source: The Inner Path of Knowledge Creation. Berrett-Koehler Publishers.

Kegan, R. (1994). In Over Our Heads: The Mental Demands of Modern Life. Cambridge, MA: Harvard.

Maturana H.R., Varela F.J (1980). "The cognitive process". Autopoiesis and cognition: The realization of the living. Springer Science & Business Media.

Mead, G.H. (1901): The Social Self. Journal of Philosophy, Psychology and Scientific Methods 10, 1913: 374-380;

Murray, T (2015 forthcoming): Contemplative Dialogue Practices: An Embodied Inquiry into Deep Interiority, Shadow Work, and Insight. In: Cohering the Integral We Space: Developing Theory and Practice for Engaging Collective Emergence, Wisdom and Healing in Groups. Olen Gunnlaugson (Ed)

Panksepp, J. (2005). Affective Consciousness: Core emotional feelings in animals and humans. Consciousness and cognition, 14(1), 30-80.

Patten, T. (2013). Enacting an Integral Revolution: How Can We Have Truly Radical Conversations in a Time of Global Crisis? Paper presented at the Integral Theory Conference 2013.

Prigogine, I. and Stengers, I. (1984). Order out of Chaos: Man's new dialogue with nature. Bantam Books

Reams, J., Caspari, A. (2012): Integral Leadership: Generating Space for Emergence through Quality of Presence. Journal für Wirtschaftspsychologie, 3, 2012, Pabst Science Publishers

Roy, B. (2014). CppIE: Collective Participatory Process for Emergent Insight: Catalyzing Insight and Collective Flow in Groups. Available from the author.

Roy, B. (2015): Open to Participate: Collective Participatory Process for Insight, Clarity and Cognitive Flow. Routledge, forthcoming

Roy, B., Trudel J. (2011): Leading the 21st Century: The Conception-Aware, Object-Oriented Organization. Integral Leadership Review, August 2011

Turchin P., Grinin L., Munck V.C.de, Korotayev A. (Ed.)(2006): History and Mathematics: Historical Dynamics and Development of Complex Societies, Moscow: KomKniga

Scharmer, C.O. (2003). Mapping the Integral U: A Conversation between Ken Wilber and Otto

Scharmer, Denver, C.O., 17 September. Dialog on Leadership.

Scharmer, C. O. (2007). Theory U. Leading from the Future as it Emerges. The Social Technology of Presencing. (2007). Cambridge, MA: The Society for Organizational Learning, Inc.)

Scott Peck, M. (1997). The Road Less Traveled and Beyond: Spiritual Growth in an Age of Anxiety. Simon & Schuster.

Senge, P., Scharmer, O., Jaworski, J., & Flowers, B. (2004). Presence: An Exploration of Profound Change in People, Organizations and Societies. Cambridge, MA: Society for Organizational Learning.

Venezia, A. (2013). I, We, All: Intersubjectivity and We Space, Post-Metaphysics, and Human Becoming: An Integral Research Project. Unpublished Masters Thesis. Available at http://newwaysofhumanbeing. com/2013/10/13/finally-my-thesisfinal-project/

Wilber, K. (1995): Sex, Ecology, Spirituality. Shambhala Publications, Boston, Ma.

Wilber, K. (2006). Integral Spirituality. Boston & London: Integral Books.

Chapter 4

In, As, and Towards the Kosmic We

Geoff Fitch

Introduction

This chapter describes the experiences, lessons learned, and essential practices of Causal Leadership communities, a form of integral transformative we-spaces central to the work of Pacific Integral. For over ten years, Pacific Integral has been exploring, facilitating, and researching transformative change in an integral, developmental context through the Generating Transformative Change (GTC) program, its own organization, and other communities of practice it has convened and participated in. While the GTC's structure has evolved over its history, it is currently a 9-month, intensive leadership and personal development program. In this time period we have facilitated and engaged with dozens of different integral collective we-spaces, involving over 200 individuals and over durations ranging from months to several years. The core of this exploration has been the GTC program, which enacts and facilitates a new way of being and relating, which we refer to as Causal Leadership. This chapter describes our intentions, theoretical orientations, experiences and learning with our experiments in integral we-spaces, as well as offers what we see as key practices for we-space development.

A foundational orientation to this work is a developmental understanding that spans the concrete, subtle, causal and non-dual worlds through which our conceptions of I and We emerge and evolve. The term 'concrete' refers to the world of the senses, of ordinary perceivable matter, of individuals and groups in their concrete appearances. The 'subtle' is the world of mind, with its conceptions, emotions, constructions and contextualization, the world of imagination and subtle contexts and systems. The 'causal' is the domain of awareness itself, of the unconditioned mind, full and empty, the witness and the manifest phenomena of all concrete, subtle and causal realities. The 'non-dual' world is that which is beyond, includes, and unifies all distinctions, the world beyond mind that also births mind and all forms.

As one's understanding of 'I' and 'We' evolves through these territories, the depth of our awareness and perspective reflects what we mean and experience as 'we-space.' The specific contours of the movement from subtle, intimately personal we-spaces to causally grounded spaces, in which the concrete and subtle I and We are fully present and interpenetrate each other, and our awareness of the ground of being represents the leading edge of most of the communities Pacific Integral convenes. In these spaces, the 'I' is not backgrounded but rather unique personal expressions are highly valued in an unattached, non-demanding way, as are collective expressions. The experience is of one arising phenomenon in the paradoxical coincidence of seemingly individual and collective consciousness. What we think of as collective intelligence is heightened, but so is individual intelligence. While this developmental understanding is mentioned at the outset, as it informs the language we use to describe we-spaces, it is not meant to essentially prioritize this perspective above others, such as the dimensions of shadow, embodiment, interpersonal authenticity, or service.

Lessons Learned

Pacific Integral did not set out primarily to develop powerful we-spaces, but rather to facilitate the transformation of individuals and collectives, and to deepen our understanding of how the process of transformative change and development occurs. As we began to appreciate how this transformation must occur in real, intimate community, this endeavor led us directly into working more broadly with we-space, which ultimately became central to our work. Early on we recognized that we had embarked on an ongoing, unfolding experiment, grounded a sense of participative collaboration with the ineffable. We consciously approached our work with that understanding in our being and in our actions. As a result, this unfolding adventure let us to several challenging inquiries.

First, as we engaged with the long-term development of the participants in the program, we began to recognize the limits of the frameworks we were holding, such as Integral Theory (Wilber, 1995; Wilber, 2006) and Spiral Dynamics (Beck, Cowan, 1996), and of our understanding of them to inform the transformative processes with which we worked. We wondered – how do people develop, really? How do they actually show up differently as they grow through stages and develop new capacities? This developed into an ongoing longitudinal research project into adult development, including growth across several dimensions and states of consciousness. This resulted ultimately in our theory and practice of Causal Leadership (Ramirez, Fitch, O'Fallon, 2013; O'Fallon, Ramirez, Fitch, 2014) as well as the StAGES model, a new, integral theory of development, articulated by Terri O'Fallon, one of the founding partners (O'Fallon, 2011; O'Fallon, 2012; O'Fallon, 2015). In this framework, we made new discoveries into how people conceive of and relate to 'I' and 'We' as they evolve, how they engage in collectives, how they connect and make sense together from diverse perspectives, and what supports healthy growth in individuals and collectives. While informed by our orienting frameworks, including integral theory, much of our discovery pushed the boundaries of and gaps in what those frameworks offered us, and in some cases exposed their limitations and biases.

Second, as we encountered the interpenetration of I and We, we began to see its implications for transformative change. To understand interpenetration, you might consider the move from either/or to both/and consciousness. In the latter, two aspects remain distinct but are understood to be in a deeper kind of relationship, more interdependent. Interpenetration is the next step in this process, to a recognition of "one within the other." The implication of this leads to an understanding of unity beyond distinctions; one is many and many is one. Understanding subtle interpenetration, for example, one can see that, because no one is truly independent of the collectives in which they appear, they cannot truly change without a change in their relationships; likewise no social system can transform without a transformation of the individuals involved. This realization took us into a deep exploration of both individual and collective transformation, as it occurs in every moment. How can we work with transformative change in I and We simultaneously?

Third, this opened the question of leadership: what is transformative action and leadership from the causal ground? What is choice, vision and motivation from the groundless ground where we find the distinction of I and We interpenetrate and become more paradoxical (O'Fallon, Ramirez, Fitch, 2014)? How does leadership and followership occur when I and We collapse into the background (Ramirez, Fitch, O'Fallon, 2013)?

Fourth, we explored how to stabilize the deep states of openness that the individuals and collectives were touching into, which represent an extraordinary potential to which we all have access. This spawned two other important paths of learning: How does shadow relate to this work, as we so often encounter disowned shadow material in this process and see that our conception of I and We is limited by our defenses against a fuller and deeper whole. And, as human beings touch into these deeper spaces, how do we integrate the universal with the personal? How do we hold our highest and deepest realization, while attending to the extraordinary limits of our personal will and resources?

Evolving Conceptions of We-Space

The developmental framework that grew from these inquiries (O'Fallon, 2015) makes several unique and important contributions that are relevant to understanding we-space. Most notably it clarifies important ways our conception of I and We change as we develop, and as such, how we define and engage with 'we-space'. The StAGES model describes 12 stages that occur through iterating patterns over three tiers – concrete, subtle, and causal (Fig. 1). These 12 stages include six important shifts in perspective taking. The first pattern and most relevant to this discussion is the pattern of I and We. Each tier consists of two I-oriented stages and two We-oriented stages. Thus, as we go through this evolution (which spans from infancy to rarer, later stages of consciousness), we go through six unique understandings of I and We, each of which has two stages associated with it. Each stage transcends and eventually includes the prior understandingts.

Our conceptions of 'I' and 'We' evolve through concrete, subtle, and causal perspectives.

Figure 1: Concrete, Subtle, and Causal I and We

Briefly, in the first person perspective, we are in the concrete 'I' stages. (In the StAGES model, these are called 1.0 Impulsive and 1.5 Opportunist). It is 'all about me' and there is no understanding yet of a 'We.' One can see others but does not have a truly unique identity separate from others, nor does one see others as unique in their own right. The focus is on one's concrete needs and wants. The second person perspective stages foreground the concrete 'We' (these stages are called 2.0 Rule-oriented and 2.5 Conformist). In this perspective, I see that others see me and that, in order to satisfy my needs, I must work with others and make and follow rules together. In these 'We' stages, the 'I' is present and understood, but backgrounded, or deprioritized, in favor of relationships and groups. The next perspective gives rise to subtle 'I' stages, where we realize we have a subtle self – the thoughts, emotions, and independent mind of rational consciousness (3.0 Expert and 3.5 Achiever in the model). Again this is an I-oriented space, but the we is present and backgrounded. The 'We' that is present, however, is the concrete we, groups and their norms and rituals, since no new subtle 'We' has yet been discovered.

	Perspective	Foreground	Background
	1st person	I (concrete) body, senses	(none)
	2nd person	We (concrete) groups, rules	I (concrete)
	3rd Person	I (subtle) thoughts, ideas, emotions	We (concrete)
	4th Person	We (subtle) contexts, paradigms, systems	I (subtle)
	5th Person	I (causal) awareness, source, emptiness	We (subtle)
	6th Person	We (causal) manifestation, Kosmos, whole	I (causal)

Table 1: Six distinct understandings of I and We. Our conceptions of 'I' and 'We' evolve through concrete, subtle, and causal perspectives.

This pattern continues with the fourth person perspective, where the subtle 'We' is foregrounded. The subtle We consists of the perception of one being situated in and arising out of a plurality of contexts (in the 4.0 Pluralist and 4.5 Strategist stages). The 'We' isn't then a specific group, but it is a space, and that space is complex. It consists not only of outer manifestations, such as the room, the systems in which the context is embedded, the cultural context and form, but also inner manifestations, such as the attitudes, beliefs, assumptions, states of awareness, and ontological dispositions we bring to the moment. Here, people begin to understand that one can have, if the context is right, an experience of the kind of deep connection to another, once thought reserved for a soul mate. It is at this level that the notions of we-space, collective intelligence, and collective evolution begin to arise, although we can say that collective intelligence takes form at concrete, subtle and causal levels (O'Fallon, Ramirez, Fitch, 2014; O'Fallon, 2010).

At the fifth person perspective, individuals awaken to their ever-present awareness as the ground of their own being. They begin to identify with this being as a new self, both empty and full, transcendent and immanent. In these stages (5.0 Construct Aware and 5.5 Transpersonal), the 'I' is foregrounded but the subtle 'We' remains as a context for this I. The 'I' is however not what we conventionally think of as 'I' – our concrete bodily self or our subtle thinking or narrative self, but rather our causal self, the limitless open horizon of awareness that we paradoxically seem to share with everyone and everything. Knowledgeable that deep subtle we-spaces are possible, individuals often desire to experience them in this causal experience, for example, by bringing the practice of witness consciousness into their collective experience (Gunnlaugson & Moze, 2012), and to provide a context in which their causal selves can express themselves and be recognized.

At the sixth person perspective, this new 'I' is again backgrounded as it lets go into a much larger, causal 'We.' In the sixth level stages (6.0 Kosmic and 6.5 Illumined), the 'We' is all of concrete, subtle, and causal manifestation itself, the Kosmos, the utterly full and empty existence, eternal and beyond time, infinite and beyond space. Here one experiences themselves as this whole, with their apparent (even causal) 'I' birthed by and birthing the whole. At this stage we see a waning of the interest in 'we-space' work as it is normally conceived, which most often is identified with the concrete groups and subtle containers in which they take place. This is suggested by the term 'space' which suggests a context. We-space is a particular space, while at the sixth person perspective, attention moves to the one manifest reality itself, that which is and births all spaces. There is a keen interest at the sixth level in living as this larger collective, which has its own sense of 'We', and in allowing the intelligence of the whole, and that which births the whole, to express one's existence. In this sense, this very much reflects the interest in collective intelligence at the fourth stage, but is no longer grounded in any specific group or context but in reality itself.

As mentioned, each of these six unique perspectives of I and We is further divided into two distinct stages: first, a more receptive stage, which is about awakening to a new perspective taking capacity and exploring the many dimensions of it; and second, a more active stage, in which one wants to move forward and create with these capacities. Altogether, this points to an extraordinary diversity of the constructions of human mind and has deeply informed Pacific Integral's seeing (and letting go) of we-space, informing this unique aspect of our work. Without developmental awareness, humans unwittingly reduce an approach to a particular developmental orientation or passage. As an example, the movements toward integral and evolutionary perspectives seem to posit a certain ideal, a 'from' and 'to' state, which from a truly developmental perspective can only be an overlay on one's unique individual and collective trajectory, and inevitably provide a limit to growth as much as an impetus to it. In GTC, we have learned to hold our collectives in a kind of meta-container, allowing for the integration of this developmental diversity. This is an orientation that reflects the perspectives that begin to arise at the sixth level and beyond; that the occasion reflects the Kosmic whole (and even this is a projection on the ineffable by the ineffable), the infinite diversity birthed through the interpenetration of the concrete, subtle, and causal worlds. This orientation also expresses a deep intuition that as the family of sentience, we must come together at a much deeper level than our evolving perspectives, and find ways to meet each other and integrate in our developmentally (and otherwise) diverse perspectives and qualities. In a recent cohort, we held a group of individuals spanning six developmental stages (across 4 levels of perspective taking), each of whom expressed experiences of being met and challenged in the space, sensing and existing in a whole, of which there could be no truly commonly held conception. Still, there was no denying its reality.

This brief description offers some orientation to the principles and practices of Causal Leadership collectives.

Principles and Practices

While holding this depth and span of diversity of consciousness in our awareness, Pacific Integral supports the emergence of what we came to call Causal Leadership collectives that consciously engage in developing their capacities for the embodiment of a causal awareness/ field, while expressing those capacities as service in the world. This allows the emergence of a deeper intelligence to flow through them and to allow their subtle collective space to reflect their causal awareness:

> A stabilized conscious causal collective begins to arise when enough individuals walk around with individual causal recognition and expression and share a collective

experience and understanding of how they can source from this infinite causal intelligence, influencing concrete and subtle collective intelligence by collectively accessing the causal field of existence – that is, they begin to "causalize" the former, unbending subtle contextual-systems and concrete community expressions that they have lived within. These communities tend to release the subtle ceilings that hold people in place and give space for the individuals within them to soar in their individual causal expressions, seated in and arising out of this empty creative potential of the infinite causal ground. (O'Fallon, Ramirez, Fitch, 2014, p. 92)

To support this, causal collectives need deep holding of the causal space and the developmental span of the individuals. The first and most important practice to mention is to develop state capacities in the individual and group that allow them to access, sustain and eventually be responsible for their causal awareness. Initially this may be as simple as learning breathing and awareness practices that allow individuals and groups to let go of energetic and physical holding and to rest in the stillness of awareness itself. Likewise, we practice bringing a constructive developmental perspective – the understanding that the mind is constructing in every moment and that those constructions are influenced in part by developmentally formed structures, helps to allow the individuals to disidentify with their perspectives and to hold in their awareness the developmental diversity that is present in the collective. The practice of holding a developmentally aware and fluid container is complex. It includes building capacity for self awareness of one's own perspective taking, developing authenticity, witnessing practice, holding an open space in which participant's perspectives are welcome and held while avoiding reflexive movement towards agreement, and learning to listen in new ways to the energetic movement of the whole.

As each developmental level emerges, it, to some degree, both transcends the limits of the previous stages and includes the previous stage's capacities. This transcend-and-include movement has been central to integral understanding, but not without its limitations at a practical level. In real terms, we see that all the stages to which we have experienced and have access are operating in us, that the transcending may happen as we move into a new stage, but the practice of including never ends, as we continually reach back and integrate shadow elements, revisit past developmental challenges, and build skills and capacities from previous levels that are incomplete. This also exposes what might be called a bias toward vertical development in integral work. Movement toward later stages implies greater maturity, but it also implies greater immaturity in that it may do nothing to address the unconscious shadow, incomplete growth and experience from earlier stages. While landing someone in a new place, even profoundly more rich and complex, this growth presents a whole new set of developmental demands. Causal collectives, for example, may touch into profound states of intuition and creativity, but may not know how to organize a meeting or resolve conflict in ways that arise out of and support this new consciousness.

Similarly, the same way modern, embodied spirituality has integrated the psychological understanding that causal states can be used to bypass (to avoid shadow and un-integrated parts of ourselves), the same is true of causal collectives. Deep states of connection, openness, pleasure, and presence that are possible in we-spaces can be used to bypass the conflict, projection, and defensiveness that can arise in relationships. The journey into deeper states and structures of awareness, therefore, must be just as much a journey to deeper intimacy, authenticity, and embodiment. This is expressed by the metaphor that growth can be upward (vertical development in states and stages), downward (integration, shadow work), outward (developing the breadth of maturity and capacities at each stage), and inward (self-understanding, soul work, truthfulness).

To support this, causal collectives attend to the concrete and subtle dimensions of themselves. The work of integration, healing, and horizontal growth is a regular focus of causal collectives. Shadow work and practices that support intimacy and embodiment are central tools of these causal we-spaces. Our collectives learn about and practice shadow work together, including understanding the dynamics of group shadow – scapegoating and marginalization, e.g. – as well as collective horizontal and vertical autopoiesis. They also practice emotional awareness and intimacy and embodied practices through play, dance, creative expression and improvisation. The inclusion of these approaches serves to expand the realization of the individual's and collective's potential, to serve greater fluidity, agility and impact of their work together. As further elaborated below, they are also held in balance with the actual living of life and work together and individually, not as an end in themselves but as an integral dimension of the life of the group and its service and being in the world.

As 'I' and 'We' are two interpenetrative perspectives on one occasion, this suggests that we can and should see our development in any moment through these two lenses, even if at different times we may have a preference for one or the other. It is useful to understand that the collective births, limits, and liberates the individual, just as the individual(s) birth, limit and liberate the collective. From a concrete understanding, we see our individual and collective autopoeitic patterns as shaping the moment. Groups have ways they come together, how they sit and interact with each other, what is acceptable to say or not say, do or not do, what energies and emotions are considered better than others, and so on. These autopoietic patterns take more nuanced and complex forms, too. At a subtle understanding we see the stream of individual and collective thought and experience shaping the moment, including the whole of human culture in its power and diversity. For example, in some groups, an understanding of development often reveals a subtle pattern of preference for more-developed perspectives and for individual attainment, which can find its roots in the deep habits of the modern Western mind.

As in all groups, the individuals bring their own hidden personal and cultural biases, which include patterns arising from race, gender, national, socioeconomic, psychological, and other historical factors. We endeavor to engage in this process in the spirit of mutual vulnerability, supporting the process to expose and learn from these patterns as is needed, in both our participants and in ourselves. Our efforts to bring diversity in to our groups, as well as hosting the program in different cultural environments, has been helpful in this work.

To respond to this, Causal Leadership collectives aim to create a developmental culture, including inquiry, radical openness to change, and an awareness of these individual and collective patterns—a transformative posture that recognizes the individual and collective as interpenetrating. In practice, this may mean, as an individual, I intend to be in a place of inquiry – asking how am I seeing the moment/situation? What perspective am I looking through? What is unseen, or unconscious in me that is shaping my experience? How am I seeing the 'We' and the other such that my seeing forms who we, and they, are? Likewise, as a collective, what patterns of perception and action are shaping and limiting who we are? Can we be aware of our unseen assumptions and agreements as to who we each are, and hold those lightly, open to revision, experimentation and exploration? This collective inquiry must be founded on interpersonal inquiry, where we develop the trust and skill to vulnerably give and receive feedback, explore authentic experience we have of each other, as well as the stories we tell ourselves about each other. This practice of self- and mutual-inquiry, letting go, and letting come of the emergent self/collective is essential to the practice of Causal Leadership communities.

Next, 'we-space' practice can become subtly disembodied or disconnected, in the same way individual spiritual practice can, if it does not include engagement in the world and life that expresses the spiritual heart that has opened in practice. A causal 'we-space' can be a space of practice, but we are also in many collectives, part of one larger whole and as the human heart is by its nature connected and giving, our service in all of our relationships, families, communities, markets, and the world as a whole is an essential part of the we-space practice. We have therefore continued to see this as 'leadership' work, and, while the construct has limitations, it reminds us that our deeper intent is to liberate expression, service and impact in the world.

To support this, Causal Leadership collectives aim to bring the world into the collective and the collective into the world. They do this by including in their scope all of the fields of connection and practice the participants are involved with, and by including an orientation to service and action. This radical inclusion of the macro and micro, individual and collective, as well as the personal and universal, arises out of a deeper global intent that springs from the later stages of awareness–that we are expressing care for the whole as we express care for the individual. In facilitation, we endeavor to both broaden our moral span of care and assist participants to learn to listen more deeply to the meaning and purpose of their lives, while stretching ourselves to engage more fully in that purpose in the world. In practice, these collectives engage in work together and mutually support each other's individual expressions in the world. They hold space for each other's deepest heart intention for the world, and out of that, a radical and audacious space of potential for each other's lives and for the life of humanity.

Engaging in this service in the world, practitioners often confront outmoded perspectives and habits on organization and leadership. Unique challenges arise as causal collectives, who may be able to sustain deep meditative and relational spaces, attempt to organize, make decisions, and create together in the limitations of time and space. To address this, Causal Leadership collectives need to learn to sustain and embody the causal in the context of transformative action. The practice of developing this capacity is complex. At an individual and collective level, it involves being able to sustain and embody causal practice in distracting, chaotic and challenging moments. Organizationally, it involves adopting or inventing practices that reflect more complex, later stages, such as those suggested by Theory U and Holacracy. Socially, it requires that collectives develop the capacity to be energetically fluid, being able to let go, shift, and transform moment to moment. "In Causal Leadership one experiences that there simultaneously is and isn't a leader, that one is simultaneously a leader and follower and neither, and the field of change is inter-systemic, holistic and complex." (Ramirez, O'Fallon, Fitch, 2013, p. 11)

These challenges, principles, and practices are some of the learning we have discovered in our engagement with we-spaces in our Causal Leadership collectives. We recognize that the deep, transformative we-spaces in which Causal Leadership is grounded are a reflection of the natural movement of consciousness to fuller expressions. In addition, as we deliberately bring 'leadership' into the work through an integration of consciousness and action in the world, these we-spaces move beyond an exploration of we-space itself, to enacting the awakened awareness of I/We as expression in the world. This occurs in context, in life, limits, time constraints and diverse environments that are realistic and embodied. It is an intention of this work that we not just experience or train ourselves, but that the intelligence of the we-space find its way into the world, beyond the rarified containers we can create. This work is very contextual and an ongoing exploration of ourselves and our graduate community. This integration requires a depth of working at multiple levels: leadership, organization, intimacy, shadow, relationship, awareness, energetics, and so on, while engaging the unity of distinct practice spaces, the ordinariness of life, and conscious creation, Divine Being itself. In this sense, the potential for we-space work that we hold is to create conditions for new 'leadership', collective action, and the transformation of human society.

Having said this, we might admit that, seeing the whole, inclusive of our multiple ephemeral constructions of each other and all of it, leaves us with no clear boundaries. There is only the wonder of Being. What is happening occurs through our concrete manifestations, our subtle experiences, and our causal construction and witnessing; each individual consciousness reflecting and refracting that perfect wholeness, shining such-ness. This might seem to lead to a sense of relativism, but it is far from it. There is something yet deeper guiding this process. In the midst of this enactment of the wholeness that is shaped through these dimensions, there is absolutely a sense of truth, goodness and beauty that shapes and guides the experience of the We-Space. Miraculously, as each of us may tell quite a different story about what occurs in our collective, we know it to be one story. Although we might have distinct individual needs and impulses, there is a deeper heart that can recognize this truth. We breathe as one and resonate with the same intelligence that animates the whole, even while we seem to hold quite different concrete, subtle and causal points of view. Any sense of irony or paradox is outshined by the beauty and goodness that is this Heart's Truth.

Author Bio

Geoff Fitch is a coach, trainer, and facilitator of growth in individuals and organizations, and a creator of transformative leadership education programs worldwide. He is a founder of Pacific Integral, where he was instrumental in the development of the internationally-acclaimed Generating Transformative Change program, now offered three continents and in it's 24th cohort. Through these programs, he has researched and developed novel approaches to individual and collective growth, and has designed and facilitated dozens of residential learning retreats. He has been exploring diverse approaches to cultivating higher human potentials for over 25 years, including somatic and transpersonal psychology, mystical traditions, innovation and creativity, leadership, integral theory, and collective intelligence. Geoff also has over 30 years experience in leadership in business. He holds a master's degree in Transpersonal Psychology from Sofia University and B.S. in Computer Science, magna cum laude, from Boston University, and has additional studies in jazz music, philosophy, and management. Learn more at pacificintegral.com and geoff-fitch. com.

References

Beck, D., & Cowan. (1996). Spiral dynamics: Mastering values, leadership and change. Malden, MA: Blackwell Publishers

Gunnlaugson, O., Moze, M.B. (2012). Surrendering into witnessing: a foundational practice for building collective intelligence capacity in groups. Journal of Integral Theory and Practice, 2012, 7(3), pp. 105–115

O'Fallon, T. (June 2010). Developmental experiments in individual and collective movement to second tier. Journal of Integral Theory and Practice, 5(2), 149-160.

O'Fallon, T. (2011). StAGES: Growing up is waking up—interpenetrating quadrants, states and structures. Pacific Integral. www.pacificintegral.com

O'Fallon, T. (2012). Development and consciousness: Growing up is waking up. Spanda, III(1), 97-103.

O'Fallon, T. (2015-in press). Stages. Albany New York: Suny Press.

O'Fallon T., Ramirez, V., & Fitch, G. (2014). Collective intelligence as a causal ground. Spanda Journal, V(2), 91-95.

Ramirez, V., Fitch, G, & O'Fallon T. (2013). Causal leadership: A natural emergence from later stages of awareness. Paper presented at the Integral Theory Conference, San Francisco, CA.

Wilber, K. (1995). Sex, ecology, and spirituality: The spirit of evolution. Boston: Shambhala.

Wilber, K. (2006). Integral spirituality: A startling new role for religion in the modern and postmodern world. Boston: Shambhala

CHAPTER 5

Trillium Awakening

Sandra Glickman & Deborah Boyar, Ph.D.

Introduction

The Trillium Awakening[1] we-space is the fundamental context for our transformational work, and arises in multiple contexts— teacher-student dyads, sittings, peer-led mutuality groups, in-person retreats, online events, organizational work groups, and informal creative occasions. Each of our we-spaces embody our collective orienting philosophy, which is rooted in deeply held trust in Being— the totality of All and all, the existential reality of any moment, in its nondual nature as consciousness expressing as awareness, silence, and unmoving potential, as well as the radiant and dynamic play of dually alternating forms in the subtle and material worlds. Through this shared orientation, we understand the individuals in our we-space as continuous with Being, progressively and uniquely unfolding in awareness, personal and cultural identity, and embodiment of their full nature, both finite and infinite.

We hold Being as an ultimate Mystery revealing itself in parts and glimpses over time, and consciously honor its wholeness. Our we-spaces are fed by the steady, open spaciousness of presence, freedom, and silence. From that basis, we surface personal accounts, listen to

---

1. The Trillium Awakening work emerged and evolved from the Waking Down in Mutuality® work founded in 1992 by Saniel Bonder. The Trillium Awakening Teachers Circle originally incorporated as the Waking Down Teachers Association in 2005, and in 2015 renamed its work to differentiate from that of Saniel Bonder. The Trillium Awakening Teachers Circle continues to embody and evolve the teachings and we-spaces described herein.

dilemmas, and are moved along undulating waves in contemplating losses, gains, pains, and triumphs. We intuit and come to accept being unable to ever completely know one another, and thus leave room for what is fresh and spontaneously emergent. We practice holding open our minds and hearts, even while internally registering our own biases, reactions, and judgments of character and personality. We continuously acknowledge the sacred *unknowability* of each person including ourselves, and why we are configured precisely as we are.

The Trillium Awakening we-space invites all aspects of a person into the room—from what is known to what is unknown. Within this mystery, our teachers and students access and anchor unshakable confidence in the unlimited nature of self and other. This trust includes a paradoxical core principle of our we-spaces: by descending into the finite—into personal story and conditions—and following themes to their resting point where attention is freed, a person and group are often delivered into the Mystery. The finite opens as rarefied, infinite, and spacious; it appears in and as consciousness, non-separate. In this vast space of full welcome, we are organically quickened to release stories to return to their ground, rather than sustaining identification with them. This occurs so reliably that we have come to trust in allowing and tolerating the most limited, frustrating aspects of experience, as counter-intuitive as that may seem.

From this conviction, our we-spaces offer catalytic support we call "greenlighting." We invite people to speak, feel, and embody their unique personal experience, and notice their growing sense of awareness itself, as they are warmly received in present time. We hold our we-spaces openheartedly, welcoming individual concerns, no matter how "unspiritual" the content might seem. Deep listening, empathic attunement, and careful reflecting facilitate shared relaxation into actual experience, and begin a healing process that allows people to drop into more easeful self-awareness and connection with others.

People sometimes initially distrust greenlighting, as they assume it would reinforce undesirable character traits or regressive coping mechanisms. While such manifestations might appear, unique healing is ultimately catalyzed in the space of tolerant listening, listening, and more listening. Here, people at last experience being fully heard and received—including their conditioning, their suffering, and the ways they reject themselves. As their experience is received in a loving we-space, participants develop the capacity to compassionately observe their patterns, and fundamentally discharge the constricted energy of those forms. They become organically attracted to practices supporting their next levels of growth. In such an atmosphere, transformation is activated from the bottom up, through spontaneous compelling insight and organismic initiative, rather than through top-down directives.

This exemplifies another core principle of Trillium Awakening we-spaces—Being prompts and presences what is next ready to surface and become known.

The process of being unconditionally received facilitates integration in the body-mind and spirit-matter interplay of each participant over time. It thus lays a foundation for further realization and more advanced work. Participation in the Trillium Awakening we-space permeates and heals the perceived split between spirit and matter, and opens the way for truly embodied nondual awakening. The principle of balance comes into play as polar opposites are integrated in an oscillating exchange of insight and activity that refines a person's whole being, and builds a group's capacity to hold a holarchy of perspectives. This process is experienced through vast conscious abiding as both form and spirit, "this and That." As the we-space effectively works its magic, the intelligence and discriminating force of Being is catalyzed, and begins to evolve, enliven, and ennoble the participants and the we-space itself.

Underlying Structures That Support Trillium Awakening We-Spaces

The intelligence of Being has also come to operate through our organizational structures. Our we-spaces are clearly and inherently stabilized by policies, principles, and enduring values we hold dear. Our teachers meet regularly to articulate and update their understandings, and reach agreements that ground our interactions in sobriety and integrity—which perhaps more than anything else enables people to drop into the depths of their divinely human nature. Our guiding principles and expectations of those taking part in our we-spaces, and in various levels of leadership, are posted on our public and in-house websites.[2] Our ethics policy is read aloud by the teaching staff at each retreat and training, and questions and comments are solicited from attendees to ensure clarity and mutual agreement. Additional policies for confidentiality and respectful exchange are regularly presented— particularly when newcomers are present—and we work implicitly to infuse our we-spaces with wisdom and compassion. With this kind of embodied, seasoned clarity about how we interact, we have not found the need in our various group configurations for specific exercises or practices beyond gazing meditation, individual sharing, and

---

2. *Professional and Ethics Policies of the WDTA*. http://www.wakingdown.org/profession-al-and-ethics-policies-of-the-wdta. Web

deep listening. Alchemical transmutation is ignited by the we-space itself, which is profoundly supported by our cultural infrastructure, forged over two decades of engagement, exploration, reflection, and revision. We regularly revisit our orientation as new learnings emerge. Facilitators tend carefully to the quality of our we-spaces to support the most auspicious levels of contact, creativity, and safety. The energetic tone of gatherings might range from expressive to receptive, depending on the living reality of varying configurations of people in time.

To safeguard our we-spaces from the potential excesses of indiscriminate greenlighting, teachers and participants bring various skills to bear, particularly (but not only) when participants request guidance. If conflict arises, dominates the field, and doesn't come to resolution at the time, participants are encouraged to meet with trusted teachers or neutral third parties. Newer teachers refine their discrimination through observing those in whom years of experience have brought mastery, and also through consultation, training, and feedback in supporting students moving through intensities of experience.

While being held with deep awareness and compassion, participants are sensitively invited to touch their underlying experience and bring awareness to their reactions; this is often far more effective than receiving feedback. To support their process, they might choose to explore various resources, therapeutic modalities, and teachers both within and outside Trillium Awakening. Applicants for teacher training undertake intensive training in self-awareness and shadow work, and learn to take responsibility for their impact on others. They are called to closely investigate their behavior, and adequate time is required for such integration to become embodied.

The following example, compiled from many typical experiences, shows how our we-space can assist participants to recognize patterns and make choices to express and honor boundaries. After many months of consultation, a mentee (student) begins to pressure a mentor to be more emotionally engaged, as in a social situation, or to act as a teacher, expressing dharma. The mentor then examines the felt sense of pressure, yet, despite the discomfort, chooses to honor our mentoring parameters by empathizing and reflecting, without interpreting, instructing, or socializing.

Although the mentee might grow more and more dissatisfied that the mentor won't shift, the mentor persists in tolerating the tension, meeting the mentee's experience, and compassionately greenlighting any frustration. The mentee might surface patterns of cajoling or complying, which would empathically be met, and then has the opportunity to find a true voice to state deeper needs and draw an empowering boundary. Such straightforward communication and action support significant growth and integration. After an authentic exchange of this type, both parties arrive at greater clarity with newfound mutual respect. Because the mentor remains in role, the mentee can grow within the we-space that contained and tested both parties.

A significant aspect of our we-space is the practice of engaging one-on-one teacher-student work within groups. In that setting, empowered by our whole-being dharma and the group's resonant field and focus, individual work can be especially potent and enduring. As our work integrates the individual and collective, and the finite and infinite, the entire spectrum of apparent opposites generally comes into play for exploration. Deep collective empathy is catalyzed as individuals work their process. Echoes of the same experience, perhaps reaching back in time or imagined forward into the future, reverberate in the rising field. Compassion, love, and understanding infuse our shared experience, liberating us from exclusively personal and separate identity into tender appreciation for our existence. We might have glimmerings of being called to serve this corner of our universe, and feel empowered to devotedly respond with care and vision. With each individual's process, the group ethos is more clearly enhanced. As feedback is offered, the voice of collective wisdom becomes more refined, evocative, and transformational. The field is activated by each contribution, and intensifies as the evolutionary potential surges for both individual and collective. The we-space enlivens people with uplift and bliss, which often burst forward at break times as refined, delighted awareness of the whole of "I" and "we."

Trillium Awakening Lineage

Our we-spaces are grounded in conscious embodiment through moment-to-moment awakening and recognition of the utter non-separateness of manifest and unmanifest realms. In traditional parlance, all appearances are understood as the unity of consciousness and form. This principle rests firmly in Indian tantra (not Vedanta), and was exquisitely clarified and elaborated in tenth century Kashmir by the extraordinary sage Abhinavagupta (Dyczkowski, 1987).

Our work received this orientation in modern times through Baba Muktananda,[3] who was a living exponent of Kashmir Shaivism and a

---

3. *Swami Muktananda.* http://www.siddhayoga.org/baba-muktananda

teacher to Adi Da Samraj,[4] the guru of Waking Down founder Saniel Bonder, whose transmission helped catalyze our we-spaces. In Kashmir Shaivism, consciousness (Shiva) is not isolated or elevated above form (Shakti). Rather, Shiva and Shakti are perpetually conjoined; as one, they generate and infuse phenomena with radiance. In Kashmir Shaivism, their eternal wedding is a metaphor for our true nature.

Although we don't use specific practices from Kashmir Shaivism, we mention it to indicate that tradition's radical non-separateness, which is foundational to the Trillium Awakening articulation of embodied awakening. This view is inherent in our we-spaces, and challenges paradigms that elevate spirit above matter. Today, our intention to live this "Onlyness,[5]" is progressively embodied over time in the ordinary rituals and gestures of our lives, and the sacred union of our true nature.

Embodied Awakening – The Second Birth

Since the origins of Trillium Awakening, hundreds of people have landed in the embodied awakening we call the Second Birth, which has a uniquely seminal effect on our we-spaces. Although difficult to explain to cognitive satisfaction, the Second Birth is recognizable as pivotal relaxation from the unrelenting search for liberation, healing, satisfaction, happiness, awakening, or enlightenment. This shift influences all the we-spaces in which an individual participates by adding the ineffable ingredient of the potential for liberation, and helps resolve the distresses of the body-mind.

The Second Birth entails descent from identity based in mind into the heart of Being, where consciousness fuses with the body-mind and all conditions. It occurs when a person is sufficiently healed of splits in their perception of spirit "against" matter, and sufficiently relieved of trying to hold everything together in the defended posture of ego-centered life. The individual can then open deeply to the tension and distortion of a set point that maintains acute separation from all it encounters, and might experience a shift downward into the body's

---

4. An Introduction to Avatar Adi Da. http://www.adidam.org

5. "Such Onlyness is ... deeply suffused with the intuitive feeling-awareness that Spirit and Matter, Consciousness and Phenomena, Emptiness and Form, are even now and at any and all times and places already as if melted into one another. Such a realized one feelingly knows the essences of these great polar opposites to be intensified into indistinguishability – even while distinctions somehow continue to appear" (Bonder, 2004, p. 80)

field. This is experienced as relief and profound opening, as tightly fixed patterns of mind and conditioning loosen their grip. This signals a major launch into a new understanding and experience of life, and is facilitated by a literal shift in unconscious attention. A new identity begins to take hold, based on the recognition that consciousness appears in simultaneous concert with phenomena—that consciousness IS, in fact, phenomena—in the ongoing unfolding of awareness and experience. The practitioner now begins to embrace divinely human existence. Although this transition might take place in a single moment or over a few years, it is culturally well understood that an ongoing process has begun, and will proceed through time and space as ever more complete recognition of the simultaneity of consciousness and phenomena is established moment to moment. In other words, the Second Birth is a birth, not a traditional completion stage; it initiates a continuing process of integration. Phases of maturation in this shift toward true and radical empowerment have been articulated and will be further clarified over time.

Certain qualities show up fairly specifically in the Second Birth, and directly attest to a new experience of life. Many such traits appear gradually, and not everyone displays each aspect. That said, the Second Birth empowerment and its subsequent impact on the we-space can manifest as:

- clear recognition of one's conscious nature, which deepens over time and can be regularly accessed as nondual abiding—recognized in our we-space as greater receptivity and flow between a wider range of perspectives;

- growing capacity to be grounded in one's body-mind, with appreciation for patterns as simple conditional structures, and compassion for oneself living the freedom amidst the limits – which is reflected in our we-space as goodwill, humor, and the sense of connecting solidly with others in differences as well as agreements;

- a great heart-opening to love, expanding outward toward the world, and in the we-space as a shared experience of unifying compassion and deeper intuitive discrimination;

- increased integration in self-holding and expression, with curiosity to investigate more deeply and transmute negativity, thus freeing our we-space from being trapped in the distress and stuck energies of participants;

- a deepening impulse to express devotion and actively serve others, while connecting to joy, humor, energetic liveliness, and embodiment;

- more refinement, clarity, and cooperative inspiration for tasks are brought to our we-space;

- a more stabilized, relaxed, and resilient sense of self with boundaries that are permeable or firm as situations merit;

- a pervasive uplift of freedom, while paradoxically honoring responsibility and commitment; greater synergistic exchange and cooperation in the spirit of the we-space;

- the we-space becomes a preferred context for growth and communion.

In our we-spaces, post second birth participants can potentiate integration of the personal and impersonal dimensions, thus raising the field to deeper and fuller expression by embodying these qualities.

Empathic Attunement and Holding

Empathic attunement and holding are foundational to our work and we-spaces. The tendencies to be self-critical and perfectionistic are pervasive in Western culture, and a harsh superego is common in traditional spiritual communities. In Trillium Awakening, participants are received without implicit or explicit expectation to look, think, or feel differently. In this welcoming field where wholeness is embraced, the unrelenting voice of the critic becomes less prominent and can self-liberate; here, practitioners naturally cultivate greater capacity for acceptance and self-love.

Teachers and other community members offer the light of radical acceptance and empathic holding—greenlighting—to each person, inviting them forward in their transcendent and immanent nature. Over time, we begin to hold ourselves as we are being held by others. We come to value our human limitations; we grow in our capacity to self-attune; we receive others with openness and curiosity. Our range of what is acceptable and valued expands greatly.

Through over two decades of experience, we've found that when our rejected, wounded, and frozen parts are empathically met and integrated in the nondual we-space of Trillium Awakening, defenses and contractions can melt. We relax at the core, no longer needing to present a good face or prop ourselves up behind masks and roles. The public personality can soften. Authenticity is invited and encouraged; people experience our we-spaces as a safe setting to be genuine and come out of hiding. Life force energy that was bound in suppressing unacceptable parts of self is now recovered and liberated. Participants regularly report feeling profoundly seen and heard, often for the first time.

Wounds around empathy might surface; in this field of encouragement to come forward in one's own time and way, it's natural to recall when empathy was absent. It can also take time for someone who has experienced a dearth of empathy to begin to accept, or even tolerate, the empathy available in Trillium Awakening.

Because our teachers and many participants have awakened to non-separateness, they are able to hold and attune from the absolute and relative fields simultaneously. This transmission of whole-being awareness deeply impacts participants, and facilitates the awakening process. Our teachers are comfortable in not knowing, in trusting a practitioner's organic process, and in being guided by the mystery of self, other, and the field. Their comfort and trust support participants to develop their own capacity to inhabit the Mystery, and they notice the need for certainty diminishing. This leads to greater confidence in Being, as well as facilitating dynamic healing and transformation. The entire process involves profoundly discriminating refinement and embodiment of multiple layers of being as the work of the we-space takes hold.

Balancing Sacred Holding and Spiritual Fire

A collective growing edge in our work is skillful use of the inherent tension and dynamic flow between sacred holding and spiritual fire. Practitioners are fully welcomed in the orientation of sacred holding, based on the understanding that all humans have vulnerabilities and have developed adaptive patterns to cope with their sense of separate existence. We recognize that the tender human self needs to be mirrored, nurtured, and honored for having the courage to persist. Teachers are skilled in supporting practitioners to identify and lean into their current needs—such as the wish to escape the tyranny of a negative pattern, or a deep desire for healing, divine abiding, or the recognition of consciousness. Practitioners who are already familiar with their absolute nature might simply long to be seen and known in their humanity.

Sacred holding fosters a field where individuals and the group can feel safe to explore new territory. The personality is supported to relax and integrate past experience, including wounds and disappointment in the awakening journey. Trillium Awakening offers a generously receptive, gentle field in which practitioners come to trust that the teacher and group will hold space and safeguard their process. Beneath much of the drive for self-improvement lie buried needs for affirmation and recognition; when practitioners feel adequately seen and held, they begin to fall out of seeking. For many in our contemporary culture of fragmentation and competition, this sense of being safely received while coming into fuller self-knowing is the first order of need.

One who has not yet personally experienced our honoring approach might wonder whether too much emoting and storytelling are encouraged. However, our experience has proven the nearly magical empowerment of this approach, which yields surprisingly rapid, identifiable results by laying a stable foundation in consciousness for discrimination and integration. Teachers are trained to discern when a student might need simple holding more than conceptual instruction or challenge. We adopt a pace that supports practitioners as they encounter their walled-off places, and gradually face them without arousing debilitating fear, which could activate defenses and prompt splitting. We believe survival strategies are inevitable, and actually attest to human intelligence and responsiveness to life's challenges. Ultimately, we see our patterns as continuous with our conscious nature. They most quickly show themselves and are disarmed in an atmosphere of trust, where teachers kindly and patiently hold and reflect. Under such conditions, students build their capacity to hold more tension, discomfort, conflict, and difference, thus empowering growth and transformation.

At the opposite end of the spectrum lies spiritual fire, where participants might find themselves orienting toward greater discriminative awareness and new forms of expression; here, they often benefit from increased direction and guidance from teachers, who might discuss the dharma, suggest individualized disciplines, challenge perspectives, comment on their process, illuminate needs for further development, help ignite visions for change and achievement, and generally inspire movement forward. This stance in the we-space helps loosen the grip of conditioning. Slowly or rapidly, the resulting heat and insecurity of dissolution begin to unravel old ways of being, and bring permeability and the excitement of discovery. Thought and habit patterns are penetrated through discernment and clarity. Guidance is important through the encounter with self, and teachers can help students navigate this transformation.

One of the significant gifts of our work is the availability of personal support and guidance from a teacher, either one-to-one or in small groups (often four to twelve people). This low student-teacher ratio is a hallmark distinguishing our we-spaces from paths with single teachers facilitating large groups.

Spiritual fire is present throughout Trillium Awakening, and is implicit within the quieter stance of sacred holding. As teachers relate from their non-separate, consciously embodied state, the fire of their wholeness flows freely into the field and quickens those poised to receive it. In this dynamic tension between holding for safety and activating for transformation, emergent aspects of personality and soul nature can be discovered, celebrated, and integrated. By remaining attuned to the field, a teacher calibrates to the needs of individuals and the we-space, steering between the stability of sacred holding and the dynamism of spiritual fire. This spectrum is also a natural polarity within any person, and contributes to aliveness altogether.

When engaging spiritual fire, practitioners might explore shadow work, inquiry, or feedback. Teachers might reflect the need for boundaries and self-responsibility, or the possibility of relying more on internal grounding than external support. Practitioners begin to release the need for others to greenlight their vulnerabilities, and begin to address them through innate wisdom. In working the fire for change, practitioners lean into conditions with discrimination, and explore patterns ripe for transformation. Openness and honesty are encouraged with regard to their experience of teachers' communications. If something feels off the mark or triggering, the work happens right there.

Practitioners drawn to spiritual fire are likely to be relatively stable and ready for change, and more equipped to integrate shadow in self and relationship. They are skilled at holding their process and listening for its energy to open and resolve. As they are also more confidently rooted in conscious recognition of non-separateness, they might show a greater intensity of expression. Having established competency to stand in their wholeness, they can engage a wider range of energies. They can be very direct while intensely feeling and expressive, yet also honor their own and each others' boundaries; this can be very enlivening.

A full spectrum of healing, guidance, and teaching is represented in the continuum of sacred holding to spiritual fire. The field created by our teachers, mentors, and newly arrived and long-established practitioners contributes to the mysterious alchemy of our we-spaces, which are replete with evolutionary potential for individuals and the collective. To participate in this culture, which is naturally always in flux, is energizing; it requires attunement to the growing edge, and following its most resilient trajectory.

Transmission

Our we-space is a rich field conveying the Trillium Awakening transmission, which can be felt as a subtle influence or sensed as a distinct current penetrating body and mind. Recognizing and cultivating transmission plays a large part in activating the Second Birth embodied awakening. Transmission occurs in a multiplicity of contexts among teachers, mentors, practitioners, and peers, and is understood as embodied Being communicated effortlessly and non-verbally through gazing meditation, verbally through various media and meetings, or by simply being together.

Our we-space is constellated by individuals with diverse histories, needs, views, and life conditions, as well as the subtle forces of awareness and Being. Each person within the collective can be seen as a unique individual field contributing to the whole. Multiple perspectives are articulated, and typically activate other realizations and discernments when received.

Transformation in our work is fundamentally organic, arising in Being, and is influenced by the collective field. Practitioners are encouraged to trust, be with, and work with what they encounter in their lives and the we-space. When they speak their truth in the moment, the field becomes more conscious, holds more potential, and informs those listening as they register the experience just shared. Greater nuance becomes available, and can prompt deeper self-reflection.

Deep relaxation and receptivity are catalyzed through the transmission of our work. Participants begin to experience coherence, which is felt as enormous support and a sense of shared well-being. As people relax into the we-space, all domains of Being are welcome to emerge, be held, and seen. The field offers shape and grounding to the potential for personal and collective integration. Like an unseen mover, it is alive and alchemical—a fertile container of healing, growth, and evolution.

Our teachers are ordinary people whose lives include the usual challenges; they profess their limitations and willingness to be impacted by adversity. And yet, as the transmission of our work becomes palpable, students gradually recognize their teachers' subtle freedom, enjoyment, and humor amidst their human struggles. This ease in Being epitomizes our transmission—we participate in the full range of experience, living deeply and meaningfully while expressing our unique gifts and talents in service to others. Gradually, expectations about spiritual practice shift as life simultaneously expresses the immanent and transcendent.

An example follows of how the transmission and potency of our we-space served to augment awareness for a woman in her mid-thirties and facilitate further embodiment, which led to her Second Birth realization. She was attending a week-long retreat after participating in our work for a year, and was familiar with the teaching.

She gazed with another woman who had been in her Second Birth for a number of years, and was close to her own age and situation. In that exchange, this practitioner found herself meeting the vastness of the other woman's conscious nature, and identifying as that vast consciousness. She later recalled that as she attuned to this felt sense, her body relaxed, her awareness expanded, and she felt herself settle. She also experienced a familiar deep human loneliness in the conditional flow, which the other woman had gracefully and vulnerably revealed. As they gazed, the practitioner simply held this loneliness with compassion and receptive neutrality, rather than becoming emotionally identified and disturbed by it. Abiding steadily in awareness, she felt capable of holding her fear of losing her intimate partner and being alone.

The practitioner next gazed with a man who was also experiencing fear and angst about losing his partner. Now, she opened and freely entered into his plight with the same compassion with which she had met herself. She was surprised to find herself capable of meeting the man's experience without collapsing into a broken sense of self. The gazing exercise came to an end, and the retreat continued. A few hours later, other participants remarked how changed the woman appeared, and how peaceful, radiant, and present she seemed, although she had earlier been absorbed in difficult material. Later still, she realized that her sense of self had fundamentally expanded to include her infinite nature. This shift in identity was later recognized as the beginning of her passage into the Second Birth and the ongoing deep spiritual transformation it makes possible.

In our we-spaces, we've discovered that the more people open to receive their experience as it is, the more steadily their perspectives begin to shift. This process is profoundly supported through consistent welcome into the awakened, compassionate, relational field, which is the very essence of our transmission.

The Core Wound of Embodied Life

A key component of our dharma that informs and empowers our transmission is our understanding of the Core Wound, which signifies the basic condition at the heart of embodiment: we appear, abide awhile, and pass away through a profoundly mysterious process. We exist at the interface of bounded-ness and openness; this tension yields inherent uncertainty, discomfort, and vulnerability. Every phenomenon exhibits perpetual movement between endlessly arising polarities—light/dark, love/hate, pain/pleasure, beginning/ending, and creation/destruction, to name just a few. To live fully, we are called to consciously participate in the endless changing flow that is our very nature.

We honor the Core Wound as the very portal to embodied awakening, with its realization of fundamental wellness and the radical non-separateness of consciousness and phenomena. Neither practice, achievement of rarefied states, nor transcending human dilemmas are necessary to enter this portal, which is a realm of letting go, surrendering, becoming present to our deep human needs and vulnerability, and apprehending how they coexist with the infinite unbounded dimension of our being.

Some people experience the Core Wound as subtle or more pronounced tension, and others register it as an underlying sense of incompleteness, separation, or existential anxiety. When unexamined, the Core Wound can drive much of our conditioned behavior. When examined, it can be an impossible, frightening koan the mind cannot hold, which the body yearns to resolve. Participants are at times invited to drop into the feeling recognition of this core paradox at the root of their being. They are invited to feel the fullness of being human, embodied, limited and conditioned, while at the same time abiding as unconditioned awareness—spacious, unlimited, and vast. Our we-spaces offer support in opening to and tolerating this core existential tension. We do not try to understand these paradoxes; we simply drop into them and feel them. Surrendering into the paradox of the absolute and relative can immediately catalyze the Second Birth awakening, although it often occurs more gradually.

To know ourselves, we must finally BE ourselves—and what we find in that process is an encounter with the radical creativity at the heart of all existence, which is inescapably present in each moment. We affirm that we evolve by embracing our utter nakedness to this dimension of our existence. This first requires encountering our suffering and limits, and descending through these layers to the felt experience of core separation. Over time, we build capacity to face into that sense of limitation. Our empathic we-space, as well as growing access to one's conscious nature, provide the deep support needed to descend, until we unexpectedly discover the Core Wound beginning to turn, dissipate, and dissolve into open boundaries and expansive freedom. At that point, the Core Wound has been integrated right through its darkest interior, and we are released from exclusive identification with our conditioned state and the separate, solid "I."

After the Second Birth, the unfathomable spectrum of opposites is perceived as both/and, rather than one or the other, thus yielding an integrated view we call the Core Paradox or Core Mystery. From this perspective, we notice our doing to be more and more sourced in Being. We find ourselves speaking and acting from the quiet source of the unknown emerging through us. When this process has matured and become recognizable, we might say, "I have entered a new life. In my first birth and life, I was such and such a person; in this Second Birth and life, I now know myself as fundamentally different, although the conditions and patterns of my life might remain the same. Most assuredly, I'm operating from new ground." There has been a shift into the heart of Being, where opposites reconverge, where tender feeling is found, and where reverence is felt for creatures enduring the journey. Love is understood and consciously lived, and those not yet awake to this mystery are held in compassion. In our we-spaces, people at all stages of exploration and realization are exposed to this transmission and have the opportunity to attune to it, resonate with it, and allow it to infuse them with awareness and warmth.

Mutuality

One of Trillium Awakening's significant distinguishing evolutionary features is Mutuality, which can be considered essential in democratizing awakening. The disposition underlying Mutuality is honoring the experience and tender heart of the other, as if placing it on a sacred altar. Human nature is inherently vulnerable, and our personal perspective and experience, however conditioned they may be, have enabled us to survive thus far, and are worthy of respect. To be honored so deeply at the core of our vulnerability is profoundly reorienting, particularly for those of us who have encountered pressure and critical feedback from well-intentioned though misattuned families, workplaces, or spiritual communities and teachers.

The practice of Mutuality is a distinct form of exchange in the self-other field. It begins with speaking and acting in integrity with our felt reality on all levels at which we are aware. While doing so, we participate with others who are doing the same, recognizing that their experience is different from our own, and remaining present with the tensions such differences can create. At times, a person might experience pain in response to our words and actions, even if we intended no harm. When this happens, we listen, honor their reality, and take responsibility for our part. Mutuality requires mature development; practitioners need to be able to take perspectives on self and other, own their part in breakdowns, and sincerely apologize when warranted. When the person apologizing is a teacher, it can be incredibly healing for students who have not experienced leaders admitting their own imperfection, insensitivity, and missteps.

At times, Mutuality requires us to bring feedback to another, sharing our honest experience of their impact. Although giving and receiving feedback might initially feel challenging, it can also be quickening for both parties. When receiving feedback, we might at times feel it's unjustified, yet in our work we have a cultural understanding that we first practice deep listening before sensing next steps.

Mutuality can require profoundly leaning into situations and tolerating many tensions, sometimes over long periods. Despite its connotations, Mutuality is not inherently mild, kind, or nice. It doesn't always lead to resolution, reunion, or shared understanding and vision. It can eventually involve the deconstruction of existing forms, and emergence of new structures that express further integration and possibility. It's an evolutionary force that invites our surrender, and builds our capacity to endure and engage with it.

The practice of Mutuality is a journey of discovery that's typically more complex and fraught with hope and fear than the experience of individual awakening. We often say that awakening is easy; the real workout going forward is in Mutuality. Moreover, people at various levels of development come together in Mutuality, and mature at differing paces as they practice. The more integrated the personal self, the greater the potential to be skillful in Mutuality. Being accelerates our understanding and development through life experience, which is at times quite painful as well as gratifying!

Evolution Through Meeting Challenge

The inherent tension and oscillation between sacred holding and spiritual fire have characterized our we-spaces from their inception. Saniel Bonder's initial dharma articulation in 1992, a fiery declaration in support of matter, the body, emotions, and ordinary people, was greatly influential in shaping our we-spaces. In it he called for a restoration of the feminine principle that required holding the space open, and restraining the dominance of traditional top-down and formulaic teachings. Trillium Awakening embodies this orientation for spiritual awakening by honoring the existential equality of its participants, as well as the functional hierarchy of those holding teaching and organizational roles. This has led to more transparent and permeable governance to distribute power and authority, and recognition of the community of practitioners as itself carrying the transmission of awakening.

Over the years, several hundred have awakened to non-separate conscious embodiment in our we-spaces, contributing to a sense of family and solidarity—a nurturing safe haven. Our organizational structures train and support a growing body of teachers (over 40 as of this writing), and develop guidelines that clarify the ethical use of power. In 2011, our teachers circle implemented Holacracy,[6] a progressive, purpose-driven form of governance that differentiates role and soul. A community network of practitioners is crystallizing, and finding its organized voice.

To further ground the democratization of awakening within the Trillium Awakening work, we continue to update the policies and procedures that govern our we-space and sustain its integrity. In alignment with this work's original impulse to evolve beyond its guru-centric lineage, the teachers circle has found it increasingly crucial to enforce our member agreements impartially, without exception.

Recently, this obligation severely tested our community to outgrow its inertia of disregarding breaches in conduct. In 2014, after frustrating and futile attempts to address problems mutually, the teachers formally called Saniel to be accountable for violations of our Teachers Circle Ethics Policy governing teachers' expression of anger and use of power. The tensions fueling this situation catalyzed intensive soul-searching and cultural assessment, including speaking perspectives from many points in a full spectrum of responses. It was a trying time for all. In the end, the efforts to bridge our differences in approach and organizational structures proved irreconcilable, leading to a separation of entities. Saniel relinquished membership in the teacher's circle, and established exclusive ownership of his trademarks. The teachers chose to rebrand and establish their own independent organization. After two rough years, the resulting groups are in a process of grounding in their own realities, having been freed from the need to encompass such an expanse of differences between them.

From the current vantage point, we teachers and leaders of Trillium Awakening see our work evolving its capacity to hold human limitation while releasing identification with obsolete patterning, and catalyzing more integrated levels of development individually and within our we-spaces. This evolutionary ordeal continues to call us toward both richer personal investigation and impersonal transcendence in service to our purpose.

Our Contribution to Collective Evolution

As we make our way through the challenges of rebuilding, we hope that our process of ongoing healing might be helpful for other groups

---

6. Holacracy is a social technology or system of organizational governance in which authority and decision-making are distributed throughout a holarchy of self-organizing teams rather than being vested in a management hierarchy. See Robertson, 2015.

as they face into common difficulties of maturing and evolving. Among our contributions to collective evolution are the many individuals who have experienced profound healing, awakening, and integration in our we-spaces, where vulnerable, authentic, heart-awakened, energized beings find their calling in all manner of cultural expressions. In their capacity to hold paradox and the Core Mystery of embodied life, our practitioners provide robust containment for a full range of immanent and transcendent experience.

Our community is revealing itself as a vital launching pad from which teachers and practitioners evolve new perspectives on their accumulated repertoires of practices, interests, and skills. This expansion, coupled with our foundational teachings, brings the possibility of awakening to growing numbers of people. Articulations of our core values now appear in various fields of creative expression, shamanic and somatic therapies, traditional and mystical spirituality, consciousness studies, and fresh interpretations of typological maps. The groundwork of conscious embodiment established through the Trillium Awakening sensibility, and the participation of thousands over the past twenty years, have provided rich, permeable soil for deep waters to seep upward, infusing all with the living spirit of transformation and enterprise, through a great diversity of individual expression and collective engagement.

Author Bios

Sandra Glickman MA, Transpersonal Psychology, MA, English Literature. A lifelong investigator of transpersonal and integrated studies, she has especially advocated exploration of Consciousness, and also study of types (through models such as Enneagram, Human Design, Somatic Experiencing) to facilitate recognition of patterns and shadow. As a long-time Senior Teacher, she has participated in Trillium Awakening from its early years, helping to found and evolve its vision and forms. She is now retired from 27 years as a licensed psychotherapist, with continued participation and focus on shepherding the training of teachers and leaders and grounding of supportive forms for emerging structures. Her past spiritual association is with Adi Da and various yogic communities. You can learn more about her work at sandraglickman.com

Deborah Boyar, Ph.D. offers an interweave of somatic awakening and transpersonal healing that continues to evolve over many years of study and practice. As a senior Trillium Awakening teacher and co-founder of The Institute of Awakened Mutuality, she supports students in an integral process of self-discovery through an open-source architecture of nondual awareness. Her we-space orientation is informed by her studies with Terry Patten, Craig Hamilton, and Patricia Albere, as well as her practice of Holacracy as a partner at HolacracyOne and within the Trillium Operating Circle. She brings to the we-space a deep understanding of post-trauma resilience through assisting multiple Somatic Experiencing trainings and volunteering at a clinic she co-founded at an integrally-inspired homeless shelter in northern California. In India, she participated with teams assisting survivors of natural and human disasters and sponsored women's development initiatives. Her lineage path includes Adi Da and Integral Spiritual Practice. For further information, please see deborahboyar.com.

References

Bonder, S. (2004). Healing the spirit/matter split. San Rafael, CA: Extraordinary Empowerments.

Dyczkowski, M.S.G. (1987). The doctrine of vibration: An analysis of the doctrines and practices of Kashmir Shaivism. New York: New York State University of New York Press.

Robertson, B.J. (2015). Holacracy: The new management system for a rapidly changing world. New York: Henry Holt.

CHAPTER 6

Uncovering Four Levels of Leadership Presence:

A Dynamic Presencing Journey

Olen Gunnlaugson, Ph.D.

My boat struck something deep.
Nothing happened.
Sound, silence, waves.
Nothing happened?
Or perhaps, everything happened
And I'm sitting in the middle of my new life.
— Juan Ramon Jimenez

Background

This chapter explores an application of my current research and emerging body of work in Dynamic Presencing,[1] which is focused on

---

1. Dynamic Presencing has developed more recently from research and practice with my MBA students internationally, several we-practice communities as well as my longer term research in presencing (Gunnlaugson et al., 2013; Gunnlaugson & Scharmer, 2013; Gunnlaugson 2007; 2006); complexity and contemplative approaches to presencing (Gunnlaugson, 2011a, 2011b); conversational leadership (Gunnlaugson, 2012; Gunnlaugson, 2015); intersubjectivity (Gunnlaugson, 2011a; 2009); generative dialogue (Gunnlaugson and Moore, 2009; Gunnlaugson 2007; 2006), Bohmian dialogue (Gunnlaugson, 2014); integral theory & consciousness development (Gunnlaugson, 2014; Boiral et. al, 2013; Gunnlaugson, 2005, 2004) and consciousness based forms of transformative learning (Gunnlaugson, 2008; 2007).

establishing presencing as a core leadership ability that is accessible in any situation, whether in solitude, a coaching conversation, community of practice, high performance team, or as this chapter describes more in depth, *a we-space collective*.

Presencing initially developed through Otto Scharmer and colleagues' *Theory U* (Jaworski, 2012; Scharmer, 2007, 2000a, 2000b; Scharmer & Kaufer, 2013), drawing upon important insights gathered from interviews with 150 thought leaders worldwide as part of MIT Sloan School of Management's *Global Dialogue Project*, as well as various consulting initiatives associated with the *Society for Organizational Learning*.

More recent perspectives have been applied from the field of management in the book *Perspectives on Theory U: Insights From the Field* (Gunnlaugson et al., 2013) as well as the international U. Lab MOOC (Massive Open Online Course) which started in the spring of 2015, where over 75,000 registered participants to date from over 185 countries have worked with applying Theory U to various societal, organizational and leadership challenges.

Before I introduce Dynamic Presencing, I will give some brief context on presencing for those readers who might not be familiar with it. Let's start with Scharmer's (2007) initial description of the presencing process:

> When moving into the state of presencing, perception begins to happen from a future possibility that depends on us to come into reality. In that state we step into our real being, who we really are, our authentic self. Presencing is a movement where we approach our self *from the emerging future*. (p.163)

Theory U is a process that helps leaders access the presencing experience at the bottom of the U^2, where Scharmer points out that we need to "let go of our old self and discover our emerging authentic self, which he describes as "our real self from the future" (p.189). Scharmer defines presencing as the "blending of the words "presence" and "sensing." It means to sense, to tune in, and to act from one's highest future potential" (p.8). The main injunction for accessing presencing is to "go to the place of individual and collective stillness, open up to the deeper *Source* of knowing and connect to the future that wants to emerge through you" (p.18). Senge et al.'s (2004) initial account of presencing in the book *Presence*, Scharmer's subsequent work with *Theory U* (2013; 2007; 2000a; 2000b) and Jaworski's more recent book *Source* (2012) have all made important inroads into identifying

---

2. The Bottom of the U identifies the conceptual location where presencing takes place in the U process.

the presencing process as being fundamentally about a way of leading from our emerging self and future

Dynamic Presencing builds from this body of work in supporting an overall creative restoration and re-embodiment of our wisdom nature in service of accessing an innate presencing perception that indwells within each of us. In this way, Dynamic Presencing is invested in developing our capacities to influence the emerging future by working directly at the inner and outer intersection points of emergence. This opens us into a generative perception of reality that is grounded in a way of being and action that are united and fundamentally aligned, in turn making presencing actionable at the very level of our perception and as a way of being in our leadership[3] and day to day life. Along these lines, Dynamic Presencing introduces a new language and process that supports engaging presencing amidst any type of leadership situation.

Senge's insight "collectively becoming aware of our inner places from which we operate in real time—may well be the single most important leverage point for shifting the social field in this century and beyond" (Scharmer, 2007, p.10) brings important clarity to a current leadership challenge. Dynamic Presencing builds upon Senge's insight by providing new insight into how to more effectively engage the underlying territory of these inner places from which our action arises.

To make this aim realizable, Dynamic Presencing introduces an updated process-method and language that begins where Scharmer and colleagues left off at the bottom of the U, establishing four new initiatory leadership journeys that continue down into this fundamental abyss and blind spot of our time, which to date has not been well understood (Jaworski, 2012). As the key deeper tacit grounds of our nature are contacted and integrated experientially via each particular journey, this brings forth an overall approach that supports presencing as an embodied generative capacity at the level of our overall perception and action.

As a whole, the approach of Dynamic Presencing draws on an active restoration of the more fundamental dimensions of our consciousness and human nature. As leaders learn how to integrate these inner dimensions of their experience as they lead, this shifts, grounds and reinforces their way of leading inside new territory. In this sense, through each of the four journeys, Dynamic Presencing clarifies an comprehensive approach for directly accessing and leading from these regions of being in order to catalyze and guide the presencing process.

---

3. Regarding the term "leader", this work draws from Margaret Wheatley's definition of anyone who is willing to help at this time.

For the purposes of this chapter, I will focus on the first Dynamic Presencing Journey which involves an excavation of the four lifeworlds: *Being Real; Being Witness; Being Essence and Being Source.* Each lifeworld introduces a particular synergistic culture of presence, relationality, self-sense and emergent we-space to engage with. I refer to each of these micro cultures of being as *lifeworlds,* a term borrowed from phenomenology that represents the immersive sensory world that each of us lives in.

Though we engage with a variety of lifeworlds on a daily basis, in this Dynamic Presencing journey, each lifeworld represents an activation site for a particular form of presence that is indispensible to presencing. As this wisdom is enacted and experienced at each stage of the journey, key transformational conditions are brought to life in the we-space both individually and collectively.

Being Real

The initial lifeworld is *Being Real,* which provides an initial reference point to begin letting go of whatever is obstructing us from a more transparent and grounded contact with our humanity. The initial focus is to get in touch with ourselves in a more centered and undefended way. Contact with this initial lifeworld makes it possible for our collective journey to begin from a place that is trustable and aligned with our actual ground. The *Real* cuts through mentalized, disembodied or spiritualized habits that otherwise obscure our immediate experience as its arising.

In the *Real,* the work involves connecting through to the places where our immediate experience is arising and discovering whatever awaits there. This encounter requires a willingness to discover where the ground of our presence lies through a discernment process at its source. The process is strengthened by a listening and sensing into this quality of our individual and shared nature, and acknowledging, mirroring and offering unconditional support with whatever content emerges.

Encountering the *Real* may involve getting in touch with our deeper nature or a troubling sense of inadequacy or inner struggle. For some, it can involve suspending our ideas of the *Real* on society's terms, inviting a more transparent meeting with ourselves directly. The details vary, regardless the exercise here is to forego analysis and judgment and to reconnect to our existential nature, inviting a transparency and fullness of being with ourselves and one another on terms that are less defined by tradition, history, personality, persona or self-image. Reconnecting with our ground of presence in a way that is not determined or influenced by these constructs invites us into a fuller contact with reality. Here, existential reality is given its place in our immediate experience, offering us a more robust and transparent ground for meeting and experiencing life as it is.

With this invitation to connect with the *Real*, first on our terms, then on its terms, we build a shared ground of presence for a collective exhaling and letting go of whatever might be obscuring this ground. As we let go into the presence of the *Real*, there is a discovery and settling into a more substantive ground of being than the personality. This reconnection facilitates a strengthening of awareness and awakens courage to stand with one another in this emerging space of individual and collective authentication. As we each increase our capacity to be with and orient from the *Real*, this brings us into the we-space in a way that authenticates the overall experience. Sensing into and orienting from the *Real* gives each of us permission to rest more fully in our nature, and activates conditions to allow ourselves to be recalibrated ontologically by the *Real* together

In the second phase, there is a shift from an emphasis on discovering to embodying the *Real* collectively. When this ground is experienced on terms of what we always already are, our imperfections and shortcomings can be met and transmuted rather than judged, managed, avoided or recoiled from. Whatever tendencies or habits prevented us from being more fully present with situations in the past, at this point, the *Real* provides a collective basis for discovering and then integrating our shared common ground as the principle basecamp for our collective journey together.

Being Witness

Following an immersion into the *Real*, we connect with the *Witness*. A principle practice to move into engaging the second lifeworld is "Surrendering into Witnessing" (Gunnlaugson & Moze, 2013). In this phase of the journey, our attention shifts from identifying with and orienting from the *Real* to relaxing into a place of noticing that we are having these experiences. *Being Witness* takes place when we let go from the *Real* and move into the *Witness*. Letting the *Real* settle into the background of our awareness, it shifts into becoming apart of the phenomenological context, which informs our exploration of *Witnessing Awareness.*

Traditionally, witnessing our experience involves noticing the content of our awareness and the respective currents of thought, emotion and the variegated impulses and opinions that arise in our mind streams. The surrendering aspect invites a deeper, willful letting go of the familiar identifications that we hold in our experience, including whatever identifications or experiences that helped us establish ourselves inside the *Real*. Surrendering into *Witnessing* involves initially noticing our immediate experience as it arises much like in awareness-based practices of meditation.

Traditionally, pointing out instructions offer an effective method for connecting with the ever-present *Witness* in our immediate experience. Becoming aware of our thoughts, feelings, and sensations as they arise releases us to be drawn deeper into the background of *Witnessing* Awareness that is noticing all of this. The nature of this experience is freeing, in that it helps us relax our hold on identifying our experience or thinking as "ours." In being less identified with arising thought, feelings or sensations, there is also a tendency to become more detached.

Surrendering into witnessing is more about becoming re-established inside the witness, not as a place for detached or non-attached seeing, but rather inside the subtle grounds of our more transcendent, released nature. Though this ground stands in contrast with the first lifeworld where we are more strongly immersed with the textures of the *Real*, the invitation here is to let this dimension of our nature influence our way of being more directly and subtly together as we give ourselves the chance to discover a released experience of *Witnessing* that is at once intimate, felt and subtly embodied.

The release from the gravitational hold and embeddedness in the *Real* invites the *Witnessing* dimension of our natures to unfold, helping us shift to a more distributed yet connected place. As we transition into collective *Witnessing* in the we-space, our self-sense shifts into this new ground, helping us discover a new baseline for being together and horizon-line of seeing that's useful for relating and orienting anew in the we-space.

Engaging the we-space from *Witnessing* collectively helps us transition into being more fully aware of the nature of our experience within the group field, which activates a more fundamental suspension of our seeing or *seeing our seeing*. This mode of suspended seeing activates new perceptual grounds from which we can experience our immediate reality and experience with a renewed perception from a distinct vantage point that again is paradoxically expansive yet connected to this distinct quality of being. This form of orienting from *Witnessing* fosters a subtly embodied yet expansive quality of inter-being, which is essential in discovering the prospects of *Witnessing* as a way of being— that is, an essential dimension of our natures.[4]

---

4. In this first journey of Dynamic Presencing, each lifeworld invites us into an immersion with an essential dimension of our presencing nature that with sufficient

Witnessing infuses the we-space with spaciousness, ease, a curiosity for what is emerging, de-centered compassion, and other welcoming and releasing transpersonal qualities of attention and presence. *Witnessing* gives us a vivid, subtly embodied yet comparatively (to the *Real*) more "impersonal" or "objective" access point to our thoughts and feelings. This is a marked contrast to the executive function of the everyday mind, superego and other psychological processes of the self that draw upon more survival-oriented action logics.

As such, Surrendering into *Witnessing* drops us into the next level of presence, and prepares the group for a deeper shift in our individual and collective identity. Released from the limiting conditions of the conventional sense of self and even to an extent, the *Real*, we let go into experiencing a basis for being that *has* but is much less identified with these needs, helping us discover a new empowered vantage point and locus of identity in embodied *Witnessing Awareness*.

When listening and speaking arise from relating and sharing from the subtly embodied *Witness* in the we-space, perception is drawn through a felt sense of unity with the Dynamic Presencing field. This fosters a shared experience of intimate yet paradoxically less personal grounds of relating. We are given more space to be more fully as we are, building on the insights and realizations of the *Real*. Exploring the subtle embodiment of *Witnessing Awareness* in the we-space gives a qualitatively distinct access to reality and our transpersonal nature. As we attune our listening and speaking from this place, Surrendering into *Witnessing* offers a rich and complimentary vantage point to the wisdom and grounds of the *Real*.

As groups learn to access and orient from the *Witness* collectively, attention is freed and can be redeployed toward discerning new knowledge, learning and discoveries in novel ways. Where the former exploration of the *Real* evoked an existential way of being and meeting reality, connecting to the *Witness* invites a sanctuary and release point for the self to grow into a fuller sense of its ground and nature. The *Witness* interrupts the intensity of the *Real*, helping us release our identification with life in a way that is less threatening as this background takes hold and begins to infuse our perception directly from a more distributed and compassionate grounds.

Here, entraining[5] from *Witnessing* helps us discover a distinct form of relational and inner coherence that expands and deepens our sense

---

practice and mastery, becomes potentially accessible to us at any moment and situation.

5. In the Dynamic Presencing process, there is an entrainment process in each lifeworld. This takes place both within and between us and generates a being-based coherence and dynamic quality of generative presence. In Dynamic Presencing, we

of the nature of what is real. In the we-space, our listening and speaking from contact with this place become our key instruments for helping us relax into discovering this particular dimension of our nature. As Surrendering into *Witnessing* becomes available in our immediate experience collectively, this opens fresh grounds for a different quality and order of emergence and insight to begin to germinate in the we-space[6].

Being Essence

Transitioning from *Being Witness*, we are invited to reconnect within, and open into *Being Essence*. Relaxing our identification with *Witnessing* Awareness gives rise to the possibility to move into the next iteration of a more subtle and receptive way of letting go into connecting with our essential nature. Orienting as *Essence* in the we-space relaxes *Witnessing* Awareness into the background. At this junction point, we explore the next level of our being as *Essence*.

By *Essence* I am referring to a multi-dimensional living dimension and quality of presence that draws from the innermost place of relating with our individual and collective experience. Inside *Being Essence*, *Witnessing* Awareness plays an indispensable unconditional supporting role in the we-space, as does the fierce yet vulnerable presence of the *Real*. The capacity to embody and orient from the lifeworld of *Essence* and to engage this dimension of presence serves us in a richer phenomenological grounds of relating in the conversation.

As we arrive into this lifeworld, questions arise: what conversational conditions optimally support our inquiry here? What does *Essence* involve as a sensemaking process for each particular group and moment of emergence? Where might participants be open or closed to in this invitation? Orienting from our essential nature deepens the center of gravity in the we-space, exploring *Essence* as our new baseline within the sanctuary and container of collective *Witnessing*.

The journey at this stage involves exploring phenomenological practices for activating our essential nature directly in the field. The

---

work with presence in a functional way that supports insight and new realizations. As we move through each lifeworld, this process stabilizes, clarifies and opens us into exploring and integrating more fundamental dimensions of our nature.

6. This article is primarily focused on the basic methodology for reconnecting with the four grounds or lifeworlds that activate corresponding levels of leadership presence. This particular method is taken up in greater depth alongside the other process-methods in my forthcoming book on Dynamic Presencing to be published in 2017.

focus here is more on ontologically re-rooting and re-acclimating to this inner, shared dimension of *Essence* and sensitizing ourselves to its nature inside the conversation. Unlike the spacious expansive *Witness* as a more fundamental aspect of who we are, *Essence* offers a distinct quality of ground as this site of our innermost sense of experience is uncovered.

As mentioned, each lifeworld provides distinct grounds for exploring particular inflections and functions of presence. Engaging our arising experience from *Essence* brings about key emergent conditions to access, embody, relate and inquire from this lifeworld directly in the we-space. Where *Witnessing Awareness* supported the relaxation of our identification with our thoughts and emotions in our immediate experience into a more meta-aware state, *Essence* Awareness re-engages us with the subtler more intrinsic qualities of being.

Learning to connect, orient and articulate from the interface of Essential Presence in the we-space shifts the group's center of gravity, bringing forth a distinct ontological resonance and sensemaking process. Through an essence-led discernment of what is, what is arising and our dynamic felt sense of this unfolding revelatory process, new ontological ground awaits our exploration and integration.

Being Source

Through the activation of these core dimensions of our individual and collective presencing nature, new presencing territory becomes available for both individual and mutual exploration. As we have explored, each lifeworld becomes a site for activating a particular mode of presence that lies at the basis of a fundamental presencing way of being.

Having arrived into *Being Source*, we draw on a mode of being that is no longer constituted by the self. Descending into this final lifeworld, our edge is to explore establishing contact with the origin point of our moment-to-moment experience. When *Source* presence is enacted in our perception directly, there is a re-orientation process from the very context and grounds from which we have come to know ourselves. Traditionally and as advocated for in the presencing literature, *Source* is accessed primarily through intentional practices in solitude (Scharmer, 2007; Jaworski, 2012). In Dynamic Presencing, *Source-based* stillness informs presence directly as a way of being when engaging presencing in the context of conversation and inquiry.

Arriving into *Being Source* involves a final letting go from the ground of *Essence*. Here we draw from *Source* as the fundamental not-yet-manifest domain of who we are as human beings and like the *Real*,

Witness and *Essence, Being Source* provides a distinct generative interface through which new sensemaking modes of being can be explored. *Source* represents the living origin point of our immediate experience and the underlying driving force of existence. As our presence grounds in *Source*, this fundamental dimension of our presencing nature opens us into direct contact with emergence.

Letting ourselves go into being with and from the *Source* dimension of reality re-connects us to this quiet still dynamism that's always already present, always listening for conditions to be more of itself through us. Exploring *Source* directly opens new ontological possibilities for sensitizing leaders to *Source* as an always present dimension of their experience.

The legacy of modernity in western culture has left us with a mostly disembodied fragmentary sense of what it means to really be, relate and know through to that place of *Source* reconnection and co-enactment. Bhaskar (2013) elaborates:

> The deep interior or fine structure of any moment of being. If you go into this deeply enough, if you just observe it, suspending all judgment, thought, emotional turbulence or anything else except that moment and, so observing, eventually you will experience identification with it, and the ground-state on which it depends, together with the love, intelligence, energy, bliss, etc. which characterizes it. The experience corresponds to what was believed by traditional religious theorists to be uniquely characteristic of religious experience, whereas I am arguing that it is characteristic of all moments of experience, aspects of being, even of the most ordinary sort, in their deep interior... So you can have the sort of experience that people normally only experience when listening to great music or possibly a moment of scientific inspiration, or certainly indeed through meditation or prayer, in any moment of life and in relation to anything. For anything to exist it must connect in some way to a ground-state and the cosmic envelope, and eventually through the power of your pure awareness, you will be able to access it.

Inside the experience of *Source* lies an invitation to open into this non-contingency and letting go of any remaining individual efforting to be someone, do something or get anywhere other than exactly where we find ourselves. *Being inside Source* recalibrates our ontological capacity and perceptual receptivity to directly being-with emergence from the inside out.

Source establishes key ontological grounds for engaging our emerging, evolving world and kosmos. Connecting to *Source* unites us with the fundamental grounds of our experience. While the *Real* connected us to our fierce yet vulnerable edge, *Witnessing* opened us into an expanded sense of self and relational field and *Essence* reconnected us with our unique innermost sense of being, *Source* awareness activates a quality of presence that is not tied to the limiting and conditioning influences of the manifest world of form.

In this way, new generative and actionable dimensions of *Source* in service of our emerging world and future are uncovered, particularly as *Source* becomes accessed as a discernable way of being. As our primary groundless ground, *Source*, contrary to certain wisdom traditions, does not lie exclusively within, and contrary to political philosophers and traditional activists, does not lie exclusively without either.

In the context of this work, *Source* serves as a dynamic interface for accessing generative ways of being that are uncovered in the depths at the very bottom of the U. *Being Source* puts us in direct ontological participation with emergence. By establishing an inner basis for leading from within, *Being Source* restores and empowers a deeper collective intuition that lies at the heart of social change processes. Meaning, that at more fundamental levels we are intimately apart of the world's constitution and its emergent process. To the extent to which our ontological constitution can be recalibrated to this realization as a way of being, is the extent to which source intelligence can guide our leadership and actions in the world. Systems awareness is not enough; rather a leadership education is needed that draws directly from the very interior source dimension that give rise to our world, culture and selves amidst this period. Making contact with *Source Presence* that constitutes our lives individually, collectively and ultimately at the bottom of the U opens up a new context to engage presencing from.

And so with practice, familiarity, and the process of discovery, each of these lifeworlds eventually becomes an embodied *homeworld*, analogous to the AQAL terms of each *state* of presence with adequate practice becoming a more enduring *stage*. With each homeworld, a more agile, intelligent, receptive whole mode of orienting, feeling and thinking can emerge and inform the first journey of the Dynamic Presencing process as we transition into learning how to steward and lead from these inner regions of our experience.

Transformative Phenomenology and Closing Reflections

The modern self, mainly for a broad range of cultural and historical reasons, has suffered as the instigator and victim of its own perceptual degradation, hence in part the restorative injunctions built into this work. This first Dynamic Presencing journey works with a phenomenological process of re-sensitizing our faculties of perception and observation to be more intimately and directly attuned with the emerging nature of self and reality directly.

Process-wise, transformative phenomenology supports the cultivation of a subtle discerning attention to whatever is arising in us individually and collectively through each of the lifeworlds. Learning to calibrate our ontological and sensemaking processes from these four grounds or levels of presence develops a felt embodied basis for practitioners to experience. This is indispensable to attending more closely, granularly and synesthetically[7] to our overall presencing experience.

Each lifeworld opens us into a particular depth dimension of being, which has a specific baring and influence on the quality and depth of our presence. With practice and familiarity, this develops an embodied meta-capacity to shift vertically between different self- or being-senses (*Real, Witness, Essence, and Source*) depending on the respective needs of the presencing moment and we-space collective.

Transformative phenomenology supports this activity by returning our attention to be with the inner territory of what is emerging in the we-space directly. Whether an idea, thought, or analogy—the underlying attitude is one of listening for and discerning essential emergence in the mundane, continuing to open into *what-is* to inform and guide our sensemaking. In this way, we are invited back into our senses to discern, engage, and discover what is new or significant in us as the whole process is emerging. Each we-space then becomes an insight-catalyzing collective medium through which individuals and groups can re-calibrate their perceptual processes from a more dynamic and embodied vantage point as it arises in the we-space.

Instead of mentally abstracting or emotionally reducing our immediate experience, the Dynamic Presencing Journey of *Primary*

---

7. Synesthetic awareness is the natural merging of sensory pathways, bringing about a deeper integration and union of the senses. Thought of as a kind of hidden sense, Synesthetes tend to be aware of distinctive aspects of experience simultaneously, which serve as a reference point for developing a more integrative generative perception.

Being returns us to nourishing our attention and curiosity directly and intimately from presence itself. Inside the we-space, this can support a more precise attunement to the presencing nature of our emerging experience as it arises.

Author Bio

Olen Gunnlaugson, Ph.D. is an Associate Professor in Leadership & Organizational Development within the Department of Management in the Business School at Université Laval, in Quebec City, Canada. He brings an increasingly inter-disciplinary approach to his current research in conversational leadership, dynamic presencing, we-space practice and facilitation, as well as contemplative management skills and coaching. His research has been published in several books as well as numerous international academic journals and presentations at leading conferences. Project-wise, he is currently collaborating with colleagues on a number of books and articles. More recently, he was the chief co-editor of the management book, *Perspectives on Theory U: Insights from the Field*, a recently published anthology featuring applied research on Theory U by 30 faculty members and associates from North America and Europe.

References

Boiral, O., Baron, C., Gunnlaugson, O. (2013). Environmental Leadership and Consciousness Development: A Case Study among Canadian SMEs. Journal of Business Ethics.

De Quincey, C. (2000). Intersubjectivity: Exploring consciousness from the second person perspective. Journal of Transpersonal Psychology, 32(2), 135-155.

De Quincey, C. (2005). Radical knowing: Understanding consciousness through relationship. South Paris, ME: Park Street Press.

Gunnlaugson, O & Meglin, C. (2015a). The All-Space. MBA 506 Conversational Leadership, Meridian University, San Francisco.

Gunnlaugson, O. (2015b). Dynamic Presencing: Illuminating New Territory at the Bottom of the U. Integral Leadership Review. Jan-Feb. 2015.

Gunnlaugson, O. (2014). Invited Article. Bohmian Dialogue: a Critical Retrospective of Bohm's Approach to Dialogue as a Practice of Collective Communication. Journal of Dialogue Studies 2(1), 25.

Gunnlaugson, O., Vokey, D. (2014). Evolving a Public Language of Spirituality for Transforming Academic and Campus Life. Innovations in Education and Teaching International. 51(4).

Gunnlaugson, O. & Walker, W. (2013). Deep Presencing Leadership Coaching: Building Capacity for Sensing, Enacting and Embodying Emerging Selves and Futures in the Face of Organizational Crisis, In Gunnlaugson, O., Baron, C., Cayer, M. (2013). Perspectives on Theory U: Insights from the Field. IGI Global Press.

Gunnlaugson, O. & Scharmer, O. (2013). Presencing Theory U, In Gunnlaugson, O., Baron, C., Cayer, M. (2013). Perspectives on Theory U: Insights from the Field. IGI Global Press.

Gunnlaugson, O., Baron, C., Cayer, M. (2013). Perspectives on Theory U: Insights from the Field. IGI Global Press.

Gunnlaugson, O., Moze, M. B. (2012). Surrendering into Witnessing: A Foundational Practice for Building Collective Intelligence Capacity in Groups. Journal of Integral Theory and Practice. 7(3), 78-94.

Gunnlaugson, O. (2012). Fostering Conversational Leadership: Re-Visiting Barnett's Ontological Turn. International Journal of Progressive Education. 8(2), 49-59.

Gunnlaugson, O. (2011a). Advancing a Second-Person Contemplative Approach for Collective Wisdom and Leadership Development. Journal of Transformative Education. Sage Publications, 9(1), 134-156.

Gunnlaugson, O. (2011b). A Complexity Perspective on Presencing. Complicity: International Journal of Complexity and Education. 8(2), 1-23.

Gunnlaugson, O. & Moore, J. (2009). Dialogue Education in the Post-Secondary Classroom: Reflecting on Dialogue Processes from Two Higher Education Settings in North America. Journal of Further and Higher Education. Routledge (UK). 33(2).

Gunnlaugson, O. (2009). Establishing Second-Person Forms of Contemplative Education: An Inquiry into Four Conceptions of Intersubjectivity. Integral Review, Arina Press, 4(2), 23-56.

Gunnlaugson, O. (2008). Metatheoretical Prospects for the Field of Transformative Learning. Journal of Transformative Education, Sage Publications, 6(2), 124-135.

Gunnlaugson, O. (2007a). Revisioning Possibilities for How Groups Learn Together: Venturing an AQAL Model of Generative Dialogue. Integral Review, (3)1, 44-58.

Gunnlaugson, O. (2007b). Shedding Light upon the Underlying Forms of Transformative Learning Theory: Introducing Three Distinct Forms of Consciousness, Journal of Transformative Education, Sage Publications (4)2.

Gunnlaugson, O. (2006). Exploring Generative Dialogue as a Transformative Learning Practice within Adult & Higher Education Settings, Journal of Adult and Continuing Education. Scotland. (12)1, pp. 2-19.

Gunnlaugson, O. (2005). Toward Integrally-Informed Theories of Transformative Learning. Journal of Transformative Education, Sage Publications (3)4, pp. 369-398.

Gunnlaugson, O. (2004). Towards an Integral Education for the Ecozoic Era. Journal of Transformative Education, Sage Publications. (2)4, pp. 313-335.

Jaworski, J. (2012). Source: The Inner Path of Knowledge Creation. Barrett-Koehler Publishers.

Peat, D. (2008). Gentle Action: Bringing Creative Change to a Turbulent World. Pari Publishing.

Rosch, E., & Scharmer, C. O. (1999). Primary knowing: When perception happens from the whole field (Interview with Eleanor Rosch). Retrieved January 23, 2015, from https://ai.wu.ac.at/~kaiser/birgit/Rosch-1999.pdf.

Scharmer, C. O., & Kaufer, K. (2013) Leading From the Emerging Future: From Ego-system to Eco-system Economies. San Francisco, CA; Berrett-Koehler Publishers.

Scharmer, C. O. (2007). Theory U: Leading from the future as it emerges. Cambridge, MA: Society for Organizational Learning.

Scharmer, C. O. (2000a). Presencing: Learning from the future as it emerges. The Conference On Knowledge and Innovation. Helsinki School of Economics, Finland, and the MIT Sloan School of Management.

Scharmer, C. O. (2000b). Conversation with Francisco Varela: Three Gestures of Becoming Aware. Retrieved January, 02, 2015, from http://www.iwp.jku.at/born/mpwfst/02/www.dialogonleadership.org/Varela.html.

Senge, P., Scharmer, O., Jaworski, J., & Flowers, B. (2004). Presence: Human purpose and the field of the future. Society for Organizational Learning. Cambridge, MA: Society for Organizational Learning.

Warren, S. (1984). The emergence of dialectical theory: Philosophy and political inquiry. Chicago, IL: University of Chicago Press.

Wilber, K. (2006). Integral Spirituality: A Startling New Role for Religion in the Modern and Postmodern World. Integral Books: Shambhala.

CHAPTER 7

We-Space, Integral City and the Knowing Field

Marilyn Hamilton, Diana Claire Douglas, Cherie Beck, Alia Aurami, Joan Arnott, & Linda Shore

The concept of morphic or Akashic fields creates the possibility that we could harness the intelligence that is concentrated in the city to generate much greater (more complex) intelligence capacities than we have ever dreamed of. If we could truly learn how to think together, we could harness the massive leverage of parallel processing that has enabled us to design modern computers and neural networks (like the linking of personal computers for the SETI extraterrestrial life search project). If we can do this, we will see a significant phase shift in human intelligence that will give cities major new incentives to create optimal life conditions to better support human existence. By the same token, in an optimistic spirit, I anticipate that when this intelligence is harnessed we will finally have the power to add value to life on Earth that is both sustainable (not over-using resources) and emergent (always creating new capacities from existing resources).[1]

---

1. Hamilton (2008) identifies that an Integral City has 5 sets of 12 Intelligences. Contexting: Eco, Emergent, Integral, Living; Individual: Inner, Outer; Collective: Storytelling, Structural; Strategic: Inquiry, Meshworking, Navigating; Evolutionary

We Begin With Mystery

In the Beginning is The Conscious Divine Mystery both creating and observing it all. And The Great Mystery comes forth as inquiry and evolution, as I and we, as humans and cities, as space inside and space outside, as intelligence and heart, as fields and possibilities, as life and perspectives, as unity and boundaries, as experience and space, as Kosmos and bees.

Discovering the Boundaries of Our We-Space: Who and What Is Integral City?

In order to frame our We-space we will start with the "strange attractor" that drew us together to explore the question: "Who and what is Integral City?" Integral City (IC) is both a new paradigm and/or archetype for the city[2] – discussed below – and a community of practice. Integral City Community of Practice (ICCOP) is the organization that has emerged in service to birthing IC into the world. At the heart of our We-space was the dream/vision of an integral way of being, such that we would transcend and include the limitations of individual bio-psycho-cultural-social modes of existence that embraced systems, complexity, evolution and spirituality into a transpersonal experience of reality that opened the boundaries of human interaction into the morphic and/or subtle realms (Hamilton, 2008, p.73; Sheldrake 1988; Wilber, 2006). Tapping into such evolving life-giving capacities and imagination skills within and for (our) cities seemed to open the eventual planetary We-space for Integral Cities. This meta-dream then became how to bring all of the Voices in the city (and its surrounding areas) into a safe space inside which we can listen to each other, learn from each other, dream together, share stories, imagine together in a life-giving We-space to create an Integral City.

---

2. Douglas and Hamilton (2013) identify multiple usages of the words "Knowing" and "Cities"

> Knowing Cities: the Knowing Field and Cities
> *Knowing: we can come to know a city, know about it, and be guided around it*
> *Knowing: the city itself as an energetic entity has a knowing capacity within it*
> *Knowing: a way of perceiving beyond the five senses*
> *Cities: are the largest human systems yet created.*

Cities: include all the dynamics of individual, family, organizational and community systems co-existing in rhythms, cycles, patterns and fields.
Cities: are collective expressions of the human species, like a Human Hive.

Our core purpose, intention and commitment now has become to work with others co-creating conditions for the emergence of the Integral City as Gaia's organ-of-consciousness enabling her to reflect upon herself. [3]

Emerging the Human Hive

Our we-space (and all Integral City work in the world) draws on the ancient ways of knowing, intelligence and resilience of honeybees (the most evolutionarily advanced invertebrates on the planet (Bloom, 2000). The honeybees and their hives are a life-form which gives rise in us to totem imagery; such imagery reminds us of being and belonging in a much greater We-intelligence that includes humanity yet goes beyond the limitations of an anthropocentric focus and experience. The metaphor is a subtle yet embodied reflector and reflection. Bees are pollinators whose activities are hugely life-giving. Symbolically, images of the bee and the hive structures are embedded in our We-space and are a reminder of serving life for Life itself.

An Integral City can be metaphorically viewed as a "Human Hive." Beehives are sustainable and emergent when all four bee "roles" work together in a natural synergistic emergent expression which some refer to as the Hive Mind. Integral City uses Howard Bloom's wording: those roles are named Producer, Resource Allocator, Inner Judge, and Diversity Generator.[4] The Integral City conceptual framework has identified those four roles among humans in cities as "the four City Voices," named Citizens, Civic Managers, Civil Society, and Business. An Integral City can be thought of as a healthy Human Hive to the extent that those four voices become coherent and resonant to one another and learn to express synergistically as the Human Hive Mind (HHM). In Integral City terms HHM arises from the demonstration of Integral and Emergence Intelligences[5]; in other words, the emergent "thinking together" capacity of the city. This combination of intelligences is how the We-space operates at the

---

3. Lovelock (2009) refers to humans as the "reflective organ" of the living system that is earth i.e. Gaia

4. Bloom (2000) identifies 4 roles in the beehive: Conformity Enforcers, Diversity Generators, Resource Allocators, Inner Judges. Hamilton (2008) extends this to the Human Hive and refers to the same roles as well as the 4 voices: Citizens, Business, Civic Managers, Civil Society.

5. Integral City Intelligences – see Hamilton (2008); Footnote 1; website www.integralcity.com

city scale, in service to a superordinate Purpose in ecological balance with the eco-region (environmental surroundings) of the city.

It is important to note that emergent deep presence of humans working together as Human Hive Mind in our 4 roles (described above) as Gaia's reflective organ in service to her wellbeing is completely different from (in fact opposite to) the stereotype of the "hive mind" as a repressive communistic autocratic state. Because Human Hive Mind involves synergy toward a shared Purpose of benefit to the Hive/city and to the Planet, HHM is one of the higher stages of We-space, an evolutionary step forward corresponding to evolution into We-space.

How We Perceive the City's Relationship to Gaia

As our relationships in ICCOP became more complex – evolving from individuals connecting as a "we" to practice groups, and now to wisdom space holders for the city, we have come to appreciate that the city is the most concentrated form of habitat created by and for Homo sapiens sapiens[6]. Cities, like beehives, are highly-populated energetic nodes linked within a global energetic body (Gaia,) which we experience biophysically, psychologically, culturally, socially and spiritually. The survival purpose of the beehive is to produce 40 pounds of honey annually and in the process to pollinate the local plant-life for ongoing renewal in the ecology. The survival purpose of the human hive (aka city) is to serve as Gaia's reflective organ[7] (while our individuals and groups act as cells and organelles in that organ) giving consciousness a means of expression at the planetary scale.[8]

---

6. Homo sapiens sapiens is the terminology used in Hamilton (2008) to designate the species. It conveys human being conscious of its knowing. Used also by Barbara Marx Hubbard.

7. See Endnote iii Gaia's Reflective Organ

8. James Lovelock (2009) and James Grier Miller (1978) both contribute to the understanding that human systems are fractal; i.e. they exhibit similar patterns at different scales.

Who Is the "We" of Integral City Community of Practice (ICCOP)?

We have grown from one person with a vision articulated in a book[9], to three of us engaging the 2010 course presented by Marilyn Hamilton, "The Map, the Mesh and the Human Hive", to Integral City's 2012 production of a 4-week global Online Conference (IC20C), which embraced hundreds of others as Thought Leaders, Designers, Practitioners and a core production team. Subsequently the IC20C Core Team converged to a group of 10 diverse women[10] from around the world. We have responded to show up in our brilliance to engage an idea, a big idea – enacting A Planet of Integral Cities, an explicitly interdependent matrix of integral cities across the globe.

Many of the 10 of us have never met in person, meeting via GoToMeeting or Skype, email, and phone. Week after week, month after month, year after year, for some for 5 years now, we have been drawn by a shared interest in exploring the possibility that the city is the natural scale of human systems from which the human species will emerge to the next level of complexity (Hamilton, 2008).

Among us is a great diversity of understanding and prior experiences of what "We-spaces" are, yet each individual has been able to let go of prior notions and enter the IC field itself, allowing its own emergence. Also, among us we represent multiple lines of relatively high developmental stages (as measured by various instruments like EQ (Goleman, 2009), SQ (Wigglesworth), sTAGES (O'Fallon, 2013), Spiral Dynamics (Beck and Cowan, 1996) or sentence completion (Cook-Greuter). Each of us brings into this we-space their history of owning and taking care of their strengths and gaps; all are willing to "own their stuff" and apply learning to themselves. These levels of consciousness-growth practices essentially operate invisibly and automatically as We-space practice injunctions, which enable our "no-holds barred" kind of engagement.

We are constantly being guided by the emergent we for decisions and choices about what to do and how to do it in our ICCOP work (constantly practicing to more clearly access and express that guidance). Laughter and playfulness are abundant; for example, riffing off others' words in word play during meetings.

---

9. Hamilton (2008)

10 No men so far, not by design or choice. We remain open to men engaging with us by attraction and/or invitation. (However, Hamilton, not altogether playfully points out that the honey beehive is made up primarily of females – who have the power to create both the reproducer-queen bee and the short-lived males, (Maeterlinck, 1954).

For the writing of this chapter we formed a working group, a small number of the core team who volunteered to carry out this experiment: writing from inside the ICCOP We-space. We came to realize in this process that a We-space had opened up through our investment in ICCOP, each other as individuals, and ourselves as a collective. We have come to trust each other's sensing, ways of knowing and inter-and-transpersonal relationships in our We-space.

We observe that our inner movements belong to the greater planetary shift moving away from the prevalent identification with the individual to a more collective sense of identity.

We see ourselves as a seed or part of a much larger collective we-space that holds space for other diverse and novel we-spaces to co-exist, and/or nest within themselves. That larger entity, to which we are in service, we call the Spirit of Integral City (which in turn is a smaller fractal of the entity Spirit of a Planet of Cities)[11].

After exploring the paradoxical nature of the relationship of individuals' awareness, collective awareness and emergent field awareness, our group came to realize that our maturing as a We-space moved from being a "we" as merely an aggregate[12] of "I's" toward being a "we" that was an emergent higher-order Conscious Presence — our emergent (with capital W) We-space.

What is most important is that we see ourselves as a prototype of the Human Hive We-space. The work we have done together – moving from individual to we to We-space – has led us to become aware of our own process as that prototype.

This We-space is still in an early stage of development. How far and fast a We-space can emerge is experientially based on the "I's" who show up in each moment. "I-work" and "we-work" are constantly bootstrapping each other, and our We-space flows and strengthens in the dynamic tensions between our sense of multiple "I's" and actual "We-space Presence."

Steps to Building our We-space Prototype

1. Crossing Boundaries: Individual transition

2. Noticing We-space as a presencing of the Human Hive

---

11. See Douglas and Hamilton (2013); Lovelock (2009) and Footnotes 2 and 3.

12. exploringsecondandthirdtier.blogspot.com/2013/04/exploring-phenome-non-of-collective.html

3. Exploring space inside, space outside, space between, and expanding our boundaries to include the Mystery and the field of HHM.

4. New stories

5. Systemic Constellation Work and the Field

Building Our Prototype: How Did We Become an Emerging We-space?

The prototype of the Human Hive Mind has gone through some noticeable stages. Each of us has noticed a form of individual transition from I to we and then to We-space. Then we became aware that our We-space had the qualities of a presencing field (discussed below) that we have come to call the Human Hive Mind (HHM). With a growing awareness of this emergent field, our boundaries began to dynamically shift, expand, and transform. New stories emerged about how we could use our We-space presence for supporting the Integral City paradigm to emerge in the world by serving city leaders, city voices and city roles in new ways. Finally we adapted the experiential process of Systemic Constellation Work to learn more about our We-space, the cities we were working with and the designs we were using to make cities aware of "integral" framings and make integral communities aware of "city" scale impact.

Crossing Boundaries: Individual Transition

Moving from contracted boundaries to crossing the boundaries to expanding into we/We has not always been an easy passage. One of our original triad described her journey as a "resolution of a war between I and we/We."

> We emerges from I. I emerges from We.
> How ironic. The evolutionary impulse that attracted us three to 'wake up the city' attracted others who were and are lit up by the same calling. We have evolved from a solitary I into a meta-connected we through building relationships and creating systems for delivering outcomes.

I just recently, though, found we in the I and I in the we. It's a profound shift, made possible from my numerous moments of engagement and change dynamics in the interior of the interior of our collective[13].

Somehow, staying open to the moment, with both the acknowledgement of the collective's existence (and longing to belong to it) and holding my own boundaries (and my desire to go back to my independent,' lone wolf 'stance) − I feel a shift, a POP, startling and settling at the same time. I sense movement through some kind of barrier. I feel joy and existential freedom. Where am I now? Oh, this is the Space of We!

I notice I am able to see and hear everyone more clearly, to receive insight about the perspectives being expressed in the discussion happening right now, I am interested and feel care and concern. I notice I am not writing for the we. I write, for the first time, from the we as I.

Noticing We-Space As a Presencing of the Human Hive Mind

Practice within our We-space is showing us the paradox that within the city/Human Hive as a We-space, the individual "I"s" don't disappear; rather they gain the capacities to come into coherence with the whole system of their We-space. Coherence arises from the internal alignment of all the elements of the Human Hive/city system/city We-space in pursuit of its Purpose in such a way that energy is optimized. At the same time "resonance" emerges when the Human-Hive/city-system/city-We-space is aligned externally in the Purpose of service to its environment: as the hive − human or bee − literally resonates with its surroundings.

We are discovering an emergent fractal evolution from me to we, then through We-spaces such as this group, and then through the fractals of we-spaces we find or catalyze within cities. Thus the leaps from me to we, to the city/Human Hive and then to all of humanity

---

13. Wilber (2006) refers to all quadrants as having both interiors and exteriors − which he calls Zones. The interiors of all quadrants have odd numbers (1, 3, 5, and 7). The exteriors have even numbers (2, 4, 6, and 8). The Interior of the interior collective quadrant (Lower Left Quadrant) is called Zone 3.

are becoming naturally bridged, with no part of the natural fractal growth sequence or scale skipped over.

Exploring space inside, space outsid[14]e, space between, and expanding our boundaries to include the Mystery and the field of HHM.

But Then a New Realization Occurs: The We-Space is in the Space In-Between!

In our We-space an attractive force has emerged that is sensed by each individual and at the same time seems to have become the container in which we think/sense, act, relate and create. This force of attraction is neither simply the energy from inside the boundaries nor the energy from outside the boundaries of our container – rather it is a force which has a palpable energy of its own that we simply name the "Space Between." The fullness of the Space Between in our We-space may have implications for cities, possibly because the nature of this we is (presently) all women. Maybe that is why we sense that one of the important developmental tasks for cities is to create we-space as a womb/container that will birth what's next for cities. Perhaps, this occurs to us because we see the city as a larger scale or fractal of our being mothers (or "I's" who have the capability of containing new life) capable of being life-givers for a new we? It is a question we pose and hold in the field of our pregnant We-space.

New Stories

As noted above, emergence (as We-space) happens through coherence and resonance – when the roles within the Human Hive have connected internally and externally to the requisite degree. We have learned that the bees "we," by feeding each other continuously. Humans feed each other through stories. "People need stories more than food to stay alive."[15] This is especially so in the city/Human Hive – in fact it appears to us that the free flow of stories is what enables and expands the capacity of the Human Hive. It is how we reflect for Gaia.

---

14. This is in contrast to some other groups where there appears to be an assumed grand leap from the group we-space to all of humanity.

15. Lopez, B., & Pearson, T. C. (1990). Crow and Weasel. Berkeley, CA: North Point Press.

One such story that we are learning from our own practice is that anybody can change a city by changing themselves – finding the energy to change by noticing what gives them energy. That energy may come from any of the 4 voices of the city – including and especially the citizens. This story is in contrast to the old story that cities only change from the center – from the decisions and actions of civic managers in city hall who work from the top down. We see this shift in our own thinking changing the way that we interact with all the voices in our own cities. Some of us have access to and interact with civic managers (e.g. conducting research on housing policies); many of us connect with civil society (e.g. giving a sermon to the church's new city role as Integrator of the Human Hive); some of us work with entrepreneurs (e.g. advising investors on how new transportation models impact the city); and all of us are citizens influencing our friends, families and neighborhoods (e.g. improving the health of the system by connecting face-to-face "unplugged" in the coffee shop; practicing the Master Code of caring for self, others and place in our meditations; or contributing to the very source of (real) food in the city by planting community gardens.

This is ICCOP's unique offering to cities as Human Hives. Within our connective exchanges we have discovered a secret key – that anyone has the power to initiate change in the city and tell the story about it. This realization transposes the simple value of stories as entertainment into the value of stories as catalysts that emerge new meaning (even a new paradigm) and shift our coherence and resonance (aka intention and meaning) from an old story (only city hall can initiate change) to a new story (we can all initiate change). As capacities expand via new stories, the stories we feed ourselves evolve through stages of purpose or meaning that span from the individual me to we to we-space. These are the story archetypes of vertical emergence. We as cells in Gaia's Reflective Organ are learning to tell, listen to and share stories so that we serve the healthy emergence of the Human Hive Mind.

Co-Creating Prototyping Methodology: Systemic Constellation Work

The Space in-Between our we-space and actual real life cities is occupied by the Purpose of our We-space to help create a Planet of Integral Cities. The tagline for some of our emails frames it this way:

> Out beyond the smart city, out beyond the resilient city,
> Lives the Integral City. There is a Knowing Field ... we
> will meet you there.

Our use of the word "Field" has more than one derivation. We embrace energetic AQAL state-structures as fields[16]. We also use "Field" to mean the "Knowing Field" — a term created by Albrecht Mahr,[17] a German physician, psychoanalyst and leader in Family Constellation Work. The "knowing field" is the constellation energy field, which informs the facilitator, representatives, client, and those observing the constellation of the underlying (often hidden) dynamics that are blocking or resourcing the flow of Life.

That "Field" is a we-space with forces, energies, dynamics and spheres of influence that are usually invisible to us. However, when we look at the scale of life on this planet, we notice that cities as human systems are in the center of the space between self and planet.[18] As we look around the world (including the work of others in this book) it appears that higher-consciousness stages of we-space at various scales are increasingly active and prevalent as the next stage of evolution for human systems, including cities which will become Integral Cities. As ICCOP, we attend to action in the world related to the integral evolution of cities, noticing where Second Tier[19] organizing principles are emerging in larger (communities and organizations) and smaller (teams and families) scales of human interaction. We are being invited to help individual cities evolve by working directly with other emergent "we-fields."

For example, on several occasions the ICCOP has been invited to hold energetic space for other city-related research projects and conference we-spaces, while not necessarily showing up physically or interacting person-to-person with these projects. We have done this for at least five city projects around the world. The experience of our We-space (connecting with the IC field) was that we could merge with the other relevant we-spaces for powerful and continuing happenings that occurred in real-time in the cities we visited to conduct a form of needs analysis; such as the engagement with indigenous peoples for whole new entrepreneurial activities; or the resolution of ancient conflicts that impacted present reality. The feedback from those situations indicated that they experienced the energy of our field,

---

16. Wilber (2006) describes State Structures, Chapter 3, p.71-83.

17. Mahr (2011) collectivewisdominitiative.org/files_people/Mahr_Albrecht.htm "Some years ago I came to name the informing energy field of a constellation 'The Knowing Field.'"

18. Hamilton (2008) represents these nested holarchy of human systems as Map 2, p.62

19. 2nd Tier refers to levels of consciousness that embrace all six of the 1st Tier levels of consciousness; looking at reality through whole systems, and one world lenses.

and that it contributed to beneficial happenings in their cities. That feedback then attracted us to the Systemic Constellation process that nurtures the We-space of our ICCOP as well as offers us a process for gaining access to the invisible we-spaces in particular cities.

Systemic Constellation Work As Process

Systemic Constellation Work[20] (SCW) was a natural choice for Integral City to use in order to do research and development to expand our ways of knowing the archetype of Integral City as a reflective organ for Gaia; and to support presencing, prototyping and processing for Integral City Community of Practice. Several of our group had previous experience with SCW, and knew its potential. Our lead constellator and Founder of Knowing Field Designs has exceptional skill in it and an adventurous spirit in new uses of it.

SCW itself is the over-arching term used by a world-wide community of constellators and coaches who practice both Family Constellation Work and Organizational Constellation Work. Originally founded by Bert Hellinger[21], a German philosopher and facilitator still working in his late 80s, SCW views problems, issues, conflicts, entanglements and designing the new from a systemic perspective, whether it be with individuals, families, organizations, or larger collectives. It is informed by a body of knowledge (based on living system design principles of belonging, balance and order) gathered phenomenologically from trainers and facilitators doing SCW's with thousands of people and organizations from around the world. It uses an experiential process in order to embody energy and information so that which underlies the issue, design or question is made visible. SCW is a change process revealing the hidden dynamics and potentials — the inner images, behaviors, challenges, and opportunities — that exist below our conscious awareness. SCW can be applied to an infinite number of issues on multiple scales, including individuals, families, organizations and collective groups like cities.

---

20. Why use the word "constellation"? SCW started in Germany and much of the original language used was translated into English from German. The nearest translation of the original German word "Aufstellung " was "constellation," which means "placement, assembly." So "Constellations" has a double meaning in this work: Constellations are groupings of elements within their home group — in families these are all the family members and in organizations, these are all the roles within the organization. It also refers to the process used of the setting up or placing of representatives in a visual way.

21. Bert Hellinger http://www2.hellinger.com/en/home/

Evolving a Non-Local, Non-Linear Process

Although SCW has historically been done in person within a group, quite recently constellators are finding ways to do this experiential process online. Our Lead Constellator developed with Integral City a way to do the process through GoToMeeting with up to nine members simultaneously in different locations in Europe and across North America on a monthly or bi-monthly basis.

The Process Steps Integral City Uses

The Context:

At ICCOP's monthly meetings, we always begin the meeting with a silent meditation and check-in ritual. The purpose is to create and tend a sacred WE space container for all our work together. When we have agreed to do a constellation during a meeting, this ritual also prepares the team – collectively – to enter the Knowing Field.

The Process:

ICCOP uses these process steps when working in the Knowing Field:

Preparation:

1. The Lead Constellator (LC) prepares herself by tuning into the Knowing Field (a sacred multidimensional space[22]) and receiving its guidance.

2. Each participant prepares themselves in their own way. Some meditate beforehand. They also prepare their own space – either desk top or floor space – placing a clock chart in the center of the space. This represents the Knowing Field, the circle or field within which we work. Using computer paper or sticky notes as place-markers on the clock chart, each participant is able to map the process visually and then share with the others so we are all working from the same map.

---

22. For example both horizontal and vertical dimensions: past-future; above-below.

Clarifying Intention & Placing Representatives:

1. LC clarifies the intention or question to be constellated in conjunction with sponsor and ICCOP.

2. LC calls in the Knowing Field which holds us in our work together. It too is a "we" space.

3. The elements (unique to each constellation) to be represented in the field are named.

4. Representatives for each of the elements are chosen.

5. The representatives for each element are placed in the field. As the representatives stand in their place, they report back what they are experiencing (as images, body sensations, emotions, thoughts or phrases) from the Knowing Field.

Observing Images:

1. This first image (which is a visual and kinesthetic map of the question or issue) externalizes what the question-holder or team is carrying internally and perhaps unconsciously. We then explore this image — noticing how all the elements represented interact with each other. Hidden dynamics begin to reveal themselves.

2. Transition images: The first image begins to shift (this is the transition image) when representatives make slow movements — sometimes big, sometimes small — showing the direction for change. Most often the different elements dialogue with each other, which is one way we gather collective intelligence.

3. Resolution image: When everyone or thing represented feels strong and peaceful and in their rightful place. When that does not happen in the time allotted, we bring the process to completion, acknowledging there is more to do.

Release, Harvest and Debrief:

1. Representatives release themselves from the element they have been representing and come back into themselves.

2. Debrief: Although the SCW protocol is to not interpret or analyze the constellation process, we find that each member may interpret or give meaning to what we have heard or seen. We ask: What can we harvest?

3. LC tracks how the SCW process is informing and impacting us over time. It is as if a seed has been planted, and its fruits blossom in their oen time!

4. We have found that we come together as a we who thinks and perceives together while each remains their own self (not thinking the same) having shifted our perspective through the greater knowing that is emerging from our SCW.

Facilitators' Roles

The LC, through her work with IC (and other organizations), is finding new ways of applying (and evolving) this experiential process — a natural emergence from the Knowing Field. She holds the palpable dimensions of SCW and through her embodiment of its philosophy and premises, she calls the we's to reflect on and trust in We-space.
The founder of IC, as a co-facilitator, invites and supports the use of constellation in IC, holds the dimensions of the city in the Field, and often sponsors the question or issue we constellate. She also applies the information received from the Field in her work with cities.

Practicing: Is Our Prototype Functional?

In an interview with Ken Wilber in 2012[23], he noted the importance of the (at least) 32 perspectives of AQAL: "The choice is to ignore these perspectives — each with their own demands, needs, desires and hopes — or start to build habitats in which different viewpoints can find a comfortable existence." Our practice in ICCOP suggests that SCW is a powerful methodology to access these different perspectives, give them voice and release energy to become more coherent and resonant.

---

23. Hamilton, M. (2013). Marilyn interviewing Ken Wilber during Integral City 2.O Online Conference

Each constellation process is an experiential experiment, where we are willing to enter the Mystery and be informed by it. We have used SCWs for two years, almost every month for many purposes, including building our own team/We-space, making crucial decisions, preparing members to take their place in working with and in cities (in Canada, USA, Mexico, Hungary, Russia), writing articles and chapters for books, testing several maps we use (Integral, AQAL, IC's 4 Voices for the city, ERAS, 4 Roles, Values)[24], and doing constellations on behalf of cities.

There are many ways that the process of SCW (placing representatives in the Knowing Field and watching their interaction) can be used. Originally, Bert Hellinger developed the process through a phenomenological (open, from the ground up, learn-through-experience) approach. The question or issue is placed in an "open field." Sometime later, Insa Sparrer and Matthias Varga von Kibéd developed the structural constellation approach. Here an already-pre-determined structure is placed in the field and the representatives interact with it and within it as well as with each other. Within the ICCOP, we have used both types of constellations with cities.

Following are two examples of our work with cities – the first an open, the second a structured constellation.

Amsterdam:

An example of an open phenomenological constellation in an in-person group setting. In the spring of 2013 the Integral City and Knowing Field Designs leaders presented (at the INFOSYON[25] conference in Amsterdam) a workshop entitled "Knowing Cities: The Knowing Field and the Emergence of Integral City Well-being." We co-facilitated a constellation on behalf of the city of Amsterdam as a demonstration of IC work. A Citizen (representing the Citizen Voice) sponsored the question: "How can Amsterdam step into its future in service of the Planet of Cities?"

The Citizen located where the Past and Future were in the room. In order to ask the Spirit of Amsterdam (SofA) permission to do the process, the Citizen placed representatives for herself and the (SofA) in the Field.

---

24. Hamilton (2008), p. 62-63 Integral City Maps

25. INFOSYON: the interdisciplinary international association for Organizational Constellation Work that sets standards for trainers and certification for facilitators.

The SofA was very near the Future and reported feeling she was in a new place, frozen and paralyzed, and yet she could see the Citizen was friendly. Shaking to release the shock, she reported that there was a need to go cautiously because there was huge energy coming from behind and that she needed a dike between herself and the Past.

Three dike representatives, a young man, a woman and an older man found their place between the Past and the Future.

Three other participants indicated they were part of the constellation and came into the Field standing near the Past. One was the Sea who could destroy everything and once the dike was in place she was not as dangerous. Another in the Past said he was an explosive force that could also destroy everything. The third was the mush/ground on which Amsterdam is built.

With these additional representatives, SofA said she could look at the explosive force (Past) briefly and she as the Spirit had been there "much longer than the Past."

The woman who was part of the dike turned from facing the Future to facing the explosive Past.

SofA (who was looking towards the Future) said she could feel a Force pulling her from behind.

A representative for this Force came in and stood between the SofA and the dike and said she was too strong for SofA and so moved further away and also turned to the Past.

The SofA collapsed on the floor as did the Force.

The Sea and the Mush, which had been in the Past (expressed as explosive forces) moved up to be by the Force.

The women-representing-the-dike turned to the Citizen and said that she needed to acknowledge and accept the energies from the Past. She repeated this several times. The Citizen said, "No it was enough to have seen the energies from the Past, not accept these energies. I am a new generation who has other work to do. I trust your generation to deal with the Past, and I will be free to move into the Future/ the new paradigm." (The energy of the new paradigm was palpable at this point).

A woman who was sitting as a witness stood up and wanted to be noticed. She was invited into the Field. She was the voice of immigrants who needed to be noticed and heard and included in the Field.

The Citizen-representative wondered who the client was. A witness said, "Gaia is the client!"

The processes ended when the Citizen-sponsor said that she had seen enough.

Although the constraints of the time for the workshop did not allow it, a period of debrief for all the representatives would enhance this process.

Post-session:

Spirit of a City is real and permission needs to be asked of any city we might work with. Since then, in the ICCOP constellations we always call in the Spirit of

Integral City and the Spirit of the Planet of Cities

A City in Mexico:

An example of a structural constellation via GoToMeeting:

A peer spirit organization was offering a major program in a city in Mexico (designated as M) and IC was invited to support their work in a variety of ways. We decided that the focus for this SCW would be to ask: "What did the Spirit of M (SofM) need to hear from all her eras (that exist at one time in a city) in order to move into her Future. What/how can she benefit from all her eras[26]?"

Each participant worked within her own "clock-diagram" map in her own home space—so we ended up with four different maps using the same elements.

The structure was a 4-quadrant model placed in the Knowing Field: Traditional (UR), Modern (LR) and Post-Modern (LL) and Integral (UL). The representative who stood for the SofM was placed in the center of the four quadrants.

---

26. M. Hamilton personal communication: I think of eras as waves of consciousness or worldviews. Let us call them Postmodern, Modern, Traditional and Integral. Let us consider that each era is the parent of the one that came before (a kind of lineage at city scale). All the eras are alive at the same time today.

Much information came from each representative for the SofM, and the SofM was able to give voice also. The Traditional Era needed acknowledgement, The Modern Era was disconnected from the Traditional Era, feeling a lot of confusion and disorder and cried for help. The Post-Modern Era said she was the heart-beat of the system and before she can connect with the SofM, needed to release in order to expand the circle of care that includes all others. The Integral Era needed more connection with the SofM and represented a vision in which the rootedness in the Traditional Era allows "there to be a dance, a dance that would draw others into the dance!" The Traditional Era was most connected with a long term vision. The Modern Era was connected to Now, and Post-Modern era was heart-oriented.

The SofM, by the end of the process, felt more whole and that she could operate as a whole when all the Eras were in alignment and communicating. "Rather than pull the Modern and Post-modern eras into the Future, they need to be re-rooted in an understanding of the traditional sense of responsibility for the Whole, caring for all beings."

After the process:

Following the process, the individual consultant who had requested IC support for city M was able to take the information back to M's city design team and help them include the Traditional voice in a significant way. The information was also used to write a proposal to sponsors for values-based city development. (The basis for identifying and aligning the values was informed by the SCW revelations of how the eras related to one another.)

What is the Outcome of SCW on Our We-Space? Appreciating Benefits and Insight

The impact we want from our SCW is the integration, alignment and synergy of multiple elements, entities, interests and motives, so the system can weave them together to create healthy, dynamic, comprehensive solutions to complex problems within rapidly changing complex environments.

Many benefits and insights have arisen from our explorations and experiments in the Knowing Field. Here are a few outcomes with particular impact:

- We practice our Inquiry Intelligence[27] by finding the clearest question or issue to bring to the field (such as illustrated in the two examples above).

- We give voice to all the elements related to an issue recognizing the Divine in all.

- We hear from all elements, often at a level deeper than our conscious mind. For example, we listen to the Spirit of IC, the Spirit of the Planet of Cities…and the Spirit of this chapter before making decisions or taking actions. We hear the 4 voices of the Human Hive.

- By listening so deeply to each other, the Old Story is opened into a new version — so that the New Story and a new stage can emerge.

- We can see the levels of change possible — an awareness of hidden dynamics; a shift in perspective; a movement either large or small that shifts direction; a resolution. The change may happen immediately or over time.

- We allow and are conscious that the Mystery is present with us in the field.

- We gather collective intelligence for the IC We-space and for the greater collective.

- Every time we tap into our We-space through SCW we learn more about our own ways of making meaning.

- We have come to trust in a Divine Order.

- Such a deep exploration enables us to experiment with AQAL maps and structures and test ideas and solutions.

---

27. Inquiry Intelligence is an Integral City intelligence (Hamilton (2008). integral-city.com defines Inquiry as an intelligence that asks key questions that reveal the meta-wisdom of the city:
- What is important to you?
- What's working in your life, family, community, school, health system, city?
- What's not working in your life, family, community, school, health system, city?
- What is your vision of the optimum in your life, family, community, school, health system, city?
- Where do your source your bio-psycho-cultural-social energy in the city?
For a truly vibrant city, each of the inquiries reveals a values system that must be healthy, in order for the whole city to be healthy.

- Through SCW, we have cared for our We-space. We have been and continue in the container with reverence.

We Continue in Mystery

Our We-space is an alive, pulsating, messy, joyful space that, at its best, is a generative mysteriously informing gathering that comes together in time and (cyber)space and is not limited to time and space. We sense our We-space is just one emergent, living, growing expression and evidence of the evolutionary wave of humanity's rapidly strengthening capacity to live, be, and relate in natural shared Kosmic consciousness.

While our We-space has become a part of, and an expression of the Spirit of Integral City, we also see this We-space scaling from the Space Inside of our prototype of the Human Hive Mind, through Spaces Outside, to the Planet of Cities, to the Morphic/Knowing Field, all in service to the We-space of the Planet, and back into The Mystery.

Author Bios

Marilyn Hamilton is the founder of Integral City Meshworks and the author of Integral City: Evolutionary Intelligences for the Human Hive. A city evolutionist, AQtivator, author, and research, Marilyn co-creates a global constellation of Integral City Meshworkers, Learning Lhabitats, Peer Associations and City Institutes. Learn more at integralcity.com

Diana Claire Douglas of Knowing Field Designs (aligning human systems with Life) is a constellator/facilitator (family, organizational, and social issues), social architect, artist, writer and explorer of the depths. She is internationally certified as an Organizational Constellation Work facilitator through the Bert Hellinger Institute of the Netherlands. Learn more at knowingfielddesigns.com

Cherie Beck sources generative capacity in human habitats, integrating Integral City intelligences within herself and emerging we-spaces as a result of those intelligences. She invites others to become co-producers of wellness at the intersection of two evolutionary ideas: that cities are both human hives and "organs" in Gaia's living planetary body cheriebeck@gmail.com

Rev. Alia Aurami is Head Minister of "Amplifying Divine Light in All" Church. Her primary ministry is fostering humanity's capacity for living in shared higher consciousness (exploringsecondandthirdtier. blogspot.com) and includes helping organizational leaders operationalize a Turquoise worldview (organizationalintelligences. blogspot.com).

Joan Arnott is an evolutionary amplifier who works with the subtle energy architecture of planetary systems, cities, and organizations. She is also known as an adept Listener and facilitator of deep reflective processes for leaders that expand world views and consciousness with a kosmocentric perspective. joarnott@shaw.ca

Linda Shore, MA is a Human Resources and Organizational Development Planner. She has served as Director of Human Resources for a metropolitan regional district and held various line and functional positions during her 21 years with the organization. She is currently working with Integral City on initiatives designed to advance sustainable cities policies and programs. She also provides coaching services to individuals and dispute resolution for groups. She has an MA in Leadership & Adult Training, and is certified with the Justice Institute of British Columbia in Conflict Resolution.

References

Beck, D., Cowan. (1996). Spiral dynamics: Mastering values, leadership and change. Malden, MA: Blackwell Publishers.

Bloom, H. (2000). The global brain: The evolution of mass mind from the big bang to the 21st century. New York: John Wiley & Son Inc.

Cook-Greuter, S. (2002). The development of action logics in detail. Retrieved from www.cook-greuter.com

Douglas, D. C., & Hamilton, M. (2013). Knowing cities: The knowing field and the emergence of integral city intelligence. [Constellations and Rituals]. The Knowing Field (22).

Goleman, D. (2009). Ecological intelligence. New York: Broadway Books.

Hamilton, M. (2008). Integral city: Evolutionary intelligences for the human hive. Gabriola Island BC: New Society Publishers.

Hamilton, M. (2013). Integral City 2.0 Online Conference 2012 Appendices: A Radically Optimistic Inquiry Into Operating System 2.0 – 36 Interviews M. Hamilton (Ed.) Retrieved from http://www.scribd.com/doc/123005653/Integral-City-2-0-Online-Conference-2012-Appendices-A-Radically-Optimistic-Inquiry-into-Operating-System-2-0-36-Interviews

Lovelock, J. (2009). The vanishing face of Gaia. New York: Harmony Books.

Maeterlinck, M. (1954). The life of the bee. New York: Mentor.

O'Fallon, T. (2013). The senses: Demystifying awakening. Unpublished manuscript. Paper presented at Integral Theory Conference 2013. San Francisco.

Sheldrake, R. (1988). The presence of the past: Morphic resonance and the habits of nature (1995 ed.). Rochester, Vermont Park Street Press.

Miller, J. G. (1978). Living systems. New York: McGraw-Hill Book Company.

Wigglesworth, C. (2013). SQ21: The twenty-one skills of spiritual intelligence. New York: Selectbooks.

Wilber, K. (2006). Integral spirituality. Boston: Shambhala Publications Inc.

CHAPTER 8

Evolving the We: A Journey and Inquiry

Miriam Mason Martineau & Stephan Martineau

Setting the Stage

In this chapter we reflect on our journey with the we-space and share the key conditions we have experimented with over the past twenty-five years as we have sought to discern a process that enables a depth of communion, a kind of collective intelligence we didn't know was possible until surprised (overwhelmed in the most positive sense of the word) and graced by it. We also reflect on the obstacles we have encountered, and the vision we hold for our collective future. This chapter is exploratory in nature. Putting words to our experiences, which are subtle even as they are deeply impactful and powerful, is not always easy. And yet, it is our hope that by articulating what we perceive as a next step in our collective evolution and how each of us can contribute to its emergence, this potential may find ever more solid footing.

The evolution of collectives is currently being explored in many different ways around the world, describing various degrees of intimacy and shared meaning making, of being heard and of hearing, of seeing and being seen by another. The deepening of these collectives depends on and enables the participants to show up increasingly as their truest selves, while opening up to that which unifies – from tasting the exquisite promise of a higher collective when we feel acknowledged and embraced for who we really are, to stepping more fully into expressing and receiving from our essential self (our soul-self), which facilitates accessing a higher mind and exploring collective intelligence together. This supports becoming available as one who listens to and expresses from Source, to the as-of-yet rare moments when we gather and, through pooling our most authentic selves, offer our highest capacity, intention, devotion, and build upon all of the above-mentioned nested layers of deepening togetherness. From here, it is our experience that the possibility of a new Being becomes present in our midst, a higher-level Being that is made up of the collective and more; a Being that, in our experience, has its own volition; a Being that is both woven together from those present and that weaves it all together, that is distinct and independent, and is more than a mergence of the many. For some readers, the emergence of a new Being in a we-space could sound anthropocentric, fantastical, utopian, impossible even. Nonetheless, we feel that this step is an important one connected to our collective evolution as communities and as a species. We base our exploration of this next step – the potential of people coming together at a higher octave to become present to what we are calling a new Being – on our experience and observations in collectives, as well as our reflections and study of certain evolutionary patterns. Rather than try to establish scientific validity for this emergence, this chapter shares the sense of a "We-Being" that aligns most closely to our experience and cross-referencing with others' experience.

Stephan's Journey: Glimpsing a Possible Future

Our explorations in evolving the 'We' began for me in India in 1991 on a walk during a meditation retreat where I experienced insight into and a deeper seeing of a possibility for collective evolution. Reflecting back to this vision, it felt like I was transported into a possible future, and experienced a distinct sense of coming home. People were living together in awakened awareness, having dissolved their attachment to egoic consciousness. They were aware of the underlying unity of everything, and were simultaneously capable of discernment of their own experience in relation to this unity in themselves and others. They emanated sincerity and a concentration of love poised at the juncture between full communion with each other and joyous autonomy. In the vision, there was a definite presence which was distinct and independent, weaving everything together. It felt like another Being was in the space, so tangible, almost visible. Like a thin, all-pervading mist or web or glue, it was between, over, around and through everyone and everything. Its expression seemed to be dependent on all the humans present, while simultaneously being an independent Being. Stepping further into this 'image' or 'film' I experienced an immediate shift in my self: a level of relaxation and breathing out, matched with an equivalent measure of heightened awareness and aliveness. Connecting with this Being seemed quite normal and everyday, even as I was aware of the new version of life this possibility offered: an existence where no one lost themselves, yet at the same time each was completely in service and available to this sacred experience.

I sat there, soaking it in. The bell rang, announcing the end of our 5-minute break – a few moments that felt more like a few hours and changed the course of my life; direction and purpose clarified and reconfigured. What became apparent to me in reflecting upon this experience was the possibility of our journey as human beings shifting more fundamentally from an 'I' to a 'We': building upon and nurturing individual awakened awareness to co-create a new level of togetherness. As I integrated this and other experiences and work related to the we-space, a new sense-making arose of the potential of coming together at a higher octave beyond the confines of the separate self, with this profound reverence toward the mystery of creation and becoming fully who we are as a basis for contributing to a greater whole. It felt like an important key to addressing the many questions and seeming insurmountable challenges we face as a human family. The vision held promise of collectively giving voice to a Being that may very well hold wisdom, which none of us can access on our own, thereby enabling an entirely different future.

Having just spent the past four years travelling around the world in search of my own "enlightenment," this glimpse of collective awakening was profound and changed the direction of my journey. I returned to Canada with a clear sense of purpose. This led to sharing the inspiration and invitation with others, searching for land in the interior of British Columbia and, a year later, the founding of Morning Star community—an integrally informed community of initially seven individuals. Propelled by the polarity glimpsed between the one and the many, the following questions guided us throughout the next decade: How can we reconcile the intrinsic human drives to, on the one hand, encourage and maintain individual autonomy and, on the other hand, come together in communion? What powers of invention and choice exist in us to discover a space where unique essence and essential oneness co-habit, thrive and lift us to new understandings of human potential?

Miriam's Journey: Beckoned and Intrigued

A few distinct threads contributed to the resonance and recognition I experienced when met with the potential of a higher 'We'. These included yearly immersion in a meditative prayer practice at a monastic community; growing up in a tight-knit family that sang and prayed together most evenings; stumbling upon profound states during Eucharist; and being hugely affected and inspired by my great aunt's visions. She conversed daily with angels, saints, Mary and Christ, receiving information, tasks and insight that brought the transcendent world very close. She also instilled in me the experience that we human beings are invited to co-create to a much fuller degree than we might often think.

Through her visions, family and close friends would regularly get tasked to pray – for countries, global matters, individuals, nature, and transformation. The notion that we could "move mountains" with prayer was seeped into my consciousness. While empowering, I was also faced with the challenge to become spiritually free and independently discerning in relation to these visions. Reading through one of her manuscripts when I was 15, I first came across her visions of a new time to come, one based on the unity of the human body, mind and spirit, being infused and becoming one with God's spirit and light; a time where a 'church' of sorts, a collective emerges that is inspired by the life of John the Beloved, who in her visions was shown as an example of the full development of the human being and the affirmation of life on earth in all its depth and breadth. I remember the wholehearted "yes" I experienced in reading of this potential to live 'heaven on earth', not putting unity with Spirit off into some far-distant future, but being invited to live into this possibility, now, here, alone and together.

When I met Stephan in my early twenties, he spoke of community with a similar passion and conviction. He also spoke of a new way for people to come together. More than an intellectual grasp of what he was saying, I got a visceral hit. It resonated and made a home in my soul. A couple of years later, during travel across Canada I engaged in two months of concerted prayer, which Stephan and two of his closest friends joined me in daily, for the emergence of this new time. This intensely focused invocation coincided with the beginning of Stephan's envisioned community.

As soon as we moved in, we began sitting together daily for an hour or two – in silence, in prayer, and in contemplative conversation – and in ways and for reasons we may never fully understand, we were gifted with a prolonged experience of higher we-states. The we-state was so palpable – drawing from the communion between us human beings as the vessel through which to come alive in our midst.

Where two or three are gathered in my name I am amongst them.

— Matthew 18:20

158

In our community, we sometimes called this higher-level collective Being 'Christ' – the experience reflecting our understanding of Christ's invitation and promise to relationally embody the Spirit of God on Earth as a humanity, and the Pentecost event whereby Christ's wisdom and presence were voiced and carried forth through a collective, individuals living with insight given and guided by the Holy Spirit.

There was something to these experiences that moved the deeper strings of our selves and felt like the most real experience we came across during that decade. The moments of 'it' stood out clearly and distinctly. What is it that happened in those fleeting moments and periods of grace? In one sense there was nothing extraordinary about them. Life was as life is – a blend of practicalities to be taken care of, relations to be nurtured, work to be done, play, prayer and meditation to sustain and inspire. Yet, at the same time, there was a distinct and undeniable sense of "finally, this is what we've been longing for and seeking – this is what we've always intuited that life should actually be like!" The birth of a new level of communion, in which we didn't lose ourselves, rather each of us was more in touch with who we really are. A sense of being lifted an octave, playing and played at a higher note, tangible joy. Uncompromised. Unhindered. Not forced or produced, wishfully projected or imagined. But real life, simple and true, experienced together with others, actually amongst each other and within. Meaning and purpose not searched for, but rather, each moment naturally infused with the sacred in our midst. At once, extraordinary and ordinary.

Key Elements to Support We-Being Emergence

> It is a wholeness that is neither pure unity nor an extrinsically gathered manyness. It is unity that is the intersubjectivity of the many...It is truly one being. It has internal differentiation, but it is one. (Bruteau, 2001, p. 35-36)

In the following section we describe the *key elements* we have experienced as essential and supportive to evolving the we-space and becoming present to the We-Being both during our first ten years of exploration at Morning Star community and since then. But first, we'd like to offer a brief description of the exterior setting, which, although not essential, was conducive and very helpful as we began our research.

The larger setting is a secluded piece of land in the Selkirk Mountains of British-Columbia, Canada, accessed by a 2.5km, unpaved private driveway that climbs steeply up the mountainside. The land is shared with cougars, bears, deer, elk and myriad other creatures. One can drink the water that flows through the land straight from the creeks. Turning to face west is a large mountain range, the Valhallas, a lake and meandering river in the valley bottom. For the first decade we would walk or ski in and out for about four months each winter. In short, it provided a quiet, undistracted exterior, supportive for focusing on inner and interpersonal research. Enfolded in a rural lifestyle, community life included individual and collective practices, retreats, and co-created seasonal rituals. We cleansed and strengthened our bodies, grew organic food, built homes, hosted and taught workshops, and worked hard to protect the valley's watersheds from commercial logging. And once in a while, this elusive possibility emerged, showing up most expectedly during our weekly we-practice that we began calling 'sacred circle.' At that stage in our exploration we also sensed that we were practicing a mode of communication that could one day become daily, that this conscious form of communication was setting a groove for the future, thus requiring extra care and attention until it became a new norm. We did taste this new norm occasionally outside of our sacred circle setting, for example, when we were in the garden, working silently, sensing the almost tangible web of sacred connection that had descended upon us – again that distinct combination of remarkable and natural. But in general, this collective Presence was more likely to convene with us in our we-practice. What was it about this particular ritual that welcomed it so often?

A *simple, specific exterior setting*: We sat in a circle, with a candle in the middle, providing both a focal point as well as a reminder of what is greater than the sum total of all of us gathered. The circle was well formed, allowing everyone to make eye contact. All distractions were taken care of (phones silenced, doors closed, chores done, time committed) and simple aesthetics considered (uncluttered space, visual beauty and ambience).

Spaciousness also proved to be helpful, which meant that when we started out, we didn't put a time limit on the practice, rather we listened for a natural closing, which varied greatly. Sometimes we sat together for a few hours, other times just half an hour. Consistently, as we listened into the collective space, there was a mutual recognition of when we were 'done,' a collective 'nod' of sorts.

And finally, *body posture*. Reflecting our intention to give our full presence to the practice, we would make a point of sitting up straight – simultaneously relaxed and wakeful. This helped us give all our attention to the co-created weave and emergence. It facilitated pouring our concentrated focus into the endeavor, while releasing effort.

As mentioned above, we imagine this emergence is possible in myriad exterior settings. Certain ingredients, however, we have observed to be essential.

Context

Reflecting on how we have collectively come to be here now as human beings, we can see that evolution has unfolded along distinct patterns for billions of years. Biologically, matter has organized at increasing levels of complexity. Atoms have organized to form molecules, molecules have organized to form cells, cells to form organisms, culminating in the blueprints of what we call life. The miracle of each of these biological evolutionary leaps is that a new form came into being and completely changed the trajectory of life. From this continued unfolding, the human family has emerged with the conscious awareness and ability to recognize the very pattern that has miraculously birthed us. Notice that every step in this process is marked by increased complexity. Notice also that as atoms, molecules or cells organize into more complex wholes, they remain distinct, vital components, fundamental to the greater gestalt. They do not dissolve to the point of becoming one amorphous whole. Rather they maintain their 'integrity' while partaking in and contributing to a further evolutionary step. Individual entities must therefore remain utterly unique and individuated, while contributing completely and perfectly to a greater whole. As part of our inquiry, we were curious about the implications of this trajectory. Could it be that this particular pattern of evolution offers a useful way to imagine and understand the possibilities for collectives, even as we as human beings are much more complex than atoms? We think so. Evolution has moved from being primarily a physical, biological and then rational affair to a movement at the noetic level, the level of consciousness itself. At this level our most essential characteristic – the authentic within each of us – is called to the fore, to come together with others who are making the pilgrimage to a fuller personhood. In our experience, coming together authentically provides the gateway to what we described as the next stage in the journey, to finding a healthy balance and interweaving between autonomy and communion.

How Did We Bring This Context Into Our Sacred Circles?

- We held awareness that our sincere and wholehearted contribution is needed for this higher consciousness to emerge in our midst.

- We invited all present to become friendly with Silence – to come into stillness and be OK with silence, not needing to fill the space with words, learning to open body, mind and heart to listen deeply into the space.

- We encouraged everyone to be present to what is emerging, to speak when moved by an authentic impulse, and to discern with a humble awareness the Sacredness of this time and opportunity.

- We reminded each other to listen carefully for the thread of truth, of resonance, and to build upon that, while gently and clearly discarding what was jarring by not lingering on it, but simply letting it pass.

In essence, we created a container to lift us out of the limitations of our respective personal stories and allow for collective wisdom to speak. It was this expanded and heightened context that consistently seemed to provide a central key for this We-Being to emerge. The integral evolutionary context within which we held our efforts and each other inspired, guided and informed us.

Grace

Our experiences showed us that another key ingredient is Grace. Grace is not something we can make happen of our own volition. Grace is a gift given. At the very beginning, in those first few weeks of community life, we felt we had just stumbled upon a treasure. We had worked hard – from purchasing the land to communicating well, to meditating, praying and invoking like never before. This is both humbling and relaxing. It is not only up to us. There is a critical point where the efforts of individual will are met by the wonders of universal Grace. We give it everything we can and there is support for this endeavor from the spiritual realm. A big resounding 'Yes' from the universe. When we are aligned and intrinsically motivated, we contact and are lifted by the force of life itself.

As we kept 'stirring the pot' and refining the recipe over that decade of community life, we found it challenging to progress from touching upon the higher 'We' as a momentary state to bringing this experience fully alive in our midst on a daily basis, as an embodied stage. We didn't seem to be making real headway in this regard. Often in our sacred circles, beautiful integration, astounding insight and healing conversation would take place. Some people, however, sat with us in these circles for years and weren't able to fully suspend their story, to release their habitual constructed self for the time we came together to practice. We ourselves noticed fluctuations in our availability to this higher consciousness, bumping against our own unconscious habits and shadows. Why was it so hard?

A huge sense of idealism drove us. Some of us questioned and doubted that the glimpses we had could last. What had seemed so simple and real slowly dissipated. Personal challenges, doubts and desires found their way back in, and we were left with the regular take-it-or-leave-it-well-intentioned intentional community. Lukewarm. The glimpses of a higher-level Being, however, would haunt us, propel us to continue the search, it would not let us go. It was too real and too precious to forget or to put aside. It resonated too much in the innermost core of our being to simply be discarded. That was the least we could do, as it "slipped" through our fingers – to honor the experience, to seek to understand and to not forget, but continue to be available for this incredible gift of full life together with others. Our inquiry around this invisible wall that we kept coming up against led us to realize more fully how important healthy individual development and capacity-building are.

Capacity and Readiness

In addition to context and Grace, we experienced and identified individual capacity as the third core key to help evolve the 'We'. Reaching a certain benchmark in individual evolution is necessary in order to consciously participate in the birth of this collective Being, since the effort requires ego awareness, and the readiness to know and dis-identify from the small self, while having a solid, healthy ego structure.

> The passion for individualism, which is instinctually in our nature as an ontological necessity of self-preservation, self-promotion, self-fulfillment, has to be superseded by the passion of ecstasy, the movement of exodus that pours us out into the space between us and other people, accomplishing in us the movement that makes us capable of real love. (Hederman, 1999, p. 63).

Coming across Ken Wilber's Integral Theory in 1997 was very helpful and impactful in this regard, bringing affirmation, clarity and articulation to what we had been sensing and bumping up against. It became evident to us that genuine focus and attentiveness are required to participate in these sacred circles. To set a new groove in consciousness together takes utter sincerity of heart and mind, as well as refined critical awareness and inquiry in the pursuit of truth. And above all, it requires in us discernment in regard to how we are showing up, who we are showing up as. Which 'I' is each of us bringing to the 'We'? In our experience, this higher-level Being needs our truest Self; it asks us to bring the most intimately authentic energy of our personhood to the table; the energies and gestures of creative thought, of choice, will and love.

Discernment between our constructed or socialized self and our essential Self is in part an act of will, and to a larger extent it is an expression of developmental maturity. Ego awareness lies beyond a theoretical grasp of the distinction between the false self and the true Self. It is ultimately an experience of seeing, of recognizing and knowing the difference, knowing which self I am residing in at any moment in time, becoming aware of the fluctuations, and humbly making discernment an ongoing practice: who am I truly? Which self am I residing in? Where am I listening and speaking from? What in me is authentic and wholesome, and what is self-absorbed and contracted? This is an effort that is humble and modest, simple and honest. With compassionate feedback, we can help each other along the way. We may be tempted to feel that True Self is inaccessible, impossible to touch. But it is not far away; it is the immediate condition of everything that is; it lies within each of us, whispering wildly and softly the secret of who we truly are.

Most important, we think, is the realization that individual awakening is a step along the way, rather than the final destination. Many of us see awakening as a lifelong journey and this becomes a self-fulfilling prophecy. If we understand awakening as a step along the journey, it puts our life into a different context, and we begin to ask ourselves what lies beyond this step.

> This inner 'I', who is always alone, is always universal: for in this innermost 'I' my own solitude meets the solitude of every human being and the solitude of God. Hence it is beyond division, beyond limitation, beyond selfish affirmation. (Merton, 1985, p. 207)

Also key is that we come home to ourselves first. Coming together with others can be challenging if we lose ourselves in the process. Many collective experiments have been unsuccessful for this reason.

Once we have individuated and found a relaxed solidity, then coming together with others is not a need and not just a choice. It is also a responsibility.

Developmental Distinctions and Trajectory

People have come together and experienced casual as well as profound moments of companionship, intimacy and togetherness for thousands of years. How did what we were seeking and experienced, both relate to and distinguish itself from other collective experiments? This question remains alive for us to the present day, especially now that we are seeing many groups offering a higher 'We' experience. Is everyone talking about the same thing? Are there important distinctions to be made? How might we cross-reference? What can we do to ensure that the various versions of We-practice are honored, and simultaneously hold awareness for the deepening layers possible?

Just as the individual evolves, so does the collective. Mapping out the development of the collective has helped us navigate and best leverage our own efforts in its evolution, as well as collaborate effectively with other groups' initiatives. It has also helped us appreciate and acknowledge the many ways in which the 'We' is nurtured and grows up, stepping stones connected along a shared path. Here's a broad stroke overview of the 'map' we carry with us:

There are a number of stages of collective experience that are well established in our world at this time. These include myriad daily events we share with other human beings, evolving from situations in which this happens by chance (listening to a concert or watching a movie in a theater or crossing a street at a major intersection together), to those that involve more intention (collaborating on a project, discussing a shared topic of interest, playing team sports, church services) and on to somewhat less common ones in which we share our interiors – how we feel, what we experience, sense and care deeply about – with one another (experiential workshops, self-help and therapy groups, social gatherings, talks in close-knit families).

Following these stages of collective experience is a mid stage that is quite readily available, but not yet fully or commonly established. It is currently the most evolved embodied stage that we have experienced or are aware of. Here a group comes together specifically to support the evolution and growth of the individuals present. It recognizes the intrinsic value of the individual as well as the value of a supportive community context. Examples are some Quaker gatherings, healthy spiritual communities, AA meetings, integral groups and organizations. In these kinds of collectives, constructive feedback, shadow awareness, empathetic listening and mirroring, and the potential of healing and transformation are encouraged.

In our reflections on this subject, we also identified three *later stages* that are generally available as states, but not typically as embodied stages. In these later collective stages, individuals have reached a certain level of maturation, ego-awareness and presence that enables the separate self to increasingly be suspended and retreat, allowing that which is greater, sacred and holy to enter the space.

In the first later stage, people begin to experience a *Collective Mind*, and express collective wisdom and intelligence. They are surprised by the depth and novelty of information and insight uttered through this greater collective intelligence. For a collective mind to emerge as a stage, individuals need to be present as and speak from their soul-self, able to rest in suspending the "known," always already curious, listening for and building on truth revealed, with the understanding that no one owns the truth, moving beyond the I-thou dichotomy, and celebrating wisdom whenever and from whomever it emerges.

In the second later stage, people begin to experience an abiding *Collective Soul*. Each individual has awakened; awakened to their Self – realizing the oneness of everything; realizing theirs and others' unique expression of that oneness. They are able to access a witness perspective on an ongoing basis, enabling their presence to deepen and grow. They become available as one who listens to and expresses from Source.

In the third later stage, the collective soul is transmuted into a *new Being*. This Being enfolds and embodies itself through the individuals present, and a profound sense of communion is experienced, with individual expressions remaining unique. Contributing to and receiving from this higher-level Being, individuals begin to engage with each other as parts, as expressions of this new Being.

An overarching insight from our ongoing experimentation with collective evolution is the state/stage differentiation in regard to evolving the 'We.' Higher 'We' states were accessible and deeply appreciated; they greatly informed and inspired us. Establishing later collective stages in community, however, proved more challenging than expected: we fluctuated in our capacity to make the inner pilgrimage from our ego to our Self. It is our person, rather than our personality, that is called upon to contribute to be a collective vessel for a higher 'We'. And so the exploration of this higher 'We' rests upon each of us making this pilgrimage over and over again. Until this becomes the 'new normal,' we touch on the potential here and there; we access it as a state. The state experiences of the higher 'We' help prepare the soil within and amongst us. They allow the necessary conditions and capacities to develop and become refined. They are without a doubt important, but, regardless of how profound and life-altering they may be, they are still states. As is their nature, they come and they go. The voice of the higher 'We' is expressed, and then it isn't. The ongoing project, and what these state experiences point to, is to offer higher We-states permanent access, in other words, to contribute to them becoming lived and embodied stages, including the development of new systems and structures to hold this evolving consciousness.

The Journey Continues: Challenges, Discoveries and Next Steps

By 2002 we had been immersed in this inquiry for 10 years. We had experienced this higher-level Being emerge as a state, but as mentioned, our attempts at stabilizing this Collective Presence as a stage had not been successful. If this phenomenon was happening in our lives, we figured it must be emerging elsewhere in the world. It was time to investigate. We packed and left on a one-year pilgrimage in search of who else was engaged in this inquiry, where else this collective Presence was emerging. We wanted to contribute, learn and partake.

We travelled through Europe and North America and met with authors, spiritual teachers, communities, families – groups and individuals interested in this next step in human consciousness. One day in Ireland, about two months into our trip, in a prayer chapel beneath an old stone church standing in presence with a few monks, there it was again, in our midst: the beautiful, exquisite, sacred Being, vast and almost tangible. It was the first time we experienced this unmistakable holy Presence outside of Morning Star Community. The significance of this event was profound for us. Having until that point not known if and where else this collective Being may be making itself known, we were elated. A few more similarly profound meetings further confirmed that this next evolutionary possibility was indeed emerging elsewhere. Along the way we also met with many people who themselves had not yet experienced this phenomenon, but resonated deeply with its implications, and one woman in particular, who had even spent years thinking about and writing about it: Beatrice Bruteau.[1]

After a year of travel, we came back home full of enthusiasm. We had learned and confirmed that what we had been exploring at

---

1. We spent hours comparing notes with her, and left renewed and encouraged. Beatrice recently died, on Nov. 16, 2014 – for a beautiful tribute: contemplative. org/a-tribute-to-beatrice-bruteau-by-cynthia-bourgeault/

Morning Star was, in fact, not just a happenstance phenomenon. We had experienced this collective consciousness emerging in other places, a huge affirmation, as well as solace. We didn't, however, encounter groups with permanent access to this higher-level Being. We, and everyone else we met who was touching upon this new consciousness, had experienced a taste, a glimpse or a state. We also returned with a clearer understanding of the obstacles in the way, the main one in our estimation being that we humans are still largely invested and wrapped up in our individual growth and development, and identified with our separate sense of self. While acknowledging the futuristic nature of the vision, Father Thomas Keating at Snowmass monastery, whom we met and interviewed during our pilgrimage (2003), shared his sense that it would be a minimum of 10-20 years before more candidates would be available for this process.

We took time to consider our next move. Should we dive back into community living, or come at this project from a different angle? How might we best serve and welcome this new consciousness? Knowing of the shift necessary in us for a high-level We-Being to arise stably – shifting from identifying with the constructed separate self-sense to knowing ourselves as the deeper essential Self at our core – we decided to put our attention toward readying the ground more fully in ourselves and with others. Next Step Integral was born – an organization to educate, learn and provide tools, perspectives and skills, and essentially work toward putting integral vision into action, especially in the areas of community, ecology, parenting and education.

The ultimate aim of Next Step Integral was and is to build a village to support the emergence of this higher We-consciousness, a place where it can become a lived stage, creating conditions conducive for ongoing health and evolution. In 2011 we felt a readiness in the collective field to bring our core focus of *Evolving the We* into the greater community, and so we began hosting seminars and retreats to this effect. Part of preparing such events included reaching out to others whom we had the impression were engaged in a related vein of exploration. This has proved to be a wonderful networking among kindred spirits.

At these seminars and retreats we practiced in various group sizes, configurations and with a number of formats. Sometimes the experience was tender or tentative or awkward, other times blown wide open and holy. Practice certainly helped. Some of these experiences allowed for spontaneous upwellings of gratitude, honoring, blessedness, healing and challenge.

Closing Reflections

Where do we go from here? Since 2012 we have witnessed a rapidly growing interest in the potential of a higher 'We'. Many groups and individuals are speaking about collective consciousness and practicing together. The increased popularity of evolving the we-space is incredibly heartening. It also calls for ongoing humility and discernment. When a phenomenon becomes more widespread, it can easily get watered down. A question that is alive for us in this regard: How may this work grow and widen, while upholding and honoring the inherent sacredness of the work? In other words, how can we collaborate to increase the breadth of its reach without compromising its depth?

The duty of privilege is absolute integrity

– John O'Donohue

It is apparent that we are in need of a more fundamental breakthrough as a human family. Our journey of individuation is beautiful and necessary, yet it can also be destructive. Every time a new level in consciousness evolution arises, it provides a platform for profound transformation on a global scale, even as it pops up in pockets here and there to begin with. Today many of the most evolved human beings are not sure where to go from here. Wait for everyone else to catch up? Teach others how to get to where they are at?

What if the more evolved individuals were more responsible for the current state of affairs of this world? In other words, what if the responsibility for humanity to navigate this time in history rested on the shoulders of those interested and capable of breaking through to a new stage in our collective evolution (people like you and us, reading this book, writing these chapters)?

How would that change your personal choices today and tomorrow, and how would your priorities shift? Our sense is that the more one knows and is capable of, the greater the responsibility for this evolutionary journey we are all on together. As those with sufficient capacity and readiness become fully accountable to something greater, with deep care and reverence, and come together with others with similar capacity and readiness, the landscape of humanity can change dramatically.

As we have shared in this chapter, our sense is that once a human being has become fully individuated and has awakened to her/his true nature, and then comes together with others who have similarly developed their personhood, a whole new stage of existence becomes possible: the birth of new possibilities for collectives. Indeed, it is in the space *between* our and other selves that this new level of integration and transmutation can unfold. A distinct aspect about this next step in consciousness evolution is that it takes us working together to build it.

Through coming together in awakened consciousness, century-old human yearnings are met: the yearning for love and connection, for embrace, for discovery and change, for growth, for accountability and expression, for creativity and collaboration, and finally and perhaps most importantly, for contribution. We can hear this evolutionary call in the whisperings of our souls, at the core of our beings, as well as in the suffering present around the planet. For us the possibilities of the We-Being we have reflected upon in this chapter hold answers and invites new questions to some of today's most pressing dilemmas that none of us can answer individually in a satisfying way. In addition, we believe that this collective Being also reciprocally needs us in order to become more fully embodied, to come alive and be an active player in the evolution of our world. This particular set-up is precise and beautiful: It ultimately points to the fact that we need each other more than we could ever imagine if we are to elegantly navigate the challenges of this time and our future collectively.

Appendix

We offer here a distillation of We-practice injunctions that combines insights and practices from various We-practice experiments, including: Morning Star Community & Next Step Integral, Bay Area We-practice community, the Quaker tradition, Olen Gunnlaugson's injunction "Surrender into Witnessing" (2012), Terry Patten's ITC 2013 paper "Enacting an Integral Revolution", and inspiration from our We-retreats. Links to many of these resources can be found at: nextstepintegral.org/resources/icWe-SpacePracticeinjunctions-invitations-invocations:

- Gather in a quiet space, in circle formation, without distractions, with a candle in the center.
- Remind ourselves of Context by asking the group to remember:
  - o Why we are here
  - o That this very moment and collective focus is an opportunity to co-create new tracks in the sand of consciousness together

- o The shared intention that this effort be on behalf of the Whole
- Open eyes / Sit up straight / Show up fully
- Ring Bells: 3 times to start
- Read, sing or speak out loud a Devotional Prayer
- Offer a spoken reminder of everyone being enfolded in the Ground of Being (God)
- Facilitate a brief guided weaving (invite participants to bring awareness to their "I" as a pillar of light. From there shift focus to the person sitting opposite and send light to this person. Following this, bring attention to all the beams of light and attention meeting, to the web created, and the We at the center of the circle. Breath into that center pillar). This can also be done through facilitated toning.
- Reading of an inspirational text
- Speaking out loud as invocations and invitations, the following:

1. May we surrender into witnessing, allowing Presence to deepen

2. May we suspend the "known", being open and curious

3. May we listen deeply to what wants to emerge, building on the truth of what has been said

4. May we engage passionately, infusing the space with life energy & expectancy

5. May we be mindful of self, especially our inner faculty of discernment

6. May we be mindful of other, attuning to the thread of truth

7. May we be mindful of the space, informed by the whole field.

- Dive fully, as awake as possible, into the emergent co-created unfolding! Focusing an inquiry, for example a question on three scales:
- Global: The koan of our time: How can we "be" the great needed change?
- Local: What's the next step that we can do?

- Medial: What's the soul nature of this circle's unique assignment?
-

Closing in a way that invokes a continuation, an onward and forward.

Author Bios

Stephan Martineau founded an intentional community at the age of 24 with the purpose of discovering the voice of the "We." Since then he has continued working toward supporting the embodiment and the expression of the voice of the "We" in the world. He is founder and president of Next Step Integral (nextstepintegral.org), an international organization focusing on individual, interpersonal, and systemic transformation in the areas of community development, education, parenting and ecology. Stephan works as a consultant for organizations, businesses and communities as they develop vision inter- and intrapersonal discernment skills and practices and seek to implement these in ways that are effective and resilient to change. He has worked in watershed management and ecosystem-based planning since 1993. He is co-founder and business manager of the Slocan Integral Forestry Cooperative(sifco.ca – a 35,000-acre community forest in British Columbia), where he successfully spearheaded an integral approach to a multi-stakeholder situation in one of BC's most contentious areas in regards to forestry practices. He recently managed the creation of a 25-family Co-Housing project in Nelson, BC, Canada.

Miriam Mason Martineau is a mother, counselor, writer, and researcher. She has spent the last 20 years studying and applying Integral-Evolutionary theory, educational frameworks, and spiritual practice. Miriam holds an M.A. in Psychology from the University of Zurich, with specialization in Youth and Child Psychology, and has been working in private practice as an integral therapeutic counselor since 1995. She lived and taught for a decade in an integrally-informed community that was founded with the specific intent and vision of evolving the We. Since then she has continued to design and offer transformative community and educational events internationally. She also teaches courses on community development and integral parenting (integralparenting.com). She is vice-president and faculty member of Next Step Integral (nextstepintegral.org), an international organization that brings an integral perspective ecology, education, parenting and community. Miriam lives near Nelson BC, Canada, with her husband, Stephan and their 12-year old daughter, whom they homeschool.

References

Bruteau, B. (2001). The grand option: Personal transformation and a new creation. Notre Dame, IN: Published by University of Notre Dame Press.

Cook-Greuter, S. R. (2002). A detailed description of the development of nine action logics. Adapted from ego development theory for the leadership development framework.

Feuerstein, G. (1987). Structures of consciousness: The genius of Jean Gebse. Lower Lake, CA: Integral Publishing.

Gebser, J. (1986). The ever-present origin: Foundations of the aperspectival world. Authorized Translation by Noel Barstad with Algis Mickunas. Athens, OH: Ohio University Press.

Gunnlaugson, O., Moze, M. B. (2012). Surrendering into witnessing: A foundationalpractice for building collective intelligence capacity in groups. Journal of Integral Theory and Practice. 7(3), 78-94.

Hederman, M.P. (1999). Kissing the dark. Dublin, Ireland: Veritas Publications. Interview with Father Thomas Keating. Early spring 2003. Retrieved from nextstepintegral.org/father-thomas-keating.

Kegan, R. (1983). The evolving self: Problem and process in human development. Cambridge, MA: Harvard University Press; Reprint edition (Sept. 14, 1983).

Merton, T. (1985). Disputed questions. San Diego: Harcourt Brace

Jovanovich. Patten, T. (2013). Enacting an integral revolution: How can we have truly radical conversations in a time of global crisis? Paper presented at the bi-annual Integral Theory Conference in San Francisco Bay Area, USA. Paper retrieved from foundation.metaintegral.org/sites/default/files/Patten_ITC2013.pdf.

Teilhard de Chardin, P. (1964). The future of man. New York: Harper & Row.

Wilber, K. (1996). A brief history of everything. Boston & London: Shambhala Publications.

CHAPTER 9

Exploring the Ego at the Boundary of the I and the We

David McCallum, Ed.D., Aliki Nicolaides, Ed.D. & Lyle Yorks, Ed.D.

Introduction

Our lived experience as facilitators, educators, leaders, and consultants has taught us that while collaboration and cooperative action have great benefit and advantage, there are myriad ways in which our individual egoic agendas, interests, and defensive routines can lead us to act against a group's greater good. While there are many definitions available, by "ego" we are referring in particular to the alienated part of the psyche which is over-identified with its individuating freedom and agency, at the expense of the participation with and for others (Heron, 1992, p. 36). While we maintain a light spirit of inquiry into the topic, we know that at times the ego's antics are not only self-serving, but often highly unhelpful for the work of teams, groups, and communities engaged in generative or collaborative processes, strategic planning, creative problem solving, or collective transformation. In such cases, instead of acting from within these "We-spaces" in a way that reflects collective purpose and empathetic care, individuals act upon or apart from the whole, often to the detriment of the group, community, or organization.

What then are the individual (and collective) conditions whereby a person or persons in a group might *act from within* the interpersonal field of relationship, rather than acting upon, or separate from that relational matrix? How is it possible for a kind of action to emerge from within the We-space that reflects the freedom of differentiated,

175

constituent selves who are each able to maintain critical subjectivity, yet also participate in an interpersonal field that interweaves collective intention, interest, and purpose? These questions have led us to explore philosophical and psychological theories that could inform our practice, and enhance the depth and skill of our work at the interface of groups, teams, organizations, and communities.

In this chapter, we present the seminal work of humanistic, transpersonal psychologist and philosopher, John Heron, whose phenomenologically rooted theories of personhood (1992) provide means of describing an *extended epistemology* (Heron, 1992, 1996; Yorks & Kasl, 2002b, 2006) that describes a holistic lens for understanding the subtle, often preconscious, interpersonal boundaries that shape the interactions in groups. Epistemology, the philosophy of knowledge, defines the ways of knowing and the methods and practices used during sense-making and knowledge creation. Heron's extended epistemology provides a theory of personhood that defines how one is holistically in relationship with different ways of knowing within one's self and with others. While Heron's work has been long understood as foundational for the new paradigm approach to research known as co-operative inquiry (Heron 1992, 1996, 1999; Heron & Reason, 2001), we continue to find relevance in his distinction between the individuating and participatory modes of the psyche and the ways these modes affect the interaction at the boundary of the self with the collective. The individuating mode of the psyche inclines toward one's personal freedom and agency while the participatory mode inclines toward relationship and cooperation with others. The tendencies of the psyche toward individuation or participation evolve in a somewhat predictable pattern as a person matures and learns to gradually balance the two modes (e.g., moving from ego-centric behavior to more socio-centric behavior, to gradually identifying with humanity itself, etc.). Heron provides a model of adult development that describes this pattern in terms of distinct levels, and each of these levels has considerable implications for an individual's ways of relating within the We-space of groups, teams, and organizations.

We propose that while the ego might contract and act in an individuating, separating manner in each of the developmental levels, there are nonetheless practices that help individuals and groups attenuate egoic impulses counterproductive to participatory, collective action. While our focus of attention is primarily the intrapsychic dynamic of the individuating and participatory modes, we maintain this focus in relation to the quality of the interpersonal field of the We-space, e.g., the condition of trust, the equitable availability of resources, the feeling of safety, etc. Heron's theory is particularly relevant to this topic as his formulation of co-operative inquiry is a prototypical form of a systemic We-space grounded in his holistic theory of personhood (Heron, 1992, Heron & Reason, 2008; Yorks & Kasl, 2002a).

In this chapter, we present a brief exposition of the relevant elements of Heron's model, with emphasis on the individuating and participatory modes of the psyche and the ways that these modes shed light on our work of facilitation, teaching, leadership, and the collective generation of knowledge and action. We will bring attention to the importance of critical subjectivity for the individual and to the role of empathic knowing for the emergence of an extended epistemology in the collective. Finally, we will explore intentional practices for helping to integrate the individuating and participatory modes of the person within the We-Space.

The Theory of Personhood

John Heron's (1992) "theory of personhood" is complex; an exhaustive summary in this condensed space is not possible. However, because our exploration of WE-space is grounded in the epistemology posited by his theory, we describe only the most relevant concepts (for more robust exposure to the theory see Heron, 1992; 1999, 2006; Yorks & Kasl, 2002, 2006). In his 1992 book *Feeling and Personhood*, Heron describes the goal of his theory of the person "to provide a seedbed for generating working hypotheses which may be fruitful in living and working, in learning and inquiry, and in helping and facilitating" (p. 6). Heron (1992) outlines an integrated theory of human psyche in which he treats experience as a process, an encounter with others and the world. He offers us a model to live and explore from within that encounter through our emotions and feelings, access to imagery and intuition, capacities for discrimination and reflection, with intention and through action.

From Heron's phenomenologically oriented point of view, he (1992) posited four modes of psyche—affective (emotion and feeling), imaginal (sense impression and intuition), conceptual (thought and judgment), and practical (action and impact)—that are distinct and interdependent. These interdependent modes of psyche produce four distinct ways of knowing: experiential (grounded felt sense), presentational (expressed in aesthetic formats such as story, music, drawing and painting, etc.), propositional (descriptions, statements, theories, and reasoned meaning making), and practical (how we do things with skill, competence). Significantly, Heron's (1992) model does not privilege any one mode of psyche or corresponding way of knowing. He does, however, suggest that the ways of knowing relate to one another in an "up-hierarchy." By, up-hierarchy, he means that each way of knowing draws from and is dependent on those beneath it in the hierarchy. Experiential knowing is at the base of the hierarchy and serves as the foundation from which presentational, propositional, and practical ways of knowing arise. His emphasis on experiential knowing is a helpful reminder to us as facilitators to help participants remain close to their lived experience, and to balance their individual, first person voices with the third person, propositional concerns they are addressing.

Heron (1992) states that "within the psyche... there is ... a basic polarity between an individuating function and a participatory one" (p. 15). This basic polarity is key to our discussion and exploration of the person in the We-space. Before we narrow our focus to the engagements of the participatory and individuating modes, we will discuss what Heron means by the affective psyche where emotion and feeling each have nuanced meaning.

Within the affective mode of psyche, emotion is an expression of the individuating function; emotion is "the intense, localized affect that arises from the fulfillment or the frustration of individual needs and interests" (p. 16). For example, group members might experience the satisfaction that comes from completing an assignment and receiving positive feedback, or members might experience the disappointment of having a collective project rejected for funding. These are examples of emotion from Heron's perspective. By contrast, feeling represents the participatory pole. Acknowledging that he assigns a "special usage" to the meaning of feeling, Heron writes that feeling refers "to the capacity of the psyche to participate in wider unities of being.... this is the domain of empathy, indwelling, participation, presence, resonance, and such like" (p. 16) – key dimensions of collaboration in the interpersonal We-space (Scharmer, 2007; Scharmer and Kaufer, 2013; Gunnlaugson, Baron, and Cayer, 2014), which tap into a generative field of unrealized potential, meaning, vision, and action. For example, one might experience a felt sense of vulnerability with other members of a group when someone shares an experience of deep sadness, or members might be moved with a sense of courage that they are ready to risk letting go of key assumptions about themselves as a group. The capacity for this resonance is not only essential for the empathetic connections with other people, but also for opening up to intuition, the subconscious, and what might be described as the transpersonal field, which stretches beyond the individual to the extended field of reality. This might take the form of a shared silence in a group that, after some time, generates an insight, or an answer to a shared problem. The other three modes of psyche also include participatory and individuating functions. We will say more about the relevance of feeling for these two modes in the section on cooperative

178

inquiry. In what follows, we discuss briefly how a person's ways of knowing are enacted at the boundary of the We-space.

Critical Subjectivity and Empathic Understanding

Heron suggests that a key developmental challenge is for a person to become adept at practicing "critical subjectivity," which "involves an awareness of the four ways of knowing, of how they are currently interacting, and of ways of changing the relations between them so that they articulate a reality that is unclouded by a restrictive and ill-disciplined subjectivity," (Heron & Reason, 1997, p. 281). In his use of the term critical subjectivity, Heron suggests that knowing in its fullness requires awareness of the sources of data, of the thematizing process of sensemaking, of the influence of assumptions and ideology, etc. For example, if a person working with a diverse team is not aware of the extent to which he is privileging his point of view at the expense of others' experiences, this will become highly problematic for collaboration by the team. Another example would be the way that a leader holds a stance that conveys urgency and challenges an organization to make deep changes while at the same time communicates care and empathy for the uncertainty and fear that members are feeling. Despite the sometimes intense resistance to, and even rejection of, the leader in that role, he or she is able to maintain a stance that simultaneously acts from within the membership of the organization and yet also exerts responsibility for moving the whole in a different direction. Critical subjectivity requires considerable self-awareness of feelings, history, patterns, values, thoughts, strengths and weaknesses. Effective exercise of critical subjectivity leads to congruence among an individual's ways of knowing and is an essential pre-condition for participatory collaboration in the We-space.

Moving from the consideration of the intra-subjective experience of the individual to the inter-subjective experience of the collective, an important corollary of critical subjectivity is the practice of empathy in the We-space. Engagement with the whole person of fellow participants in the We-space of groups, teams, organizations and communities requires interacting with others through the same balanced mix in ways of knowing – through affective and imaginal modes of psyche, as well as the conceptual and practical. This involves engaging in what Kasl & Yorks (forthcoming) describes as whole person dialogue that "creates opportunity for empathic connection. Empathy is the ability to encounter the other's feelings, ideas, and actions from within the other's experiential perspective." This empathy entails a space where the first person experience is welcomed in the form of storytelling, or other forms of presentational expression. For example, in a conversation between peer stakeholders who have leadership roles in an organization, can those with more positional or informal influence empathize with those who have less, and work in such a way that equality in decision making is maintained? This might require the persons with less influence taking the risk of sharing their vulnerability or need with those who have more power through the use of a story, metaphor, or image. Or in a community dialogue about access to public resources such as education or health care, can separate interest groups come to understand the distinct perspectives and needs of one another, despite the resources being limited? This might require creating space for each interest group, especially the most marginal, to communicate expressively, perhaps with considerable emotion, without rejection by stakeholders who have more access. Having perfect understanding of the other's experience is, of course, impossible; yet, the power of empathy is demonstrated in the willingness to understand someone else's distinct experience, and the vulnerability of being open to change through dialogue and relationship.

Living within the point of view of the other is the essence of empathic understanding and can create a space in which individuals can engage in critical discourse and meaning making that supports action from within the We-space. Heron's extended epistemology asserts that only through authentic epistemic and political participation is it possible for people to be present as real persons, as both distinct and united, capable of both differentiated, critical subjectivity and of participatory, collaborative action. This extended epistemology is built upon an ontology, or philosophy of being that situates the self and the other/collective in a radically interconnected relationship which we will treat briefly, though essentially.

A Radical Ontology

Heron (1992) presents a radical ontological rationale for his theory of the person that is germane to the consideration of the self in relation to the collective:

> Reality, I believe, is both One and Many. The Many are a real Many, a genuine Multiplicity with Mind, spiritual monads, differentiated centres of consciousness within a cosmic presence. Personhood is one such centre, a particular focus of development within the field of universal consciousness, unfolding a unique perspective within, with people emerging from the

> progressive differentiation of the person from germinal to transfigured states… The isolation and alienation of the human mind is an egoic illusion born of our use of language, psychological wounding, and the deep tensions within the human condition. Dismantling that illusion means that personal consciousness uncovers its true heritage – that it is both distinct within, and one with, a universal presence (p. 10).

In this quote, Heron addresses the ontological basis for understanding consciousness in terms of a differentiated, yet unified reality. He holds this radical notion of individual/collective consciousness lightly and is careful to avoid a transcendental reductionism that collapses the individual into the many, preserving the real distinction between the differentiated self in relationship to the whole without the necessity of a subject/object split. In fact, much of Heron's intellectual project is to offer a unitive, phenomenological approach to personhood which sees and experiences the subject and object as "distinct, interpenetrating, and non separable," (p. 9). Further, Heron (2006) suggests that the person can enter into communion within an integrated, open, and committed group such that each individual can access the energy, and indeed, the "destiny of the whole group," (p. 69).

Why is this issue of ontology so important? Such a project is helpful to any consideration of the self in/with the collective, and to this conversation about the way in which deep and effective collaboration occurs within the We-space of groups, teams, organizations, and communities. For us as practitioners, this philosophical view of a differentiated and yet unified field of consciousness provides a way of understanding the radically interdependent nature of relationships between parts and whole, individuals and groups, and sub-groups within larger and larger collectives. For example, when an individual whose rights have been violated brings this experience to a community for redress, the collective has an opportunity to see itself represented in the person, and so, act in the interest of that person and itself by supporting justice. Likewise, in the instance of individuals who are recognized with genetic or social "frailties," the degree to which a community understands these individuals, not as "other," but as being integral parts of a larger whole will determine approaches to care, allocation of resources, etc. Heron's ontology creates a theoretical foundation for a deeper appreciation of interconnectedness in the We-space that is beyond mere relationality, but which rests upon the inter-being of persons and the wider reality. Such a foundation creates a claim on individuals to act in a way that is distinct, but not separate, from the collectives of which they are a part, lest they exercise a kind of unilateral power which can be destructive. The relationship between the self and the whole of which the self is a part brings our attention to the principle boundary of the person and the collective, specifically the dynamic function of the ego.

Heron on the Ego, the Role of Feeling and Emotion, Individuation and Participation

Heron (1992) describes the ego as a "busy contraction together of action, discrimination, imagery and emotion," (p. 18). He portrays the ego as an alienated part of the psyche that is, at times, over identified with the individuating modes at the expense of the participatory. This alienation stems from a variety of potential sources: the subject-object split in language which suggests a dualistic, either/or pattern of meaning making and a self concept that may be overly separate; the suffering produced by forms of psychological and emotional repression of the (wounded) child; and the widespread anxieties that arise from the radical tensions within the human condition (p. 36). The alienated ego strives, for example, to compensate for perceived inadequacies, to identify with external values in pursuit of power, and to defend against the suffering that comes with vulnerability, or the fear of being engulfed by others. These tendencies of the ego create obvious tensions when individuals are invited into intimacy, community, or collaboration. At the same time, Heron points out repeatedly that the individuating modes are not necessarily egoic, except when they entirely exclude the participatory mode (p.18). In other words, a person who has reached a sufficient degree of maturity and integration maintains these two modes in proportion, neither merging nor over-identifying entirely with an other or the collective, nor separating entirely. Heron suggests that the whole person has all eight of the functions of the psyche in a more comprehensive and conscious balance: action and intention, discrimination and reflection, imagery and intuition, emotion and feeling (p.19), and therefore, is able to balance both the individuating and participatory modes through the exercise of critical subjectivity, and a grounding in one's feeling of empathic resonance with the whole/We-space.

For Heron (1992), it is feeling that is the participatory mode par excellence, a sense that as an individual, I "indwell in the world, participate in its being, resonate with how it is," (p. 23). He continues, "and while thus identifying with its presence, I am at the same time aware of my own distinctness, individuated by an emotive state that correlates with my participatory experience," (p. 23). For an individual in a group, this felt sense of resonance with others facilitates a balance of one's interests, desires, and agency between the self and others. For example, in the context of a small group session, a member of the group dealing with his own sense of inadequacy made a passive aggressive attack on another member, but the recipient of the attack maintained both his personal boundary and a sense of empathic sensitivity for the attacker; this allowed the group to hold both the energy of the aggression and, simultaneously, the sense of intimacy, mercy, etc. This appreciation of the sense of differentiation and participation is what allows an individual to maintain freedom and critical consciousness while also experiencing the feeling sense of connectedness with the We-space. While feeling allows for an empathic resonance with others and the whole, emotion is often triggered by agitation or distress, and can at times lead to overemphatic individuation that separates one from the group at the expense of conscious participation.

Yet, when in balance, emotion is simply the primary, basic locus of human individuation, grounding a person in their sense of distinct being. In the course of a single interpersonal interaction with a group a person might experience many oscillations in and out of the feeling/participatory and emotional/individuating states, depending on the content of the interaction, the context, etc. For instance, in an inquiry group established to explore the congruence of member's intention and action, one member expressed anger with another for not expressing more gratitude and reciprocity in response to her generous hospitality toward the group. She seemed to be calling out what she perceived to be an attitude of entitlement that she took quite personally. Instead of making space for her and the other member to pair off in a tangled, interpersonal conflict, another member invited her to explore where this anger was coming from, and how it might have triggered a memory from her past. When she quieted down to take this question in, instead of more anger, she came to a place of vulnerability and tears as she recalled how her father's generosity in his community had been abused. When she expressed this in the form of a brief story, the whole energy of the group shifted toward her rather than away and the member she was addressing was able to join her with empathy and understanding, allowing her to rejoin the group at a deeper level of trust and mutuality. While a distinct being can become overidentified with a sense of separation, resulting in egoic alienation, Heron (1992) suggests that true individuation can emerge through the many states of development into the context of participatory feeling and resonant action in the world (p. 24). He (1992) writes, "full participatory unity is interdependent with a full-distinctness (not separateness) of individuation" (p. 35). It is to these distinct states of development of personhood and their implications for participatory collaboration in the We-space that we turn next.

Heron's States of Personhood

Due to his respectful, even reverent regard for the dynamic, oscillating nature of personhood, Heron avoids the usual language of linear, sequential "stages" of development and uses instead "states" as a means of describing the less predictable manner in which distinct states may occur for any individual. While he admits that broad generalizations can be made about stages of development, Heron writes, "people have a way of making some very idiosyncratic journeys toward self-realization," (p. 52) as they integrate the individuating and participatory modes along the way.

While there is much to say about the way Heron uses each term to describe the distinct qualities of being at each state of personhood (see Table 1) and their similarities and differences to the corresponding stages of other theorists including Maslow, Kohlberg, Loevinger, Torbert, and Wilber, our focus here is on the path of integration that progressively unites the individuating and the participatory modes. This progressive integration of the individuating modes of emotion, imagery, discrimination, and action with the participatory modes of feeling, intuition, reflection, and intention allows for personal action that is at once increasingly differentiated and more capable of action in union with/from within the collective. As an example of this degree of integration, Martin Luther King Jr. practiced an uncanny ability to be in relationship with people across social boundaries, to connect with the minds and hearts of those he led and with those who opposed him, who threatened and who joined him on behalf of a more inclusive good that transcended any one group's interests. Heron suggests that this process of integration unfolds in three stages; that of the Creative Person, The Self-Creating Person, and the Self-Transfiguring (see Table 1 and read from the bottom to the top for the ascending order of consciousness).

State of Personhood	Corresponding Stages	Distinct Qualities of Psyche and Ego
Charismatic Person	Ironist (Torbert), Causal (Wilber)	The psyche is a continuously transfigured, living presence; full integration of the individuating and participatory modes; "no ego" (in the sense of the alienated, illusory self; though we suggest that temporary regression is possible as it is in all stages).
Self-Transfiguring Person	Self-Transcendence (Maslow), Alchemist (Torbert), Subtle (Wilber)	The psyche realizes its psychic and spiritual potentials; realizing capacity for integration of the individuating and participatory modes; dissolving ego.
Self-Creating Person	Self-Actualization (Maslow), Autonomous/ Integrated (Loevinger), Strategist (Torbert), body-mind self (Wilber)	The psyche is autonomous in healing and actualizing itself; early capacity for temporary integration of individuating and participatory modes; open ego.
Creative Person	Self-Esteem (Maslow), Conscientious/Individualistic (Loevinger), Post-Conventional (Kohlberg), Achiever (Torbert), Mature Ego (Wilber)	The psyche is autonomous in external behavior; tendency toward individuating pole; open ego and closed ego swings.
Conventional Person	Belongingness (Maslow), Conformist (Loevinger), Conventional (Kohlberg), Diplomat (Torbert), Membership conscious (Wilber)	The socialized psyche adopts cultural roles and rules; tendency toward individuating mode; closed ego.
Compulsive Person	Opportunist (Torbert), Shadow (Wilber)	The wounded psyche has defensive splits and repressions; individuating mode; closed and potentially extreme ego.
Spontaneous Person	Safety (Maslow), Impulsive (Loevinger), Pre-Conventional (Kohlberg), Impulsive (Torbert), Body Self (Wilber)	The uninhibited psyche expresses its innate impulses; open ego.
Primal Person	Pleroma (Wilber)	Primordial fusion of the psyche and its foetal world; pre-ego

Table 1: Heron's States of Personhood, Based on Heron (1992, p. 53)

Of the varying capacities that unfold in each state, Heron (1992) writes, "the Creative Person begins to open up the participatory modes as a part of his or her creativity, but often shuts down again at other times," (pp. 65-66), and while that person might be in the early process of opening his or her ego, the access to the participatory modes is not integrated. The second stage is that of the Self-Creating Person who is consciously seeking to integrate empathic feeling, intuition, and reflection into their new autonomous way in the world (p. 66), developing and exercising participatory capacities in personal and interpersonal interactions, in organizations, and in wider social and ecological contexts. In the third stage, the Self-Transfiguring Person includes the prior two stages and attempts to "launch resonant feeling, intuition and reflection into the wider reaches of being: the hidden depths of the imaginal mind, subtle domains, archetypal consciousness, and unitive awareness," (p. 66).

Of the varying capacities that unfold in each state, Heron (1992) writes, "the Creative Person begins to open up the participatory modes as a part of his or her creativity, but often shuts down again at other times," (pp. 65-66), and while that person might be in the early process of opening his or her ego, the access to the participatory modes is not integrated. Of the varying capacities that unfold in each state, Heron (1992) writes, "the Creative Person begins to open up the participatory modes as a part of his or her creativity, but often shuts down again at other times," (pp. 65-66), and while that person might be in the early process of opening his or her ego, the access to the participatory modes is not integrated. The second stage is that of the Self-Creating Person who is consciously seeking to integrate empathic feeling, intuition, and reflection into their new autonomous way in the world (p. 66), developing and exercising participatory capacities in personal and interpersonal interactions, in organizations, and in wider social and ecological contexts. In the third stage, the Self-Transfiguring Person includes the prior two stages and attempts to "launch resonant feeling, intuition and reflection into the wider reaches of being: the hidden depths of the imaginal mind, subtle domains, archetypal consciousness, and unitive awareness," (p. 66).

Admitting that this description is "far too neat and tidy," (1992, p. 67), Heron describes how this path of integration is marked by anomalies and variations and should only be taken as conjecture rather than prescription. He proposes that at each stage of the three states of trans-personhood, "the psyche is undergoing transfiguration from separateness to pure distinctness within the One-Many Reality," (p. 68). This distinctness of being is not to be confused with separateness of being, nor to be conflated in practice with states at the pre-personal or personal stages, where personal distinctness can "get lost in alienation from the wider unity of the whole," (1992, p. 68). Further, the later transpersonal states of personhood gain increasing capacity for the integration of the individuating and participatory modes, yet are not entirely exempt from regression into temporary experiences of alienation, over-individuating separation, or unilateral action. Current developmental studies suggest that into the most mature stages, we continue to have blind-spots related to the operations of our own egos, and research suggests that even in the later stages, temporary regressions or "fall-back" is possible when conditions do not support us showing up as our best selves (Livesay, 2013; McCallum, 2008). We suggest that a positive corollary to fall-back is possible for persons operating out of pre-transpersonal states—that with the right external and internal conditions, such persons might experience the balancing of the individuating and participatory modes as a kind of grace/gift (rather than personal achievement) during the process of building community and collaborating in the We-space. In other words, the environmental and interpersonal conditions of the We-space can be so conducive that even if a person has not yet matured into the later states, he or she can become relaxed, open, willing to trust and risk, non-competitive, etc. It is for precisely this reason that we as practitioners find it helpful to gauge, to the best of our abilities, the relative developmental maturity of a group's participants in order to know how to support them through the challenges of collective work.

Next, we will discuss in greater detail some of the practices that can promote the integration of the individuating and participatory modes of the psyche as a person engages in mindful action from within the intersubjective field of the We-Space.

Mindful Action From Within the We-Space: Intentional Practices for Inquiry and Collaboration

When we speak of individual mindful action within the collective, collaborative space, we describe how the dynamics of being, knowing, and doing are interwoven and integrated through the holistic and immediate intentional attention described by Heron as "radical practice, a skill of paying heed to the process of action," (1996, p. 122). This intentional engagement includes being aware, while acting, of: 1) the motives of action; 2) the strategy adopted; 3) the actual behaviors and performance; 4) the context of action and beliefs about it; 5) and the outcomes of the action (1996, p. 118). Of particular relevance here in the discussion of the boundaries between the individual and the collective, we explore in brief the skills that Heron proposes to support the balancing of the individuating and participatory modes, allowing for the relaxing of the separating tendencies of the ego and for deep levels of collaboration. These skills include: being present, imaginal openness, bracketing, reframing, and several dimensions of what he calls, "radical practice," (1996, p. 122).

Being Present

"Through empathic communion, harmonic resonance, attunement, I feel the presence of people and other entities. I participate in their inner experience, their modes of awareness, their ways of giving meaning and being affected," (1996, p. 119). Without the practice of being fully and consciously present to the other/ the collective in a state of empathic connection, truly collaborative action that flows from within the We-space is not possible. By way of illustration, while one of the three co-authors was serving as a facilitator in an Action Inquiry (Torbert, 2003) project with an institute for community leadership development, *being present* opened up past wounds in the group. Key members of the leadership development team at the institute volunteered to join this Action Inquiry project. The purpose of the research project was to explore and understand the role collaborative action inquiry could play in addressing issues of community leadership engagement. The facilitator invited the group to be present with each other and the system as a whole as co-inquirers open to new learning and new knowledge, to initiate the collective space for inquiry. Almost immediately, members of the group expressed how ill at ease this form of joining made them. This expression revealed a culture of mistrust and individual protectiveness and as a result the facilitator brought attention to these dynamics in a third person mode of self-reflection with the group. As a result we took more time to renew our commitment to the collective inquiry and learn how to develop a deeper sense of trust before moving more deeply into the We space.

Imaginal Openness

This practice involves the conscious vulnerability and sensitivity to the total process of "enacting the forms of other persons by imagining them;" in other words, "perceiving others in an unrestricted way so as to attend to all levels of their reality," (1996, p. 119) in manners that prescind, to the extent possible, from bias and preconception. Said more simply, this is the skill of being open to others and reality in a way that is free from language/concepts, judgments, and prejudice. To illustrate this practice we share an experience one of us had serving as a co-investigator in an action research study. The co-investigator was unfamiliar with the studies context and practiced a vulnerable and open stance in order to be disposed to the potential learning that was sure to come. This openness also seemed timely as an approach to help build a relationship with the institute's co-investigator. The co-investigator was a retired lawyer and established long time member of a historical African American community in the region. This joint project was aimed at generating a space of resonance for community members to address structural racism that was crippling the community. In spite of being partnered with a trusted member of that community, a woman of color who had authority and credibility as a mediator, we were unable to move past the community members' perceptions that one of us was a white woman and therefore incapable of intervening. After the first collective inquiry sessions, the co-investigators decided to work with this dynamic. The co-investigator, a woman of color, invited participants to explore their reactions and judgments separately before inviting the second co-investigator back into the collective space – a brave move by the co-investigator that provided a place for more inclusive participation and space for collective insight.

Bracketing

This practice involves the intentional dis-identification with the cultural and linguistic conditioning that predispose us to understand the world and others in determined and conventional manners; for instance, as through the lens of a mechanistic worldview, or the filtered, wounded perspective of early childhood traumas, our conceptual frameworks of everyday perception become charged with threat, negative expectation, and disempowerment. The capacity for bracketing involves the willingness to see a situation in a new light, or a new frame of reference. The following provides an illustration from one of us who was hosting a group of community leaders to introduce them to skills of collaborative action inquiry (Torbert, 2003) as a way to develop a mutual space for collective visioning of a new future. These leaders were esteemed members of a community, sharing the desire for co-visioning a future on behalf of the larger community. As the co-investigators invited participants to engage with the practices of inquiry, they began to encounter each other's distinct and sometimes conflicting conceptual frameworks, which almost derailed the work of the collective. The frameworks were heavy and fixed, interacting like sharp points rather than permeable boundaries. The introduction of a new lens, Collaborative Action Inquiry (Torbert, 2014), had the unintended consequence of triggering participant's defenses and instigated more fixed identification with their pre-existing frameworks. The saving grace of this slow progress towards generating a We-space was the continuous reframing capacity of the facilitator. By continuously making open, visible and self reflexive the process of exploring judgments and frames of interpretation, the community leaders relaxed enough to take in that "there may be other ways to see".

Reflective Inquiry

We suggest that an additional practice, reflective inquiry and adaptation, can help us as individuals to consciously balance the individuating and participatory tendencies of the psyche in order to support the simultaneous experience of critical subjectivity and deep collaboration with the collective. Reflective inquiry is focused on aligning action, i.e., *how* we are attempting to accomplish our goals, with "knowing," i.e. discerning *what* the right goals are, and understanding the mental models and assumptions undergirding our strategies, with our "being" and will– the intentions, purposes, and motives that explain *why* we are doing what we are doing. Intention may have explicit or espoused dimensions that we can easily articulate, and it may involve unconscious motives as well, including subjective or intersubjective needs, fears, and desires. In the consideration of the role of the will, we recognize the way that the individuating mode of the psyche orients the will in a manner that is primarily acting for oneself, while the participatory mode orients the will in a manner that is with and for the other and the larger whole. There is obviously a place and time for each. At the boundary of the We-Space and the individual, a person might inquire:

- As I explore my intention for action in relationship to the We-space, am I primarily self focused or other focused? Or more specifically, is my intention in service to the larger whole?

- What is the purpose behind the results I am seeking? Is this vision aligned with the values, mission, strategy and action of the collective?

- Am I exercising mutually transforming power to achieve my goal, meaning that I am willing to be vulnerable and to be changed through relationships with others?

- Do I sense attachments or over-identifications that are undermining my relationships with the collective?

- Am I experiencing emotions that incline me toward differentiation from the collective (individuating mode) or feelings that connect me with a felt sense of union and relatedness to the whole (participatory mode)?

• If I am honest, are there unconscious fears, needs, or desires influencing me? e.g. fear of failure, of looking bad or incompetent; fear of losing control; fear of losing relevance or of being not needed; fear of getting lost in the crowd and not standing out; fear of conflict or loss; fear of my power, or of responsibility?

Heron (1996) describes four further reflective practices: dynamic congruence; emotional competence; non attachment; and self-transcending intentionality.

Dynamic Congruence

Heron (1996) describes this as a "radical paying heed to action at the interface between the conceptual, reflective mind, and the intuitive, imaginal mind. Simply stated, this practice involves attention to the way in which a specific action or behavior is a part that does or does not contribute to the imagined or intended whole. For example, how are the edits we are making to this chapter contributing to the final product that we have envisioned together? Paying heed at this level entails a comprehensive view of the self-in-action (with others) toward an intended goal or outcome. To illustrate we offer an example from an action research project where one of us was the lead facilitator. In this situation, the facilitator was debriefing the action research team after an early intervention with the larger participant group. During this after action review the research team focused on the interplay of power between the research team members and the participants. One member of the team observed that anytime a member of the research team intervened, the participant group resisted. When we openly discussed our observations with the group, becoming vulnerable to the group's critiques and inviting their influence, the more resistance we encountered. As we inquired further into this dynamic, we understood that our attempts at sharing power and giving power away were mistrusted based on prior experiences. The We-space container was not yet ready for sharing power. By paying heed to the action within our action as a team, we were able to slow down and give more time for mutual trust to deepen and the authentic sharing of power emerged.

Emotional Competence

The ability to identify and manage emotions. The capacity to be aware of one's own current emotional state, owning and identifying and accepting the state through self-awareness, is the basis for managing it by expression control, transmutation and catharsis (Heron, 1992). This radical skill is an antidote to moments when defensiveness may arise in the process of human inquiry. An example where this emotional competence came into play occurred when one of us was leading a strategic planning session, and several key participants called at the last minute to say they were not going to attend. Even up to the last ten minutes before the full-day session, I was feeling intense irritation and a foreboding sense that this day was going to be a wasted exercise sabotaged by these three participants, each of whom had a vested interest in maintaining the status quo. As I was approaching the room where the meeting was going to take place (aware of my negative state, yet feeling powerless to shift into a more positive frame of reference), I heard all those who had gathered in loud and energetic conversation, punctuated with several outbursts of laughter. When I took my place at the table, these energetic interactions continued and I began to see my colleagues in a new light – with increasing appreciation and even affection. As I quietly observed them, it occurred to me that in the minutes before, I had focused on who was missing to the complete exclusion of who was present. When this insight dawned on me, I felt a whole new attitude open up toward the work ahead, energized by those around me, and a genuine appreciation of them and their presence – trusting that the people we needed were the ones who did show up that day. This emotional change within me happened within the span of twenty minutes, but I believe it created conditions for me to lead and facilitate in a markedly more effective and energized manner through the rest of the day.

Non-Attachment

One can be fully open to what is going on in the situation without being too caught in one's current view of it (Heron, 1992) or in the outcomes of one's actions. This skill demands that one cultivate the ability to wear lightly the purpose, strategy, behavior and motives which have been chosen as the form of action. When facilitating collaborative action inquiry, one of us described a time that this light holding was transformative. At the boundary of the We-space, we agreed that there was an experience of continuous inquiry as to the permeability of the space. In the action research project team, we joked about how we often thought of ourselves as jello poured into different molds daily based on the disposition and needs of the group. This holding lightly of means and ends, while at the same time remaining in tune with the intention and the group itself, required patience, tolerance of ambiguity, and this spirit of non-attachment.

Self-Transcending Intentionality

The capacity to have in mind, during action, a range of alternative purposes, strategies, forms of behavior, and motives; to consider their possible relevance and applicability to the situation and to have an adaptive willingness to adopt any of these to reshape action with and on behalf of the greater whole. By way of example, one of the authors is currently involved in an interfaith, community based organization aiming to develop an interfaith youth network. At every step of the process, it has been necessary to hold a balance between critical subjectivity and the sensibility of the whole group in order to align intentions, balance commitments, and harmonize our interests so that we are genuinely serving both our own constituencies and the wider whole. This process has demanded that we each avoid leaning toward fixed positions along the way, but instead, advocate for interests and then inquire about the interests and needs of others.

These intentional practices can support the extended epistemology of the We-space by helping individuals to balance personal will with the collective will. They can attenuate the individuating grip of the ego that impedes us from being present and undermines our empathetic knowing in relationship with others. Inquiry through these practices helps us hold the ego lightly in our awareness. This awareness can support the intentional integration of the individuating and participatory modes and promote a balance between critical subjectivity and collaborative relationships within the We-space.

Conclusion

In this chapter we offer Heron's framework on how to develop deeper awareness of the individuating and participatory modes of the psyche along with examples of how we have experienced and practiced its implications. This framework provides a structure for reflecting on felt experiences, reactions, thoughts and actions when working within the We-Space of groups, team, organizations, and communities. We propose that the practices as described above can help us recognize the oscillating movements of the individuating and participatory modes of our psyches, offering us greater capacity to act from within rather than apart from the We-space. We also bring attention to the essential co-relationship between the individual critical subjectivity and the participatory, empathetic knowing and relating that unfolds within the We-space. Our hope is to promote a means of deepening freedom from some of the ego's less helpful antics, for building capacity for more conscious personal awareness, greater mutuality in relationship and collaboration, and more skillful and creative means in the face of uncertain and dynamic environments, i.e. mindful, participatory action.

Author Bios

David McCallum, S.J., Ed.D. is a Jesuit priest who serves as the Special Assistant to the President for Mission Integration and Development at Le Moyne College. He is an assistant professor of Management and Leadership, and served as both the interim dean of the Madden School of Business at Le Moyne, and the interim Vice President for Institutional Advancement. Fr. McCallum serves as a facilitator for non-profit and educational strategic planning, provides executive coaching, and delivers leadership development programs internationally. His research interests include adult learning and development, group relations, leadership and organizational development, collaborative action research, and mission integration.

Aliki Nicolaides, Ed.D. is Associate Professor of Adult Learning, Leadership and Adult Development at the University of Georgia. Dr. Nicolaides' seeks to optimize vital developmental conditions for adults, groups and systems to learn. Through years of research and teaching, she has developed a theory of learning-within-ambiguity called "Collaborative Generative Learning." The results show how adults may also learn from within the complexity so prevalent in this period of liquid modernity. Her work suggests that encounters with persistent ambiguity evoke learning from potential hidden within complexity. Dr. Nicolaides pedagogy is grounded in Collaborative Developmental Action Inquiry (CDAI); a methodology which consciously develops adult's collaborative capacity to better respond to the fluidity and complexity of the early 21st century. The complex demands of a rapidly changing, interconnected world require new skill sets. CDAI is part of an emerging learning pedagogy that deliberately helps adults adapt to (and ultimately benefit from) this new global paradigm.

Lyle Yorks, Ed.D. is Professor of Adult Learning & Leadership in the Department of Organization and Leadership at Teachers College, Columbia University where he teaches courses in adult learning, strategy development as an organization learning process, strategic human resource development, and research. He is also a lecturer in the Executive Master of Science Program in Technology Management at in the School of Professional Studies, Columbia University where he teaches a course in Strategic Advocacy. His research interests include action learning, learning transfer, and developing strategic mindsets for addressing the challenges of learning through complexity. He has also served as visiting faculty in various EMBA and Executive Education programs in the United States, Europe, and Asia.

References

Argyris, C., & Schön, D.A. (1974). Theory in practice: Increasing professional effectiveness. San Francisco: Jossey-Bass.

Gunnlaugson, O, Baron, C., and Cayer, M. Eds. (2014). Perspectives on theory U: Insights from the field. Hershey, PA: IGI Global.

Heron, J. (1990). Helping the client: A creative, practical guide. London: Sage.

Heron, J. (1992). Feeling and personhood: Psychology in another key. London: Sage

Heron, J. (1996). Cooperative inquiry: research in the human condition. London: Sage.

Heron, J. (1999). The complete facilitator's handbook. London: Kogan Page.

Heron, J. & Reason, P. (1997). A participatory inquiry paradigm. Qualitative Inquiry, 3, 274-294.

Heron, J. and Reason, P. (2001). The practice of co-operative inquiry: Research 'with' rather than 'on' people. In P. Reason and H. Bradbury (eds), Handbook of Action Research: Participative Inquiry & Practice (pp. 179–188). London: Sage Publications.

Kasl, E. & Yorks, L. (forthcoming) Do I know you? Do you really know me? And, how important is it that   we do? Relationship and empathy in differing learning contexts. Working Paper.

Livesay, V. (2013). Exploring the paradoxical role and experience of fallback in developmental theory. Unpublished dissertation, University of San Diego, San Diego, CA.

McCallum, D. C. (2008). Exploring the implications of a hidden diversity in group relations' conference learning: A developmental perspective. (EdD), Teachers College, Columbia University, New York, NY.

Nicolaides, A. (2015). Generative learning: Adults learning within ambiguity. Adult Education Quarterly, 1-17

Nicolaides, A., & McCallum, D. (2013). Accessing the blind spot: The U process as seen thru the lens of developmental action inquiry. In O. Gunnlaugson, Baron, C., & Cayer, M. (Eds.), Perspectives on Theory U. Hershey, PA: IGI Global.

Nicolaides, A., & McCallum, D. (2014). Inquiry in action for learning in turbulent times: exploring the connections between transformative learning and adaptive leadership. Journal of Transformative Education, 1-15.

Senge, P. (1990) The Fifth Discipline: The art and practice of organizational learning. New York: Doubleday

Scharmer, O. (2007). Theory U: Leading from the future as it emerges. The social technology of presencing. San Francisco: Berrett-Koehler.

Scharmer, O., & Kaufer, K. (2013). Ego-system to eco-system economies. San Francisco, CA; Berrett-Koeh

Torbert, W., & Associates. (2003). Action inquiry: The secret of timely and transforming leadership. San Francisco: Berrett-Koehler.

Yorks, L. & Kasl, E. (eds.). (2002a). Collaborative Inquiry as a Strategy for Adult Learning. New Directions for Adult and Continuing Education, 94. San Francisco: Jossey-Bass.

Yorks, L. & Kasl, E. (2002b). Toward a theory and practice for whole-person learning: Reconceptualizing experience and the role of affect. Adult Education Quarterly, 52(3), 176-192.

Yorks, L. & Kasl, E. (2006). I know more than I can say: A taxonomy for using expressive ways of knowing to foster transformative learning. Journal of Transformative Education, 4(1), 1-22.

CHAPTER 10

We-Space Practices: Emerging Themes in Embodied Contemplative Dialogue

Tom Murray, Ed.D.

Introduction

There is increasing interest and discovery regarding "we-space practices" within the community of integrally-informed theory and practice. Unlike purely contemplative or purely dialogical practices, we-space practices offer the hope to support transformative development through their attention to the inter-development (tetra-emergence) of whole systems (individuals, groups, and action-processes).

For integralists, the ultimate motivation of we-space practices (and all practices) is the moral/ethical imperatives of liberation, sustained happiness, and/or (Kosmic) evolution. Bhaskar (1993) formulates liberation (self-emancipation and social justice) in terms of the elimination of the *demi-real*—ideas and thought patterns that cause harm because they do not sufficiently match reality. I will frame we-space practices in terms of shadow work and the insights that come from exposing the demi-real to the cleansing sunlight of individual or collective awareness. [1]

---

1. This chapter contains excerpts from a much longer work to be published titled "Contemplative Dialogue Practices: An inquiry into deep interiority, shadow work, and insight" in Integral Leadership Review (integralleadershipreview.com), and references will be made below to additional material in that article.

Influences from Three Domains: Dance, Meditation, and Group Processes

Somatic We-Spaces and Facets of Collective Embodiment

There is much about we-space-practices and experiences that is "embodied"—originating in pre-verbal aspects of experience as opposed to the content of discursive thought. Many of the important themes are identical in the two domains, and focusing first on a somatic practice allows us to ground the investigation, to separate the *embodied* experience from the *social* elements of the experience and from the *cognitive* elements of the experience; and to gain some clarity where *spiritual* and metaphysical themes enter into considerations of we-space.

In the extended version of this article I give a detailed description of a collective movement activity (or "somatic ensemble score") of the type practiced within the improvisational dance community of which I am a long time participant. I describe a group movement activity in which 30 seasoned participants are following the rules of a rather simple "score"—to remain standing and facing the front of the room, avoid physical contact, and move only in linear directions of forward/back, and left-right relative to the walls of the room. In my description of a typical 30-60 minute improvisational enacting of this open score, one observes an entire universe of possibilities including stillness, flow, repetition, mirroring, swarming, eruption, quiescence, and log-jamming.

Based on the extended description of this ensemble activity, here are some of the themes that arise in collective somatic practice, which I will call "Facets of Collective Embodiment":

1. *Autonomy and communion.* The example illustrates the nuanced interplay between the individual and the collective; leading and following; listening and acting. One can be completely autonomous, yet still fully immersed in and participating with the whole. One is leading and following simultaneously, and experiencing the play of or erasure of the polarity.

2. *Awareness and sensitivity.* The desired state is one of openness and attention. What Bonnie Roy calls "still hunting"— an objectless awareness (2014). There is an attunement, sensitivity, responsiveness, and non-clinging quality to attention and intention.

3. *Egolessness and the transpersonal.* If one is fully in a flow state in such movement scores (Csikszentmihalyi, 1990), one's pre-rational body-mind is making most of the decisions; there is no conscious or verbal thought involved, and no self-judgment or self-consciousness. One is not attached to or overly identified with one's position or socially constructed relationship relative to others.

4. *Equanimity and trust.* The flow states associated with group practices require high levels of trust and surrender: trust in self, in other individuals (including the facilitator), and in the process (and, some might say, the larger whole or "the universe"). This involves a belief, or perhaps a stance forged of suspended judgment, that: I am OK—my errors and limitations are natural and acceptable—it is all just "what is" as it flows from who we are.

5. *Deep time and space.* The experiences of time and space become altered and/or heightened. The mind, no longer perseverating on past and future, roams the space of the now; attuned to moment-to-moment arising. One can experience emptiness yet fullness, the expansiveness yet one-pointedness associated with flow states.

6. *Expansive bliss.* As indicated in several items above, collective somatic activities can arouse peak states of rapture, expansiveness, unity, and focus—which are characteristics of what is called "flow states" as applied to a collective activity.

What does this show us? First, as mentioned, even though dialogue is central to we-space practices, much about the experience of we-space practice is about embodiment and is pre-language (or non-linguistic). Second, I want to suggest that much of the non-ordinary or "peak" experiences of we-space practice draws on our ("lower") animal nature, as opposed to a higher or spiritual nature or a meta-cognitive capacity. Certain elements of these practices are shared, albeit in a primitive form, with social (including herd, schooling, and flocking) animals.

The implication is that, though human experience and capacity is not equivalent to or as simple as that of other animals, there is much to be gained by exploring how much of human nature draws upon our animal nature. What we interpret as sublime, divine, transpersonal, or esoteric experience may in large part be what happens when we disengage the discursive or symbolic mind and allow more embodied pre-linguistic and pre-conscious aspects of the mind-body, which are generally culturally suppressed, to animate and permeate experience.

As integral and developmental theories teach us, how we make meaning of these experiences depends in part on developmental level. Indeed, human cognition includes layers of reflection or meta-thought that *operate upon* lower level phenomena, so that our experience of more "primitive" layers can include an awareness, reflection, or witnessing of those lower layers. But, as each experience is a unitary whole, it is possible to conflate higher capacities such as awareness or witnessing with the lower-level phenomena that they are aware of. I am claiming that, for example, the open sense of alert awareness and the boundary-less sense of merging with others are using animal-level cognition. An awareness *that* one is having these experiences, or reflecting *on* the qualities or purposes of these experiences, constitute higher level functions. This is an important distinction in understanding we-space phenomena.

Meditative Practices

I will attempt a summary of what is shared among contemplative (meditation) practices as commonly understood in the West. The goals or outcomes of meditation practices can include the following, which I will refer to as "Facets of Contemplative Practice:"

1. At a minimum a state of *relaxation*, and perhaps physical and psychological *healing* or relief from suffering (Mindfulness-based Stress Reduction, for example), as a result of simply stopping the ongoing reinforcement and reproduction of patterned thought activity.

2. A set of peak *experiences* and refined *capacities*—Shinzen Young (2011) frames these capacities in terms of concentration, clarity, and equanimity. Others speak of advanced states or feelings of bliss, one-pointedness, expansiveness, emptiness, oneness, or openness; still others speak of powers or siddhis[1].

3. The development of *love, care, connection, empathy and compassion*, which are sometimes described as natural outcomes of contemplative practice, and sometimes described as capacities to intentionally develop through contemplative practice.

4. The *liberation* from or *healing* of mental/psychological/ cultural conditioning—this includes shadow work and sometimes catharsis as a goal. (Shadow work will be discussed in later sections.)

5. A deepening understanding of the *nature of the self* (or ego)—which ultimately includes a realization that the self, as usually understood, does not exist. It may also include insight into the nature of human suffering.

6. A deepening understanding of the *nature of reality and/ or being* (and the relationship between self and reality)— including: the realization that much or all of what we experience as real is constructed by the mind; and the realization that all phenomena are impermanent.

7. An experience of, understanding of, or merging with, a *non-dual source*—which might be interpreted as God, complete emptiness, the origin of all being, etc.

The point of delimiting these goals for meditative practices is the following. I propose that these are *not* the essential goals of we-space-practices—otherwise why not just meditate (or meditate within a community or "sangha")? I propose that the relationship between contemplative meditation practice and we-space practice is: (1) we-space practices build upon the Facets of Contemplative Practice; the deeper one's experience or capacity in these facets, the more capacity one has for we-space-practices. Conversely (2) (dialogic) we-space-practices *do* tend to support all of the above goals and outcomes of meditative practices, though that is not their primary aim or significance. And, importantly, there are certain aspects of the self, the ego, the shadow, and reality that are specific to social reality and interpersonal relationship, such that we-space-practices can add significantly to healing, learning, shadow-work, and capacity-building in these areas. But, as I will discuss later, even *that* may not be the most important outcome of we-space-practices.

Group Processes

Next I will describe what is in common among non-contemplative group practices. What group process adds that is mostly missing from both the somatic and the contemplative practices mentioned above are the *social and cognitive* layers that come with *language* and social interaction (for our purposes verbal communication is a central component of group processes/practices, though there are exceptions such as Systemic Constellation work[2]). Whereas the facets of collective embodiment and the facets of contemplative practice are found *within* *we-space* practices, and in a sense underpin them, group process can be thought of as *surrounding* we-space practice. That is, a we-space practice can be a component within, or an approach to, a larger group practice frame that sets the context and the purpose for the we-space practice.

The National Coalition for Dialogue and Deliberation (NCDD), of which I am a participating member, sponsors gatherings and resources for practitioners and academics interested in a wide variety of group practices. One reason for including an overview of group-processes/ practices here is to facilitate the integration of we-space practices and principles into the larger world of dialogue practice. NCDD frames the space of methods as having four types of goals (visit NCDD.org for explanations of the specific methods listed):

1. *Exploration*—People learn more about themselves, their community, or an issue and perhaps also come up with innovative ideas. (Approaches include World Café, Open Space, Bohm Dialogue, brainstorming methods.)

2. *Conflict transformation*—Poor relations or a specific conflict among individuals or groups is tackled. (Includes Sustained Dialogue, mediation, Issues Based Bargaining, compassionate listening.)

3. *Decision making*—a decision or policy is impacted and/ or public knowledge of an issue is improved. (Includes Citizens Jury, Deliberative Polling, Formal Consensus process.)

4. *Collaborative action*—people tackle complex problems and take responsibility for the solutions they design. (Includes Study Circles, Appreciative Inquiry, Future Search.)

In addition, there is a vast expanse of academic and theoretical work related to group process in sociology and social psychology, which I will barely mention here, but which may be quite relevant to we-space practices. We-space-practitioners and process designers can learn much from research and best practices in all of the (non-

---

2. https://en.wikipedia.org/wiki/Systemic_Constellations

contemplative) group practice areas mentioned above, and in fact have in many instances. We-space-practices explored within the integrally informed community might have any combination of all of the goals and methods mentioned above. They might be used to support self-reflection or healing skill building, relationship building, mutual understanding, and idea and insight generation—all of which can later lead to actions, decision making, transformation, or large scale capacity building.

What is specific to we-space practice vs. other group processes is the movement into what I will call *"deep interior space"*.[3] Deep interior space is the psychological and somatic space opened up in contemplative practices as applied to groups (though one can gain access to it through other means). At a group level, deep interior space has all of the elements described in the Facets of Collective Embodiment above. The group process frameworks mentioned above do not normally venture into the silent, spacious territory of deep interior space, but they can be modified with elements of we-space practice to do so. Thus the study and development of we-space practice in part involves the study and development of deep interior space in dialogic group practices. Framed in this way, practitioners have only begun to explore the vast array of possible we-space-practices. One can start with any type of group process described in this section and redesign it to include experiences of collective deep interior spaces. We are just beginning to understand how to do this in a general sense, based on the most well-known we-space practices, as described next.

We-Space Practices: Bohm Dialogue, U-Theory, and Deep Interior Space Letting Go, Be, and Come and Sensing the Future

In the extended version of this paper I give overviews and comparative analysis of Bohm Dialogue Process (Bohm, 1996, and see Gunnlaugson, 2014) and U-Theory/Process (Scharmer, 2007, and see Reams, 2007). See other chapters in this text for overviews of these methods.

U-theory frames its process in terms of letting go and letting come. Letting go points to processes and states of opening, release, trust, and

---

3. Deep interior space is related to what Andrew Venezia (2013) calls "inter-subjective self-reflexivity"; and what Dustin DiPerna (2014) calls transpersonal "inter-be-ing."

surrender referred to in meditation and in Bohm Dialogue. Letting come is the emergence of content from deep interior space that can manifest as creativity, vision, new intentions, enthusiasm, insight, etc. It is only through experimental and playful interactions with the world, setting up feedback loops and learning from mistakes that we learn and increase capacity (in what Geoff Fitch et al. call "failing forward" [2010])

This is an advance over Bohm's framing, which focuses on the experience of the now and vaguely suggests that the process should lead to transformation. Scharmer's injunction to "act from the future that is seeking to emerge" (2007, p. 8) activates a search space within the empty but alert mind that primes for possibilities that are both *possible* (as opposed to fanciful) and associated with one's *moral* instincts.

Gross, Subtle, and Causal Collective States and Vision-Logic

The deep interior spaces opened up in practices such as Bohm dialogue and U-Process can involve all of the Facets of Collective Embodiment above, including experiences of transpersonal autonomy-within-communion, deep trust and equanimity, euphoria, and enchantment. We-space phenomena can be described in terms of the "gross, subtle, and causal" categories of experience or "states" used by Wilber (2006) and elaborated upon by O'Fallon (2015). In collective somatic experiences, these phenomena arise mostly in relation to *gross* physical modes of interaction. When people are engaged in linguistic/symbolic modes of participation such as dialogue they are called upon to reflect on more *subtle* modes of being, such as thought processes, assumptions, social emotions, and shadow—as they arise in the moment. Furthermore, in deep interior space one becomes aware of the contours of awareness itself, and of the meaning-making process itself—which is called *causal* awareness.[4]

Thus, in we-space practices, the phenomenological aspects of the Facets of Collective Embodiment relate to subtle and causal object of awareness, as well as gross objects. The felt-sense of the state experience is not necessarily different, however. As Wilber (2006) notes, a given state of consciousness can be experienced from different developmental levels, while additional objects of awareness and interpretations are available at each successive level.

---

4. See O'Fallon's StAGES model (2014) for a good explanation of gross, subtle and causal modes of experience and development.

Venezia distinguishes the "subtle we space" as operating "on the inter- and intra-personal subtle boundaries that make up our personalities," from the "causal we space [of] shared awareness and 'compassion *as* awareness' [which includes an] interpenetration and mutual emptiness of boundaries and categories" (2013, p 11-12, 23).[5] Venezia continues with "it may even be fair to say that awareness, love, and presence are the mind, heart, and body of causal realization" (p. 24).

Drawing from O'Fallon's (2012; 2015) and Kesler's (2012) work I would propose that the causal state can be described as *objectless awareness, objectless seeking,* and *objectless compassion*—in terms of the body, mind, and heart (and the it/I/we of sacred presence). Roy's notion of still-hunting captures the states of objectless awareness and objectless seeking, and work in contemplative studies speak to the development of objectless compassion as a general state experience, independent of a particular recipient. Causal level We-space practice might be described in terms of establishing the conditions for the senses, the mind, and the heart to roam with super-fluidity through the widest and deepest spaces of possibility that a group can muster.

Other Contemporary Contemplative Dialogue Projects

In the extended version of this paper I give an overview of contemporary we-space projects that have been inspired by ideas from Bohm-dialogue (Bohm, 1996), U-Theory (Scharmer, 2007), spiritual activism, and theories of collective consciousness. These include projects led by M. Scott Peck (1997), Arnold Mindell (1995 & 2002), Thomas Hübl (2011), Saniel Bonder (2005), Terry Patten (2013), Steve McIntosh and Carter Phipps at the Institute for Cultural Evolution (www.culturalevolution.org), Sara Ross (2005) and Jan Inglis' (2007) TIP framework, Thomas Jordan (2014), Gary Steinberg and Gregory Kramer (www.metta.org, and see O'Fallon & Kramer, 2008), Ria Baek and Helen Titchen Beeth (2012), Dustin DiPerna (2014) and the WePractice community, Next Step Integral (www.nextstepintegral.org), and Pacific Integral (www.pacificintegral.com).

---

5. Venizia (2013) describes a further "Awakened we space" as exhibiting an "emergence of a shared self-aware and self-reflexive interpersonal mind." Though this description may be pointing to something important I will not use it because it spills into territory more speculative and metaphysical than our scope here.

Emerging Themes in We-Space Practice

Let us go deeper into the questions of "what are the intended *goals and outcomes* of these practices?" and "what do we know about the factors that contribute to success?"[6]

Insight, Elimination, and Other We-Space Goals

Collective intelligence and collective consciousness are intermediate goals for we-space practice, but what about the final goals? We-space practices include more than meditation practices and more than collective somatic practices because of the added element of *dialogue* (and, in some models, fuller integration with praxis). Thus, what is unique about we-space-practice in this context relates to the *meaning-making* aspects of being human together. I will suggest, following Roy (2014), that the most important goal of we-space-practices is the generation of *insight*. The term insight is related to creativity and intuition, but includes an emphasis on depth that I am exploring in this paper. Though I will claim that insight generation is the primary goal, there are many other valid goals for we space practices, including (each is explained in the extended version): action outcomes, community-building, transformation, uplifting, and morality and metta (loving kindness). Bohm's description of Dialogue (1996, and see Gunnlaugson & Moze, 2012) and Scharmer's description of U-Process (2007) also locate insight as the central purpose of we-space practice. For Bohm Dialogue the goal is insight into the nature of thought and cultural or collective shadow. As was mentioned, Bohm Dialogues are not debates, therapy groups, social gatherings, or conflict resolution sessions—the goal is the transformation of thought. For U-Process, the goal is to generate insights that lead to action-reflection cycles.

We-space-dialogues are about the playful (even if sometimes painful) generation of ideas and insights. The deeper the interior space, the greater the potential for radical ideas and profound insights. In my definition, insights do not come simply from additive or gestalt combinations of ideas, nor from creatively brainstormed ideas. They come from the lifting of a veil of ignorance from a concealed, suppressed or denied truth.

---

6. In the extended version of this paper I give an overview of contemporary we-space projects that have been inspired by ideas from Bohm-dialogue, U-Theory, spiritual activism, integral theory, evolutionary enlightenment, and theories of collective consciousness.

Shadow

We-space practice is oriented toward insight, which in turn is based on the eradication or integration of so-called shadow material. Much has been said of the nature and healing of shadow material within fields related to psychotherapy and transpersonal psychology, starting of course with Freud and Jung. We can draw from this, but the insights we are after in we-space practices involve the ablation of *collective* shadow, not individual personal shadow (though personal transformation can happen as a side-effect of a group session). Bohm made this clear in his description of Dialogue as uncovering cultural bias, irrationality, and incoherence through the "collective proprioception or immediate mirroring back of both the content of thought and the less apparent, dynamic structures that govern it" (Bohm et al., 1991). What do we mean, then, by shadow and collective shadow? I will start with individual shadow and extend this concept to collective shadow.

As mentioned above, thoughts and beliefs can be thought of in terms of connections. Through various processes, including painful experiences and cultural conditioning, some ideas and some pathways become occluded. We will use the word *occlusion* to stand for the many metaphors that can be used for shadow or the dynamic it creates, including: bias, distortion, blind-spot, lacuna, rigidity, knot, obstacle, barrier, wound, trauma, baggage, fog, and numbing. Related words used in psychotherapy include: pathology, dysfunction, repression, suppression, defense, neurosis, resistance, and denial; and related words from contemplative traditions include: contraction, fear, attachment, illusion, ignorance, and conditioning. Related processes and outcomes include: oppression, projection, dis-identification, alienation, and regression. This barrage of terms and metaphors attributes to the scope of what we mean by shadow, and attests to the complexity and breadth of the topic, yet there is a single basic notion underlying it all. This is of pernicious stuff lodged within the thought system and body that hampers the process of making *connections* between ideas or information that could potentially be related, or has hampered the *perceiving* of something that would otherwise be available to perception.

Due to its active nature, much human energy and potential gets bound up in the maintenance of shadow material. When and as shadow is freed up and made transparent, not only are the occluded ideas or aspects of self revealed, but they are suddenly made available to make *new* connections throughout the mind, in a flood of reorganization, unlearning, insight, and freed up energy. New modes of perception may also be freed up, deepening the quality of awareness. Reorganization happens quite naturally and this has important implications. First, it supports our notion that insight is mostly about the eliminative processes of unlearning or habit-breaking. The "work" of insight is in the often demanding process of trying various strategies to release the stubborn knots of shadow material or reveal what has been hidden as a matter of habit. Once occlusions are removed, new connections and perceptions are available for the rather automatic processes of cognitive (re-) organization, which produces insight. Therapeutic, reflective, and critical forms of dialogue and personal process usually bear fruit only through substantial motivation and skillful means. But it often appears that once the knot is untied or the dam is broken, what follows is a flow of new information, energy, and possibility, which, again through effort, must be integrated into the life-world.

What was said above about individual shadow can be said about "collective shadow." By collective shadow I mean either the occlusions (un-seen truths, connections, or data) shared by most or all individuals in a group, or the structural (socio-cultural) aspects of a group that result in systemic occlusions. Above we noted how shadow can be thought of in terms of occlusions or inhibitions among various types of connections.

At the individual level, shadow is about what cannot be thought about consciously, while at the group or social holon level, shadow is simply what is not *talked about* (or communicated, explicitly represented, or enacted). To reduce or heal collective shadow is to speak (or demonstrate or represent in some way) a truth (or apparent truth) not previously consciously known to oneself and the rest of the group (or the majority). This might be in the form of "now I understand that *I...*"—a revelation about self that others can relate to; and it might be of the form "I now understand that *we...*" (as a group, culture, or species). Note however that we are focusing on revealed intuitive insight, not intellectualizing analysis (not that these are mutually exclusive categories).

Additive vs. Eliminative Development: On Being Born in the Middle

In the integral theory community, discussions of development are sometimes confusing around the downward movements into evolutionarily prior (pre-human) capacities vs. upwards movements into evolutionarily advanced (post-rational) capacities. We have touched on this theme above in noting the difference between tapping into what I called "the open sense of alert awareness and the boundary-less sense of merging with others," which are lower level capacities, while awareness, witnessing, and meta-thought use higher level functions. Lower level functions are available to us from birth, though accessing or experiencing them is often occluded or repressed (and they, like all capacities, can be refined with practice). As we have said, shadow work (and thus also spiritual/ego development) largely involves dealing with the occlusions and their reduction (through eliminative movements).

Development, on the other hand, as usually understood, is a process of accumulation and complexification. Each developmental change operates upon lower level capacities through differentiation to create wider fields of nuance, or through integration to create higher gestalts of unity. The confusion between lower-level and higher-level functions comes in part because, as Roy puts it, "we are born in the middle" (2014). Born into a pre-given life-world of culture and language, surrounded by various forms of oppression and ignorance, one can not help but develop the occlusions, neurosis, biases, etc. characteristic of the human condition. Development up to the culture's (or family's) center of gravity happens through effortless assimilation of the habit patterns one is surrounded with. Development beyond this requires personal motivation, unusual experiences, or life stressors that propel one to build higher level skills and capacities.

Accessing and rebuilding *lower* level occluded capacities does not usually happen by itself or easily—doing so requires *higher* level capacities such as reflective awareness and self-understanding. Thus one must often reach developmentally up into greater hierarchical complexity to build the motivation or skill to gain access to developmentally lower capacities whose occlusion has thus far limited one's "human potential."

Heart-Based Development and Wisdom

The above discussions help clarify a question summarized by the title of my 2009 article "Intuiting the Cognitive Line in Developmental Assessment: Do Heart and Ego Develop Through Hierarchical Integration?" I've said relatively little thus far about love, compassion, and one-ness, which are central goals in some models of individual or group contemplative practice.

In the standard AQAL interpretation, morality develops along separate developmental lines—vs. cognition, ego, spirit, and emotional/social skill. These lines are assumed to influence each other but their relationship is underspecified (indeed it must be quite complex). However, spiritual, ego, and social-emotional skill development are all aspects of what we might call Wisdom Skills, which combine cognitive (post-rational) development and heart-based capacities related to compassion, empathy, care, and feelings of mutuality and union. While the (cognitive) reflective reasoning and perspective-taking skills associated with wisdom-skill clearly involve advances in hierarchical complexity, the expansion of the *heart-space* that comes with increasing wisdom and spiritual development seems to have a very *different* developmental topology.

Using our upward vs. downward arcs of development, we can say that the heart-based aspect of development is eliminative (downward toward embodiment). Through the negation or transmutation of shadow material there can be an opening to an underlying or primal sense of unity and oceanic love that has been occluded through conditioning, but is available to the infant and at the mammalian levels of human being. We don't learn to love so much as unlearn our fears and alienation. However, as described above, the upward developmental arc is usually needed in tandem with the eliminative side, both to produce the motivation and skillful means to navigate the deep dive, and also in how the insights and new capacities that are uncovered are integrated, interpreted, and put to use. This helps explain the reason why late stage ego development seems to lead to profound commitments to compassion and service across ever wider extensions of time and space.

An Evo/Invo-Lutionary Model for Group Shadow-Work and Insight Generation

We have postulated that insight is the key outcome of we-space practice, and that this insight involves removing or seeing through occlusions, usually from evolutionarily/involutionarily lower layers of the self. In this section I propose a specific layered model for the downward involutionary arc (and the middle-out process of development) that has already been hinted at above.

In recent years I have been inspired and influenced by Bonnitta Roy's work on Collective Insight. An emerging model developed by Roy in collaboration with others situates shadow work within a stratified evolutionary developmental biology (evo-devo) framework. Different sources of shadow are associated with each phase of evolution as recapitulated in development: from matter to life to animals to early and then late human cognition. Related to each layer are truths that can be pressed into the demi-real of shadow through denial, resistance, pathology, etc. Liberation and insight for each layer involves revealing what was occluded at that layer.

There are numerous possible models of evolution/development at different levels of granularity. Here I will present one that is simpler than that used by Roy.[7] Such models that add a structure to shadow-work can be used both diagnostically and prescriptively in we-space group work. Knowing the layer of shadow that a group is struggling with or producing insight from can inform process design and leadership decisions; and can help we-space practice groups auto-reflect and self-regulate to deepen insight. An existential crisis awaits the practitioner at each layer. A significant amount of what is hidden remains so because a truth revealed would threaten the self one is identified with. For some of these layers, the occlusion is deeper than psychological in nature, and constitutes conditioning that stems quasi-universally from one's basic humanity (or animal-ness), independent of cultural immersion or personal history. Figure 1 illustrates these evolutionary layers on the left (which are described in detail in the extended paper).

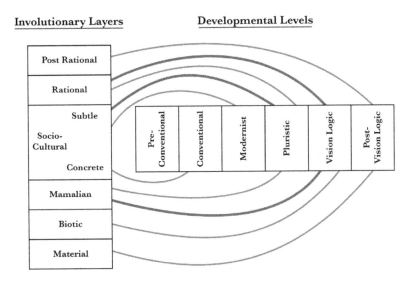

Figure 1: The Middle-out relationship between involutionary

---

7. Roy's work incorporates elements from her process-oriented integral framework (Roy 2010 & 2014). Her theory draws on recent neuroscience showing how brain activity unfolds through these layers of being. Her structural model for shadow work includes layers for the Latent self (sub-personalities, etc.), collective (cultural) unconscious (world-views), myth-o-poeia (archetypal ideas, languages), archetypes (norms, taboos), animal realms (shamanism), biotic realm, abiotic realm (primordial elements), and formless realm (energetic primes).

layers and developmental level

In this figure "involutionary" refers to the layers of evolution that subsist within the individual. I.E. there are aspects of one's being and functioning that come from being a Homo Sapien (i.e. that which differentiates us from other animals), aspects that come from being mammals, etc. Depending upon one's personal history and cultural surroundings, one may achieve capacities above the cultural norm and develop rational and post-rational skills. The "developmental levels" in the figure represent capacities to *reflect on* and consciously *transform* one's capacities in increasingly sophisticated ways (through processes of hierarchical complexity, as described by Fischer, 1980 & Commons et al., 1984). Through developmental processes increasingly more complex and/or subtle aspects of the self are transformed from "subject into object" (Kegan, 1994), as processes that compose the self are brought into awareness (as in meta-cognition, meta-affect, etc.). The involutionary layers are aspects of the "subject" or self, and the developmental levels indicate what has become "object".[8] The arrows in the figure show the relationship between the involutionary layers and the developmental levels. Thinner lines represent emerging awareness and heavier lines represent fuller awareness.

Some of the involutionary layers are generally more difficult to gain awareness of than others, and certain layers usually need to be "cleaned up" or "opened up" before others can be worked on. It appears as though the order of re-integration (the shadow work of the healing of wounds, untying of knots, and exposing the occluded) has a "middle-out" ordering starting with Conventional consciousness, because of our "born in the middle" nature. We (in Western cultures at least) are naturally socialized to a conventional developmental level of behavior and cognition. At this level one has some capacity to reflect on and expose shadow material at the concrete sociocultural level of involution. At this level, though one possesses rational thought capacities, one has little skill in reflecting on one's thought process (as the figure shows, it is not until the Pluralist developmental level that reflection upon this aspect of self begins).

Development stems from reflection on not only the "higher" aspects of self but also the "deeper" aspects of self. And this also seems to follow a middle-out path. Awareness of one's behavior as a social being tends to develop before awareness of one's emotional

---

8.vThe figure illustrates an emerging model still being refined. One of its limitations is that it can be confusing that the post-socio-cultural involutionary layers point to higher *developmental* capacities. All humans share capacities below the socio-cultural level, and only more developed individuals have higher level involutionary layers.

state, which in turn tends to develop before one is aware of the generic limitations of knowledge and language (at construct aware). This map can help describe the shadow-work aspects of group processes.

What does it look and feel like for a group to gain awareness and see through the occlusions at each of these layers? I will sketch out some possibilities below in an approximate order of accessibility, from easier to more challenging, in a rough developmental sequence. Each developmental step illustrates the involutionary layers that can be seen or seen through, and the type of shadow work that might be most appropriate there. Note that in this section I am using "layer" for the involutionary layers listed above, and "level" for developmental levels of consciousness being enacted by a participant in any given moment (which is not necessarily their stable center of gravity).

Pre-conventional level – any group work is difficult.

At this level the individual, or the group on average, does not have awareness of the Adult Self (or any other layers). There is barely sufficient intelligence or cohesion to do any type of group or collaborative activity. Group processes may involve a fair degree of blaming, defensiveness, projection, posturing, or non-participation. (Note that these levels can be used to describe an individual, a group's performative center of gravity, or a group's ideal peak capacity. They can be used to describe a momentary state or a more established stage.)

Conventional level – stable social collaboration.

With Adult Self (concrete socio-cultural self) awareness established, participants in a group activity can maintain basic levels of respect, composure, and awareness of the group context. Outbursts or actions that dominate group space, or withdrawals from group relationship, are possible at this level but are done from choice. As is described in various developmental theories, dialogue at the conventional level contains a fair amount of right vs. wrong and us vs. them language. A reachable goal for participants at this level might be to let go of posturing and personal story, gross defenses and neuroses, to create a basic level of trust and congruence of intent.

It is not uncommon for participants in Conventional (and Modernist) groups to at least occasionally drop into reactive or regressive (pre-conventional, child-like) modes of being; we are all vulnerable to such occasions, each having our own emotional or limbic trigger points.

Modernist level – productive, efficient, rigorous, and/or creative collaborative outcomes.

This is the level of awareness assumed (or hoped for) in most group processes including brainstorming, organizational meetings, citizen dialogues, group therapy, meditation retreats, etc. At this level, participants are entering what Cook-Greuter (2000 & 2005) calls "context aware"—they have a minimal understanding of how culturally reproduced ideas can bias thought. They have a post-conventional freedom to think independently, and they make good faith efforts to minimize personal and cultural bias as they engage. They are good listeners, logical and creative thinkers, somewhat in touch with their feelings, and can take the perspectives of others. Participants can reflect upon the quality of information and information sources, and the logical validity of claims. At this level one begins to gain awareness of the shadows of the Socio-Cultural Self, but insights are attached to specific ideas, cultures, or situations (as opposed to a phenomenon in general). All of the "group processes" described in the subsection with that title assume, and usually operate at, the Modernist level of consciousness.

Pluralist level (or post-modern level) – interest in and early capacity for we-space practices.

We-space practices, as we have defined them as contemplative dialogue, begin to have relevance at this level. Participants can share curiosity about and deep inner exploration of not only specific culturally biased content (as they do in the Modernist Level), but about the very nature of such systemic bias; observing how it arises inside one and within group contexts. Participants have moved from "I disagree" to "I see it another way." A familiarity with contemplation and deep inner observation begins. Participants start to explore shadow within the layer of the Rational/Symbolic self through reflective practice guidelines such as those in Bohm Dialogue and U-Process which support the apperception of the limitations of concepts and models. Insights about shadow related to the Mammalian Self may begin here also, as embodied practice leads to increased in-the-moment awareness of how instinct and emotion arise.

Vision Logic level (or second tier or integral level) – full capacity for we-space practices.

This is the level that most we-space practice aims to achieve, and is usually experienced as a "peak experience" (until practitioners become physiologically accustomed to it). It contains the maturation of shadow-awareness begun in the Pluralist level, and begins exploration into the layers of the Biotic self and the Material Self. The Mammalian Self's drives to impress, defend against, control, please, befriend, blame, take care of, or attract others in the group are seen through. They are enacted so minimally that they do not influence the flow. When these things do arise, there is no (or little) embarrassment or judgment—everyone understands that we are human (and animals) and the dialogue moves on without skipping a beat. When shadow material from the Social Self or Mammalian Self does manifest it is appreciated for its gifts, learned from, and/or compassionately chuckled at.

Participants are construct-aware and don't let the limitations of language and concepts constrain them (or rather they minimize such constraints). They know words and concepts are sliding signifiers whose meaning cannot be nailed down precisely—they don't get into arguments about definitions. They look for shared meaning and have moved from "I see it another way" to "what might she mean by that?" and "let's play with that idea." Each thing said is taken to be one perspective of many, and it is not assumed that the speaker of an idea is attached to it. Ideas and concepts are at play, not in competition. Participants have full "negative capability" (see Murray, 2013), i.e. a high tolerance for uncertainty, unknowing, and paradox. With the other involutionary levels seen through, deep insight at the levels of the Biotic self and Material Self are increasingly possible.[9]

Post-Vision-Logic level – the future of we-space practices.

I include this level for the sake of completeness, though I have only the barest glimpse of what group functioning at this level might be like, and don't want to build models beyond my experience of the territory. I don't even dare give it a more descriptive name, though, following models of Wilber, O'Fallon, or Cook-Greuter it could be called, Unitive, Third Tier, or Illumined. Roy points to the possibility of post-dialogical participation at this level. It is probably exceedingly rare (in Western society) to encounter group practice in which the participants have reached a mature level of awareness at the levels of the Biotic Self and Material Self (though it is likely that many individuals within the integral community have a post-vision-logic center of gravity, this does not translate directly into group work at that level).

---

9. My only personal experience with a group operating stably at this level has been two meetings with Bonnie Roy's working group on Collective Insight.

Conclusions

Martin Keogh, a movement teacher in the contact improvisation community, writes, "when myriad possibilities appear in each moment, the opportunities for self-criticism go down...the pathway you end up taking is simply what you are contributing to the dance...how do we increase our capacity to live in the unresolved?...Let the animal brain and body have a stronger voice...letting the river flow [and as James Hillman suggests] 'learn to accept a self that remains ambiguous no matter how closely it is scrutinized' " (2010, p. 15).

This is also a wonderful description of the openness, fluidity, trust, and panoramic simplicity-within-complexity that describe successful we-space practices as well. In this chapter I have described we-space practices, and the causal spaces of deep interiority that they aim for, from embodied and phenomenological perspectives. I have also tried to put them in context with related practices in ensemble somatics, meditation, and dialogue-and-deliberation processes, to help us gain more clarity about what is unique about we-space practices, and to situate these other domains in a way that allows we-space practitioners to draw more from what the other domains can contribute. I have proposed that the core purpose of we-space practice is the collective generation of insight; that insight is primarily about elimination and shadow work; and that what is of deepest interest are insights that pertain to the group's shadow, including insights about broad cultural and even species-level shadow material. Finally, I offer a layered involutionary model of shadow work (drawing from Roy's work) that helps differentiate the downward arcs of ablation (elimination) toward source, and the upward arcs of development. It can be used as a diagnostic tool assessing the states and types of content arising in a group practice, and as a guide for the most appropriate fulcrum points for process structures and interventions.

My hope is that this chapter will nudge us a bit further toward a type of clarity that will both accelerate the inquiry into we-space practices and, in taking a non-metaphysical tact, allow us to share what we learn with communities of theory and practice outside the integral communityvand to better learn from them in the exchange. This cornucopia of perspectives on we-space practices is only a small part of "the story," and, despite its attempt to use an embodied and phenomenological stance, it is still a rather theoretical one. What I have not covered in any detail are the practical questions in designing we-space practice groups and activities. A practical manual for process design might answer the following important questions:

What methods, principles, and structures *support deeper dives* into interior space, more collective resonance, and deeper collective insights?

What are the *diagnostic markers* of processes going well and going off track?

- What are the *difficult situations* and choice points in we-space practices, and how can these be navigated?

- How does one tailor *invitations* to we-space activities, and adjust we-space *process* structures based on considerations of:

  o *Diversity* (and homogeneity) of *developmental* level,

  o Diversity of *worldview*, culture, expertise, gender, intention, and prior familiarity and trust.

  o *Scale* of the interaction (number of participants; length of time).

  o Required *commitment* levels.

- What *leadership* style, from minimal and participant-centered, to more fully facilitated, is best for various process goals?

- What additional factors are involved in creating we-space community within a *dedicated community* meeting regularly over an extended time period?

- How do *facilitators train and prepare* themselves cognitively, emotionally, and spiritually for various types of engagement challenges?

- When and how should we-space practices be used within *larger projects* of organizational development, action inquiry, and social change?

- What does rigorous (or quasi-rigorous) *research* look like in this field—in terms of demonstrating outcomes and determining what preconditions and process structures produce desired results?

- What are the pros and cons of *virtual* we-space practices?

Of course, the answers to all of these questions will vary based on the we-space practice context and underlying theory. Practitioners have developed answers to these questions within the fields of group processes, deliberation and communication theory, and/or collaborative education, but we are only just beginning to apply these to we-space practice. All of the pioneers mentioned in my overview of contemporary we-space practice projects are working hard at the leading edge of these questions, and many do have partial answers to some of these design questions.

Dialogue invokes ideals of equality, participation, freedom, collaboration, responsibility, diversity, creativity, and adaptation. Open, free, authentic, and richly iterative communication and feedback loops are seen as essential to generating acceptable life conditions in our world of dizzying global change and challenge, and disastrous social inequities and tragedies. However, as practitioners in fields as diverse as family therapy, management consulting, and geopolitics are well aware, high quality dialogue can be a very difficult thing to foster. The ideal of open, free, authentic communication includes assumptions about human nature that, it turns out, are not easily realized. Though there are no clear practical solutions to these thorny issues, contemporary explorations into contemplative dialogue practices, or "we space practices," are fleshing out some key principles for supporting a radical depth in authenticity, group field coherence, and insight generation. One of the most important questions yet to be answered is the extent to which these methods can bring status-quo participants into new states of vibrancy and synergy "for the masses," or whether the entry conditions for these types of processes limit them to relatively developed or skilled individuals, in which case the "average" participant may need preliminary processes that first (and slowly) build capacity.

Author Bio

Tom Murray, Ed.D., is a Senior Research Fellow at the University of Massachusetts School of Computer Science, and Chief Visionary and Instigator at Perspegrity Solutions. Murray's projects include research on: supporting social deliberative skills and deep reflective dialogue in online contexts, using text analytics to estimate developmental levels, and using artificial intelligence methods to create responsive learning environments. His understanding of contemplative dialogue practices comes from many years of experiences in Bohmian dialogue, insight meditation, conflict resolution mediation, and the design and leading of various embodied group practices. He is an Associate Editor for Integral Review journal and has published articles on integral theory as it relates to education, contemplative dialogue, leadership, ethics, knowledge building communities, epistemology, and post-metaphysics. Info: tommurray.us@gmail.com, perspegrity.com

References

Baek, R. & Titchen Beeth, H. (2012). Collective presencing: A new human capacity; and The circle of presence: Building the capacity for authentic collective wisdom. Kosmos Journal, Spring 2012 and Fall 2012.

Bhaskar, R. (1993/2008). Dialectic: The pulse of freedom. New York: Routledge.

Bohm, D. (1996). On dialog (L. Nichol, Ed.). New York: Routeledge.

Bohm, D., Factor, D. & Garrett, P. (1991). Dialogue – a proposal. Available at http://www.david-bohm.net/dialogue/dialogue_proposal.html.

Bonder, S. (2005). Healing the spirit/matter split. Extraordinary Empowerments Publ.

Cohen, A. (2004). The art of enlightened communication. From www.andrewcohen.org/teachings/art-of-ec.asp (downloaded July 2010).

Csikszentmihalyi, M. (1990). Flow: The psychology of optimal experience. Harper & Row.

Cook-Greuter, S. R. (2000). Mature ego development: A gateway to ego transcendence. J. of Adult Development, 7(4), 227-240.

Cook-Greuter, S.R. (2005). Ego development: Nine levels of increasing embrace. Available at www.cook-greuter.com.

Commons, M. L. & Richards, F. A. (1984). A general model of stage theory. In M. L. Commons, F. A. Richards & C. Armon (Eds.), Beyond formal operations: Late adolescent and adult cognitive development, (pp. 120-

DiPerna, D. (2014). Streams of Wisdom. Integral Publishing House.

Fitch, G., Ramirez, V., & O'Fallon, T. (2010). Enacting Containers for Integral Transformative Development. Integral Theory Conference, 2010.

Fischer, K. (1980). A theory of cognitive development: The control and construction of hierarchies of skills. Psychological Review, 87(6), 477-531.

Gunnlaugson, O. (2014). Bohmian Dialogue: A critical retrospective on Bohm's approach to dialogue as a practice of collective communication. Journal of Dialogue Studies. Spring 2014, 2(1), p. 25-34.

Gunnlaugson, O. & Moze, M. (2012). Surrendering into Witnessing: A Foundational Practice for Building Collective Intelligence Capacity in Groups. Journal of Integral Theory and Practice, Volume 7 No.3, pp. 105–115.

Hübl, T. (2011). Transparence: Practice groups – an adventure in seeing yourself and others more clearly. Germany: Sharing the Presence.

Inglis, J. (2007). Matching public interaction skills with desired outcomes. International Journal of Public Participation. Volume 1, Issue 2, 2007.

Jordan, T. (2014). Deliberative methods for complex issues: A typology of functions that may need scaffolding. Group Facilitation: A Research and Applications Journal, Number 13, 2014.

Kegan, R. (1994). In over our heads: The mental demands of modern life. Cambridge, MA: Harvard University Press.

Kesler, J. (2012). Integral Polarity Practice. Available from the author through www.johnkesler.com.

Keogh, M. (2010). The art of waiting: Essays on the art of contact improvisation. Available from the author at http://martinkeogh.com.

Mindell, A. (1995). Sitting in the fire: Large group transformation using conflict and diversity. Portland, OR: Lao Tse Press.

Mindell, A. (2002). The deep democracy of open forums: Practical steps to conflict prevention and resolution for the family, workplace, and world. Charlottesville, VA: Hampton Roads Publishing.

Murray, T. (2009). Intuiting the cognitive line in developmental assessment: Do heart and ego develop through hierarchical integration? Integral Review, Vol. 5 No. 2, December 2009, p. 343-354.

O'Fallon, T. (2013). The senses: Demystifying awakening. Paper presented at the Integral theory Conference, 2013, San Fransisco CA.

O'Fallon, T. (2015, in press). StAGES. Albany New York: Suny Press.

Patten, T. (2013). Enacting an Integral Revolution: How Can We Have Truly Radical Conversations in a Time of Global Crisis? Paper presented at the Integral Theory Conference 2013.

Reams (2007). Illuminating the blind spot: An overview and response to theory U. Integral Review, Vol. 5, 2007, pp. 2-20.

Ross, S. (2005). Toward an integral process theory of human dynamics: Dancing the universal tango. Integral Review, 1(1) 64-84.

Roy, B. (2010). Evo-devo and the post-postmodern synthesis: What does integral have to offer? Blog post on Beams and Struts, at http://www.beamsandstruts.com/essays.

Roy, B. (2014). CppIE: Collective participatory process for emergent insight: Catalyzing insight and collective flow in groups. Available from the author.

Scharmer, C. O. (2007). Theory U. Leading from the future as it emerges. The social technology of presencing. Cambridge, MA: The Society for Organizational Learning, Inc.

Scott Peck, M. (1997). The road less traveled and beyond: Spiritual growth in an age of anxiety. Simon & Schuster.

Venezia, A. (2013). I, we, all: Intersubjectivity and we space, post-metaphysics, and human becoming: An integral research project. Unpublished Masters Thesis. Available at http://newwaysofhumanbeing.com/2013/10/13/finally-my-thesisfinal-project/.

Wilber, K. (2006). Integral spirituality. Boston, MA: Shambhala Press.

Cohering the Integral We-Space

Cohering the Integral We-Space

CHAPTER 11

Why "We" Matters:

Transformational Potentials of Evolutionary Intersubjectivity

Terry Patten

This chapter reviews three primary dimensions of my work—Integral Practice, Trans-Rhetorical Practice, and Integral Soul Work and in the process summarizes the inspiration, context and historical trajectory of my ongoing investigation of integral we-space, which I regard as groups of individuals co-creating the intersubjective conditions for the emergence of important new awareness and new ways of being human together. This chapter then describes some key principles and practices of integral we-space as expressed in both the overall field and in my work.

Integral Life Practice

In 2004-2007, with Ken Wilber, Jeff Salzman, Diane Hamilton, Bert Parlee, Huy Lam, and other members of the core team at Integral Institute Seminars, I participated in the development of both a post-metaphysical approach to Integral Life Practice, and also an integral pedagogical praxis for group processes. We challenged and invited participants to "fly a little higher" and go beyond 1st-tier relational habits in order to participate in "2nd-tier We-space." We set a context by describing the characteristics of a "2nd-tier We-space," teaching integral theory and communicating an integral, post-metaphysical approach to life as practice, including leading strength training and subtle energy practices. We led participants into deep interior experience (1st-person experience of "I-space") via spiritual practices such as guided meditations and various shadow processes, including journaling and intimately enacting the perspectives undone by reclaiming our projections, as well as the voice-dialogue Big Mind process (which has both subjective 1st-person and intersubjective 2nd-person dimensions). We led people in deep intersubjective processes (in 2nd-person "We-space") including structured conversations based on participants completing sentence stems, dyad practices using repeated questions, nonverbal embodiment practices, and an integral "lifeboat" process that heightened awareness of unspoken subtextual values and dynamics. We experimented with many sequences and permutations of 1st, 2nd, and 3rd-person processes, refining the art of clarifying and deepening individual consciousness, understanding what we were doing in the most expansive context possible, and learning to sense, facilitate and optimize the intersubjective field.

Integral Evolutionary Practice

From 2008 to the present, I deepened my engagement with these Integral pedagogical principles, exploring the depth that can be evoked by moving among 1st, 2nd, and 3rd-person processes. Drawing from what I had learned during my years (1973-1988) as a student of Adi Da to expand and deepen the ways Integral Practice can address an effective transformation at the level of *feeling*, I took into account that "each function of the human body-mind is tending toward emotional dissociation from experience" (Da Free John, 1980, p. 307). This dissociation is not only emotional but also psychic and spiritual, and is expressed globally, existentially (as the anti-ecstatic mood of our "consensus trance") and in human relationships. I offered (and continue to facilitate) devotional practices, helping people arrive not only in 2nd-person spirituality, gratitude and love, but also in territory I have not seen facilitated elsewhere in trans-rational spirituality — literal practices of prayer, spoken intimately, to the unknowable Source of Grace in the presence of others. This both requires and facilitates vulnerable sincere depth, crossing a threshold of discomfort into a transformational deepening of the subtle and intersubjective fields. In both in-person and virtual group teachings, my work, although continuing to embody an integral range of forms, has progressively emphasized the cultivation of devotional, intrapersonal and interpersonal depth and intimacy.

The Heart

Central to my approach is the active practice of exercising heart-based feeling-intelligence to help individuals make the moment-to-moment rediscovery of and connection to the Mystery of existence. This builds the capacity to rest attention at the level of feeling, and also develops capacities for intuitive *receptivity*. This receptivity progressively illuminates not only additional dimensions and dynamics of the conscious Mystery of being, but the many subtle contractions, compensations and identifications that tend to obstruct or attenuate full consciousness. It can also mature into an ongoing living participation with the principle of Grace, through which the individual navigates life devotionally—by gratefully always *giving* to the source of everything he or she receives. This is a self-regenerating process that builds the individual's connection to a reservoir of almost limitless inspiration and energy. Importantly, it is both self-renewing and intelligently self-correcting and evolving. In the past, religious and spiritual practitioners have accessed aspects of this powerful dynamic source of energy and inspiration, but traditional expressions have nearly always been grounded in fixed religious beliefs, and were thus incapable of the ongoing self-correcting evolution that is so necessary under current conditions of accelerating change, and especially in moment-to-moment intersubjective dynamics.

I have been exploring how groups can achieve more profound coherence by preceding We-space processes with exercises that guide participants in tuning in to their heart intelligence, which is expressed through a spectrum of virtues that range from self-care to appreciation to enjoyment to care for others to generosity to courage. Feeling receptivity to heart intelligence can be expanded not only into a living relationship with Grace, but also to humble patient receptivity to the subtle intelligence and guidance of the soul. When individuals are practicing in this manner, that receptivity can also be directed to the subtle information and the intersubjective fields. This builds a quality of We-space that can learn and develop and become more elegant over time. This kind of intersubjective intelligence is powered by depth — deep contact with self and other — and the field spontaneously expresses profound *care*, capable of both supportive resonance and loving challenge.

Trust

The fruit of serious Integral Practice, necessary to deepening the coherence of the intersubjective field, is trust. My work with Integral Spiritual Practice has from the beginning emphasized how regularly refreshing our commitment to practice makes us trustable. It was a more profound relaxation into radically trusting the process of my own life that led to my exploration and clarification of Integral Soul Work (to be explored below). The transformation of culture largely depends on trust — upon groups of people becoming both *trustable* and *trusting*, an aspiration that has no limit, and can keep us growing forever.

Intersubjective Practices

During these years I naturally adapted many integral We-space practices that rapidly evoked intimacy. These took many forms. Some dyad practices invite two participants to make natural eye contact and narrate their present-moment experience, completing simple sentence stems like "what I'm sensing now is…" or "what I'm noticing now is…" or "what I'm experiencing now is…" or "what I'm feeling right now is…" or "what *we're* experiencing right now is…" or even "what we're learning right now is…" Some invite participants to share whatever information they sense in the subtle information matrix. Others invite them to enter into devotional intimacy with source and speak as the intelligence of the mystery of existence or the impulse of evolution, or *to* that mystery, intelligence and love.

Integral Trans-Rhetorical Praxis

From 2011 to 2013 I spontaneously began doing something I later called "Integral Trans-Rhetorical Praxis." It unfolded not when I was teaching Integral Practice, but when I was discussing the world crisis at speaking events. I tried to have a new kind of conversation that was neither merely objective, dry and abstract, nor merely subjective or overly passionate, exhorting alarm. I didn't want any of the known, familiar conversations about environmental and political activism; instead, I wanted to quicken a communal process of facing an existential confrontation with that confounding challenge and opportunity in a way that might spark genuinely new ways of being and new outcomes. I framed a *Genjo Koan* (Dogen's word for life situations that present an impossible disorienting transformational riddle that cannot be solved via our usual consciousness), and then began breaking the stream of my discourse to speak directly, passionately and vulnerably in a confessional mode. I brought forward the feeling depth I had been cultivating and exercising in my teaching of Integral Practice. I was disclosing my own feelings and what I was learning, along with the questions I was asking, and even my inspiration, confusion, existential anguish, and personal struggle in the face of this situation, as well as my trust of life, sense of well-being and curiosity about the deep paradoxes involved. And I was speaking about all this not as something I had already experienced and resolved, but as a present living inquiry. I was even narrating my internal debates — not apologetically, but as an invitation for my listeners to join me in their own version of similarly passionate inquiry. This simple shift had a dramatic effect; it broke through a certain detachment and immunity that had previously prevented the conversation from implicating us and catalyzing a transformational existential confrontation.

In that heightened intersubjective field, I then spoke directly to the nature of our current shared experience. As we held various paradoxical tensions, injunctions and inquiries, I pointed out the discomfort I sensed as we became more existentially exposed. I described the energy I felt being released, and acknowledged how edgy and alive it was to do that in full view of one another, how intimate it could enable us to become, and how it suggested a new kind of shared practice and responsibility. And I invited others to respond. I found that when I did all this skillfully, in a way that balanced serious urgency with lighthearted essential well-being, it often reached people, catalyzing their own vulnerable engagement, releasing intense, apparently contradictory passions — including heightened consciousness, intense discomfort, fierce protective love, deep grief and anguish, unreasonable happy faith, dark suicidal despair, fierce determination, rage, and a noble, sacrificial willingness to ride into the adventure with a sense of transcendent commitment and joyous abandon.

The essence of the experiment and process (Patten, 2013) was that I said to my conversation partners something to the effect of this: "even if we can't see how, we must presume that we can redeem the cliché and actually be the change that unlocks the stuck game in which we're all co-creating this horrific global crisis. And there must be some way that we can shift right now that can more authentically enact that change; it's right here in this room between us. We usually don't believe this and almost always act as though that's not true, but it is; logically it must be—do you see this too? If so, how can we show up more authentically right now?"

My methodology followed a natural progression from 3rd-person to 1st-person to 2nd-person — "3-1-2." I had begun these experiments by framing, as a 3rd-person objective communication, our shared *Genjo Koan*, generating a shared understanding of the raw existential confrontation at the root of our human situation. From there, I spoke in 1st-person, subjectively, in real time, authentically exposing my relationship to that confrontation and koan, unguardedly and boldly (*parrhesia*, or "ragged truth-telling" in ancient Greek), as well as intimately and tenderly (*sohbet*, the Sufi term for "speaking with the tongue and ear of the heart"). On that basis, in the third step, I spoke directly to my conversation partners, in 2nd-person mode, making vulnerable contact with them, and opening up a space for our very way of being related to one another to shift in a way that might more authentically respond to our shared existential koan. I did this in large groups during public talks, in medium sized groups gathered for workshops, and intimately with groups of 2-5 people. I have sometimes been able to engage this conversation intimately with mature integral practitioners, and have discovered that this praxis has the potential to unfold into two additional steps beyond the 3-1-2.

In the first additional step, a dialogic 'dance' among the three (1st, 2nd, or 3rd-person) domains of experience can open up, uplifting both individual and intersubjective consciousness. The We-space is charged by the immediacy and power of an individual's vulnerable 1st-person confession, which sparks clarifying 3rd-person insight in another, opens a field of existential depth that makes possible a new level of tender 2nd-person contact, provokes new 3rd-person insight, and catalyzes deeper 2nd-person intrapersonal intimacy in another person, thus sparking 1st-person awakenings, and on and on. Each perspective feeds freely upon something that has gone before, in no particular order, producing an "uplift of our individual consciousness as well as an intensification of our intersubjective contact with one another and thus a continual uplift of the quality of our intersubjective field" (Patten, 2013, p. 26). The intersubjective field itself can, on rare occasions, begin to become sensitive to its own condition. This sensitivity enlists all participants into the practice of sustaining the depth and intensity upon which it depends. If that learning is sustained, the field begins to learn not only how to sustain itself but also to intensify and evolve itself, and then how to get better at doing so.

In the second additional step, which I still have experienced only rarely, and with very mature conversation partners, this positive feedback loop of intensity builds to cascade the illuminative power of the subjective and subtle energetic states of the intersubjective field and everyone in it. In 2013 I hypothesized that "this engenders a subtle field phenomenon that can function like an antenna or open nerve ending, opening into the larger noosphere and offering itself as a vehicle for the 'strange attractor' of yet-unmanifested creative emergents to find their way into form through us" (*ibid.*, p. 27). I am speculating, essentially, that extraordinary conversations can sometimes create a subtle energetic field in which new subtle structures can emerge — cultural potentials that might on occasion come, over time, to be lived more broadly, becoming new morphogenic habits and changing our ways of being human together. This would have significant implications for cultural evolution in an intersubjective analogue of the consequential scientific and artistic insights that have appeared in the awareness of people experiencing dreams or other nonordinary states of consciousness.

I've subsequently participated in a deepening dialogue between the two poles of that enduring polarity: urgency and trust, in general, and specifically in relation to our privileges and the world crisis. What has emerged is a deepening "both-and" orientation. Urgency is entirely healthy as an expression of love and commitment, but healthy urgency is not a fear-based orientation located only in relative reality. Trust in prior perfection, the non-problematic nature of "what is", and the miraculous power of evolutionary emergence is entirely appropriate. Yet healthy equanimity is not complacency, denial or passivity; it coincides with responsible caring participation in relation to real world suffering and crisis conditions—and grateful appreciation of every blessed moment of life. What emerges is an uplifted human spirit that can frame a living trans-rhetorical praxis: a fierce inspired lighthearted sobriety, not a mediocre splitting of the difference between two polar attitudes, but a heightened disposition that combines profound seriousness and commitment with profound trust and joyful well-being. This work is continuing to advance into new existential territory, becoming an inquiry into nuances of this "both/ and" attitude, and bringing forth new ways of being with maximal transformational efficacy.

Integral Soul Work

Since 2013, I've become more and more interested in taking my trans-rhetorical experiments far enough that I can engage the last two additional steps beyond the 3-1-2. As an activist, I find myself feeling less and less faith in the ability of human beings, myself included, to conceive and engage strategically, based on our limited understanding of the increasingly complex dynamics of our fast-moving world. I've meanwhile been participating actively in many explorations of integral We-space of various leaders in the field. All of this has enriched my awareness of subtle intersubjective fields and my knowledge and ability to work with them skillfully. I feel more and more open to the possibility of coinciding, or syncing up, with the hidden dynamics of life — the many things we do not and cannot understand about the workings of the world. I realize it might be possible to connect with others in a fresh and powerful mode of coherent intersubjective relatedness such that our subtle energetic field dynamics might coincide with a larger, non-linear, self-correcting and self-harmonizing intelligence.

My trans-rhetorical and intersubjective explorations have been increasingly informing my deepening personal practice, and continue to be informed by it. Both intimately and publicly, I feel called to speak ineffable truth from the most innocent, delicate and profound levels of my being with enough clarity, directness, patience and courage to penetrate and awaken the hypnotic numbness of our consensus trance. I feel drawn to open into feeling-communion with those with whom I am related in a way that can help us become a community of conscious practice that expresses higher wisdom than any of us could possibly embody as individuals. This implies dropping even more deeply into trusting the subtle and causal sources of that alignment.

In 2013, I was making an ever more radical choice to trust the deepest dimensions of my heart and psyche, thus allowing my soul to guide and inspire my life, moment to moment. I was arriving at a new level of appreciation for and participation in the profundity and importance of subtle, soul-based spirituality. Because subtle realms are not amenable to objective measurement and verification, and especially because subtle experiences are inherently vulnerable to subjective influence and appropriation by egoic motives, there are innumerable examples of distortion and delusion. Consequently, subtle experiences have most often been categorically critiqued and rejected in Advaita Vedanta, Theravada, Zen, and many other nondual teachings. While already grounded in these critiques, I began clarifying a theoretical understanding of how to integrate integral and subtle spirituality into what I called "Integral Soul Work." A healthy integral nondual view is also pantheistic, post-metaphysical, evolutionary, non-hypermasculine, and lived in awakened mutuality (Patten 2015). It can establish a self-transcending embrace of full participation not only in gross human experience, but also in the subtle dynamics of our lives. It can not only *transcend* but also profoundly *reinclude* subtle mysticism.

I began (and continue) to guide others in active conscious exploration of their relationship with their soul or *daemon*, both via long-term online courses and at in-person events. I invite Integral Soul Work participants to recognize the vital importance of activating their self-transcending connection to the source of truth, beauty and goodness so that it expresses itself *functionally*, and opens subtle pathways through which they can metaphorically hear the voice of their soul. On the basis of that recognition, I give them an opportunity to make a choice, and declare an existential stand to begin living from a new level of depth. I give them an opportunity to metaphorically ask, at the deepest level of their beings, to discern the guidance of their Soul, and align with their deepest nature and purpose at an entirely new level.

A cognitive framework and a daily integral practice create the essential context for beginning Integral Soul Work. The profound feeling and devotional depth engendered by Integral Spiritual Practice and the conscious intersubjective aliveness engendered by integral we-space practices create an intersubjective cultural context conducive to authentic soul exploration. This is further activated by the evolutionary telos that charges the intersubjective field in trans-rhetorical praxis. Soul Work then entails receptive opening and conscious participation in the dynamics of the subtle realm. A trans-rational approach acknowledges the potential for self-delusion, while remaining open to intuitive guidance, synchronicities and archetypal dynamics. Subtle mysticism is a sprawling territory replete with subjective distortion and even a fair bit of fraudulent nonsense, yet it also contains the serious study and engagement of the actual subtle pathways through which energy and information reach the soul from the transcendent causal ground. Authentic trans-rational soul work proceeds via intelligent surrender and self-transcendence, rather than through mentally focused attempts to objectively measure subjective realities or any of the myriad strategies for manipulating or otherwise controlling or influencing subtle energies in the interest of self-fulfillment.

All these transformational processes help participants move into open, curious, experimental, and progressively more intimate relationship to the subtle dynamics of their individuality and shared We-space. The foundation of the work is a deep existential confrontation that operates not primarily at the level of ordinary consciousness but the deepest levels of the psyche or soul, the place from which experience, choice, agency and meaning are sourced and recognized. Engaging these levels intersubjectively requires creating conditions of profound safety, modeling my own process, and inviting everyone into a sincere ongoing inquiry about how their self-transcending surrender to source can enable them to coincide not only with consciousness itself, but with its conditional subtle expressions and intentions. This deepens the exploration of heightened shared states of subtle energy that I described in my experiments with trans-rhetorical praxis.

I've been exploring how to create the set, setting, and intersubjective space that provide people the supportive conditions that can allow them to authentically choose to invite forth their own soul nature or *daemon,* and to wait attentively, silently and receptively, while truly listening for an authentic answer. I'm exploring how to invoke and enact subtle ritual and ceremony in a trans-rational intersubjective space. Even so, my experience has made it clear that this kind of process can never be reduced to or identified with any events in time and space. Nor is it authentic for post-postmodern practitioners to pretend to be traditional priests, monks, nuns, peasants, or hunter-gatherers. So these processes, whether virtual or in person, require economized authentic rituals and ceremonies. In designing and facilitating these learning experiences, I draw on my years of convening higher orders of We-space, so they progress naturally through a sequence of get-acquainted exercises, insights, emotional and existential confrontations, invitations, spiritual transmissions, and ceremonial rituals, including 3rd-person talks offering distinctions and frameworks for understanding the process, 1st-person movement processes, meditations, journaling and insight processes, and 2nd-person structured or spontaneous somatic, dyad and small group processes.

The necessary context for trans-rational ritual is for each individual to subjectively engage the process being ceremonially enacted — authentically, existentially and decisively. When life becomes an ongoing question or request, and the space in which there is ongoing receptivity, listening and growing into resonance with the soul's call or voice, ritual makes sense. All of this, of course, builds access to higher subjective states. It is an intuitive feeling yoga mediated by various levels of the intelligence of the heart and whole being. My experience draws upon and validates the Sufi teaching that declares "the ear of the heart" is the organ through which we can hear "the voice of the soul." Such group processes depend on each individual reaching an adequate depth of contact with his or her heart's feeling-intelligence, which means a profound depth of sincerity, tenderness, care and contact with one's feeling and attention, from the heart. Ongoing development of heart intelligence and trust are essential to Integral Soul Work.

Key Principles That Shape Evolutionary We-space

The field of integral we-space has emerged within an ecosystem or network of overlapping communities of practice. Although many significant influences ripple through the network, no single approach, teacher or facilitator is dominant. This gives this field of inquiry great inherent dynamism, vitality and strength — which I think will probably enable it to subsume and survive each of its particular embodiments, and continue to evolve and expand its cultural influence.

I am grateful to be able to contribute to that larger ecosystem and its evolution. Nevertheless, I am interested in this field for particular reasons, in service of particular higher values, so I am making original contributions based on my unique sensibility. Accordingly, in the sections that follow I will draw conclusions in two ways. I will (a) make general observations that apply to the field as a whole, while I (b) describe the practices, intentions and directions of my own work and/or identify those that I feel are most valuable, significant or promising.

The Invitation

The nature of the original invitation shapes participants' perceptions of what they will be doing together and what is possible. What does it explicitly and implicitly suggest are the attractive reasons to participate? Is it an opportunity for social connection, intimacy and fun? A personal growth opportunity? A social experiment? Is it an invitation to play and be entertained, or to work and to practice? Does it have a higher spiritual and evolutionary purpose? Does it evoke a safe container for uncommon vulnerability, intimacy and feeling depth? Are people being invited into a proven process, or an exciting experiment in something new and emergent? What's the intended outcome? Will participants simply have fun and develop stronger friendships? Will they build their capacity for a higher level of relating, and grow personally and spiritually? Will they actually contribute to an experiment with larger social significance? Is this a single event, a series of events, or is it building toward more ongoing commitment? Is there a contextual intention to help spawn a socio-cultural spiritual movement? Can anyone participate, or must people apply? Or is the invitation offered only to selected individuals who have demonstrated they are adequate to the practice?

As an ecosystem, integral we-space has room for many kinds of invitations; this diversity gives it flexibility and strength, and extends its appeal. It has niches across a spectrum of virtual and in-person events with different durations, prices, levels of commitment and aspirations. The invitations that excite me most have a high, open-ended aspiration. Although they might appeal to needs for social connection, they are serious about generating personal and spiritual growth, and about opening into a utopian social experiment, sociocultural movement and/or cultural transformation. That requires a context, which means that a much larger number of less ambitious offerings are needed to create the necessary context. Still, I am most interested in experiments that intend to break into new territory, as they have larger transformational intentions, and also presuppose an extended commitment to a life of ongoing transformative practice. Certain innovative experiments can proceed only with participants capable of certain levels of psychological health, integrity, responsibility, development and awakening, so this foundation must somehow be established, either via prerequisites or a screening process, which in turn strongly affects the nature of the invitation.

The Introduction

The way a We-space event is convened and how participants are welcomed and introduced to one another shapes the origin point for the arc of their intersubjective experience. Where does the event take place? By phone? Skype? At a hotel? Church? Yoga studio? Private home? Has the room been cleaned and decorated? Are there flowers, sage or incense? Is background music playing — and what does it evoke? If it is a virtual event, how does it establish contact, depth, and enlist engagement? How coherent is the feeling of the relationships among the staff handling registration and greeting and facilitation? Is the mood loose, informal and spontaneous or is there a sense of a more formal container? Are new people made to feel warmly welcomed? Are participants given name tags? How does the event begin? With introductions? With a presentation of principles, intentions, practices and ground rules? With meditation? Is the group field led by a strong teacher with a clear, distinct vision and unambiguous authority? Or are there multiple facilitators or assistants? Is the dynamic loose and spontaneous, or more formal and contained? What is the quality of the subtle intersubjective field? Are practices introduced early on to establish it? All these factors communicate innumerable subtle cues that start shaping participants' feelings, attitudes, beliefs and assumptions before the first formal We-space practices even begin.

As noted, the We-space ecosystem is more robust because it manifests in a wide variety of formats. Elegant touches and structure add value, yet they tend to add costs, creating a barrier to participation and appealing more to older, more moneyed participants. A spectrum of offerings addresses a range of individual needs and capacities, all of which are important. Elegance and attention to detail are expressions of excellence that need not be associated only with high-end events.

The Intention

The single most important factor is the shaping power of intention: when We-space is generated with a clearly stated shared intention, that intention powerfully influences the character, texture and direction of what emerges. Skeptics might regard this as mere suggestibility — the placebo effect. Suggestibility and placebo dynamics certainly pertain. However, all subjective experience is powerfully and primarily shaped by intentions, beliefs, shared agreements, state of mind and context. Taking these factors into consideration is essential to structuring subjective experiences, so it is no wonder that this applies equally, and perhaps even more powerfully, to intersubjective practice.

We-space practices sometimes set their intentions explicitly or implicitly on a particular subset of a wide range of values, and they usually achieve what they most value. Below is a list of some of those primary intended values, from roughly the most local to the most transcendent to the most global:

- Personal authenticity and intimacy
- Opening up higher intuitive faculties and accessing information from subtle domains
- Becoming aware of, transparent to and expressing the emergent intelligence of the shared field, moment to moment
- Intimacy with oneself, one's soul, the soul of the world, transcendent Source and one another
- Awakening together into higher states of consciousness, subtle, causal, and/or non-dual
- Becoming transparent to and voicing the intelligence of awareness itself, the ground of being
- Becoming transparent to, articulating the intelligence of, and coinciding with the nonlinear intentionality of the impulse of evolution to evolve culture amidst the global crisis

I have participated in and co-facilitated processes in which every one of these values was at least temporarily paramount. I am currently most inspired by work that stays radically attentive to what is real and really possible in each moment, cherishing all these values while aspiring to prototype ways of being that might replicate themselves in consequential cultural transformation. Paradoxically, that can mean "slowing down to speed up." Practicing more basic values like moment-to-moment aliveness and presence can sometimes generate more grounded and authentic results than reaching for the most transcendent values, such as entering shared high states of consciousness with transparency to awareness or the evolutionary impulse. Although many integral We-space practices go directly into transpersonal territory, I've found that the most deeply personal values can be a strong bridge to the transpersonal. In fact, in order to explore the larger, self-transcending possibilities I care about most, it seems necessary to include the totality of participants' humanity. I've discovered that personal authenticity and intimacy is often a necessary bridge to the vulnerability and trust required for a field of deep soul-level intimacy with self, Source and one another. And such soulful self-and-other intimacy is in turn the basis for the integrated intra- and inter-subjective states of energy and consciousness that conduct the larger self-correcting intelligence necessary for influential impact on the broader culture. Therefore, without abandoning any of the other values listed above, these are the values by which my current work is most inspired.

One of the most powerful presumptions that can engender powerful intelligent We-space is the shared acknowledgement that something genuinely novel, vital and important can happen at any time. This intention generates a crucial attitude of positive expectancy, curiosity, spontaneity and attentiveness for the most powerful We-space work. Much can happen when this attitude is coupled with a paradoxical combination of (a) lightheartedness and deep well-being, rooted in personal maturity and spiritual practice, and (b) a profound sense of urgency, engendering self-transcending willingness to be of benefit to others, in service to a greater principle.

A "Community of the Adequate"

A real praxis depends on *practitioners*. Whether it's smart physicists who can discuss a new theoretical breakthrough or football players who are athletic enough to keep up and contribute to the level of the game, communal practices require a community of the adequate. But very few of our current We-space explorations address adequacy, except perhaps to affirm it as a given. Most often, participants are invited in a way that passively allows them to self-select, and only certain people will be attracted. This generally establishes a baseline of sincere willingness and intelligence, and participants are oriented and educated into shared norms that usually elicit levels of engagement sufficient to allow a group field to form. Importantly, We-space processes inherently uplift sincere participants, and produce dynamic learning opportunities that are significantly self-correcting. However, they do not magically erase the profound constraints presented by individual limitations. Still to be explored are the possibilities for higher We-space that are possible among participants with more consistently high levels of consciousness, practice, development, psychological health, and intelligence.

There is no single definition of adequacy since we see a spectrum of integral we-spaces. Dustin DiPerna has theorized "a 'We' Line of Development" in which "the self-reflective conscious awareness of the We" progresses through "Conventional, Personal, Impersonal, Interpersonal, Transformational, Awakened, Evolutionary and Kosmic" levels (DiPerna, 2013, p. 209-212). Clearly, there are different qualifications for participating in higher levels of We-space. In my 2013 ITC paper I wrote:

> Among the components of adequacy for authentic Integral Trans-Rhetorical Praxis are: stage development in the self-related lines to "Exit Orange," "Exit Green," "Teal," or, for higher expressions of the praxis, "Turquoise" or "Indigo" levels, in state-stage growth, the relaxation of strict fixation of attention in the gross "waking state" levels of mind and emotion, a basic inner witnessing capacity, an ability to focus and direct attention and thus to stably rest it on others and the intersubjective field, some insight into shadow dynamics and ongoing sincere non-defensive inquiry into ongoing shadow dynamics, a basic capacity to endure discomfort and delay gratification, the integrity and courage necessary to transcend "looking good" in order to "make subject object" transparently, sufficient existential depth to be capable of remaining self-responsibly grounded while facing the world crisis and taking it seriously, and enough emotional intelligence, health, and compassion for self and others to be able to hold high levels of cognitive and emotional dissonance while remaining present with others in a fundamentally non-problematic manner as a mostly friendly benevolent presence. (Patten 2013, p. 33)

To that description I would now add some additional characteristics and capacities, such as an open-ended commitment to moment-to-moment practice and growth, basic sensitivity to the numinous nature of the mystery of existence, an existential stand for deeper contact and congruence with one's own soul and the soul of the world, and profoundly developed capacities for receptive listening and attunement to subtle fields. I also now put more emphasis on heart intelligence, benevolence, light-heartedness and well-being. I am most interested to see the emergent character and levels of efficacy that develop over time in We-spaces comprised of committed communities of particularly adequate practitioners.

Injunctions

As mentioned above, the nearly universal injunction is to keep redirecting attention to what is actually happening in present time, and to relate directly here and now, enabling whatever is alive to emerge. Closely related to intention and values are the higher principles explicitly or implicitly associated with the universal injunction "*to stay present.*" What exactly are participants enjoined to "stay present to?" Sometimes it's "witnessing awareness," "emergence," "the subtle information field," "the We-space," "awakening," or "the evolutionary impulse." In trans-rhetorical praxis I ask people to open to "the *Genjo Koan* of our global crisis." Once the most local, global, and transcendental contexts are placed into the field, I find it more useful to focus on the *how* of staying present, and here I point to "feeling intelligence."

In the context of our global *Genjo Koan*, in order to release attention from anxiety and dualism, it can be useful to stay present to reality self-actualizing itself through us. Sometimes practitioners set aside all higher principles, and avoid imposing any predetermined intention on the process. They instead simply allow whatever is authentic to be expressed, and thus awaken and evolve. Although this often fails to provide needed focus and contact with *telos*, in more refined contexts it leaves room for spontaneous expression of values and the emergent.

It's important to note that some communities of practice overtly or subtly emphasize injunctions that privilege or de-privilege certain kinds of content. For example, some We-space practices urge people to go beyond all "personal stories" and even any interest in personal healing, whereas others emphasize deepening interpersonal vulnerability and intimacy. Others urge people to presume that at any moment they can and should break through to a "higher" level of consciousness and connection. Still others recommend releasing all agendas. These polarities need not be seen as mutually exclusive, and can even have a developmental relationship. As mentioned above, a process can first deepen personal intimacy and later build upon that foundation to progress toward self-transcending practice and transpersonal coherence. Premature transcendence can lead to idealization and subtle spiritual bypassing, qualities that sometimes creep into immature We-space.

Other Important Factors

Amidst these wide-ranging diversities there are two obvious major distinctions:

1. *Virtual vs. In Person.* Virtual We-space (practiced via phone or Skype in groups) is very different from in-person We-space. Many of the most enjoyable aspects of intersubjective experience are only possible when people are in the same room: this includes direct eye contact, the sensing of etheric energies, and touch. However, it can be logistically challenging for groups to sustain a commitment to meet regularly in person over time. Virtual We-space enables people to more easily meet over a period of months or years. The virtual format is initially more challenging and seemingly distant, but a range of subtle fields, subtler than the etheric energy associated with the physical body, can be evoked and sensed in virtual space with people even on different continents. Virtual We-space meetings are often supplemented by intimate practice groups of two or three, and also with online forums. The voice can be a powerful medium for intimate, soul-level contact. In contrast, in-person encounters can be more conventional and subtly evoke self-consciousness and personality-based social dynamics. These are more easily bypassed in virtual settings where interaction can focus purely on the deepest dimensions of felt experience, awareness and intention. I've actually seen virtual We-space go very deep, often deeper than commonly achieved through in-person We-space practices. Some We-space communities make use of both formats. Virtual intimacy is enhanced when people have also met and gone into deep resonance in person, and vice-versa.

2. *States vs. Content.* We-space is roughly divided between practices focused on creating various shared experiences of higher intersubjective states, and practices focused on creating innovative meaningful conversations that focus on content to advance shared understanding, creative innovation, team cohesion or problem solving.

Potentials for Social Transformation

What is most interesting to me currently are the factors that deepen and strengthen We-space to make it more robust, dynamic, and sustainable, with strengths ultimately building upon strengths in a virtuous cycle. I hope this enriching praxis will eventually have cultural, social, and political significance. If highly developed people can become truly coherent, and profoundly trustable, they can be a force for social change. This is one of the ways I currently understand the organic *telos* of this spontaneous cultural experiment.

Historians have noted that exceptional individuals become focal points during times of rapid social transformation, even when such shifts are the inevitable outcome of larger forces. When colonialism declined in India, Mahatma Gandhi served as an inspiring example of moral and political leadership. As racial segregation ended in the United States, Martin Luther King functioned similarly. When the apartheid system fell apart in South Africa, Nelson Mandela was the wise focal point and leader of a benign transition.

At this time, we face a crisis that is vastly more complex and multidimensional, which will require far more challenging transformations of our behaviors and worldviews. Great leaders are a valuable source of inspiration, but I don't believe we can focus on individual heroes in the time ahead. Instead, along the lines of Thich Nhat Hanh's oft-quoted saying that "the next Buddha may be a Sangha," our global crisis may require and constellate around heroism and leadership from *groups* rather than individuals — groups that represent a new kind of human collective. That creates an inspiring possibility for our communities of practice. I hope our current experiments in higher intersubjectivity will contribute to progress toward this remarkable and needed possibility. My 2013 ITC paper emphasized the intersubjective nature of:

The inquiry that responds to the existential koan of our time is not merely a knowable skill or developmental capacity that can be taught or coached. It rests on existential seriousness, and the capacity to be profoundly self-responsible and vulnerable, and also to dare, vision, risk, and extend into the unknown. So I teach a process that leads to a glorious sanity capable of the level of sincerity, practice, openness, intimacy and authenticity required to participate in this ongoing inquiry, which by its nature must be ongoing, open-ended and paradoxical. (p. 32).

And I joined it with other praxes that "also cultivate capacities that help build adequacy for participation in a higher level of intersubjective discourse, for co-creating a profound emerging Sangha through which the "next Buddha" may come into being" (Patten, 2013, p. 33).

That takes a village of villages — an ecosystem — which we are! I see all the pioneering We-space mystics prototyping new forms and praxes for being together in deeper and more coherent ways. Our global crisis-opportunity is generating a context of urgency, capacity and potential that is fertile ground to sprout the seeds of radical transformation being sown in our We-spaces. Perhaps our shared experience can interweave diversity that liberates the evolutionary urge to converge, and the intuitive systemic synergy to pull it off. We needn't fear grandiosity to dare to be inspired by the outside chance that we can make a difference. We have only to do a good job of learning better ways of being us together, while intending innovations that turn evolutionary corners into emergent new territory. Whatever the future holds, we can tend that wild hope like a tiny nascent sacred fire, cherishing whatever it sparks, knowing that genuinely awakened mutuality could be profoundly consequential in its unfolding.

Author Bio

Terry Patten is the founder of *Bay Area Integral* and a key voice in integral evolutionary spirituality, culture, leadership, and activism. He co-developed *Integral Life Practice* with Ken Wilber and a core team at Integral Institute and was the senior writer and co-author of the book *Integral Life Practice: A 21st-Century Blueprint for Physical Health, Emotional Balance, Mental Clarity, and Spiritual Awakening.* He hosts the online teleseminar series *Beyond Awakening:* where he has engaged over a hundred leading-edge conversations with many of the integral world's most renowned thinkers and teachers based on the question "How can higher consciousness enable human beings to better meet the crises and challenges of our time?" He speaks, consults, and coaches on four continents via the web. To learn more about his work, go to: terrypatten.com.

References

Albere, P. and Carrera, J. (2013) Mutual Awakening: opening into a new paradigm of human relatedness. Evolutionary Collective

Armstrong, K. (2006) The Great Transformation: The beginning of our religious traditions. New York. Alfred Knopf

Aurami, A. (2014) Leadership on the bleeding edge of humanity's evolution. Notes from the field. Integral Leadership Review. January-February 2014. Retrieved from http://integralleadershipreview.com/11117-integral-living-room-boulder-colorado-usa-october-31-november-3-2013/

Bayer, B. (2014) The Art of Circling: 37 practices for deepening your relating skills. Authentic World Publishing. Available at http://www.lulu.com/us/en/shop/bryan-bayer/the-art-of-circling-1st-edition/paperback/product-21798467.html

Beak, S. (2013) Red Hot and Holy: A heretic's love story. Boulder, CO: Sounds True.

Bohm, D. & Krishnamurti, J. (1986). The future of humanity: A conversation. New York, NY: HarperCollins Publishers.

Bohm, D. (1996). On Dialogue. London, Routledge

Da Free John (1980) Scientific Proof of the Existence of God Will Soon Be Announced by the White House. Clear Lake, CA: The Dawn Horse Press

DiPerna, D. (2013). Streams of Wisdom: The core vectors of spiritual development. Occidental, CA: Integral Publishing House.

DiPerna, D., & Augustine, H.B. (2014). The Coming Waves: Evolution, transformation and action in an integral age. Occidental, CA: Integral Publishing House

Foucault, M. (1983). Parrhesiastes [lecture notes]. University of California, Berkeley. Retrieved from http://72.52.202.216/~fenderse/Parrhesiastes.htm

Gunnlaugson, O. (2009). Establishing second-person forms of contemplative education: An inquiry into four conceptions of intersubjectivity. Integral Review, Arina Press, 4(2), 23-56.

Gunnlaugson, O. (2011). A complexity perspective on presencing. Complicity: An International Journal of Complexity and Education, Volume 8, Number 2, 1-23.

Gunnlaugson, O. (2012). Collective intimations of the future: A recent inquiry. Beams and Struts Online Journal. Retrieved from http://beamsandstruts.com/essays/item/789-collective-intimations-of-the-future-a-recent-inquiry

Gunnlaugson, O. & Moze, M. (2012) Surrendering into Witnessing: A Foundational Practice for Building Collective Intelligence Capacity in Groups. Journal of Integral Theory and Practice, Volume 7 No.3, pp. 105–115

Gunnlaugson, O. (2015) Deep Presencing: Illuminating New Territory at the Bottom of the U. Integral Leadership Review, January-February 2015. Retrieved from http://integralleadershipreview.com/12783-215-deep-presencing-illuminating-new-territory-bottom-u/

Harvey, A. (2009) The Hope: A guide to sacred activism. Carlsbad, CA;

Hay House Publishers

Harvey, A. (2014) Reckless love and friendship at the edge. In T. Patten. Beyond awakening: The future of spiritual practice [Teleseminar series]. Retrieved from http://beyondawakeningseries.com/blog/archive/

Harvey, A. (2014) The ways of passion and illumination. In T. Patten. Beyond awakening: The future of spiritual practice [Teleseminar series]. Retrieved from http://beyondawakeningseries.com/blog/archive/

Hübl, T. (2011). Transparence: Practice Groups—an adventure in seeing yourself and others more clearly. Germany: Sharing the Presence. http://www.thomashuebl.com/en/mediashop/book.html

Hübl, T. (2012). Birthing a new we: Evolutionary ways of creating community, society, spirituality. in T. Patten. Beyond awakening: The future of spiritual practice [Teleseminar series]. Retrieved from http://beyondawakeningseries.com/blog/archive/

Louchakova, O. (n.d.). The experience of Sohbet. International Association of Sufism. Retrieved from http://www.ias.org/spf/sohbet.html

Macy, J. & Brown, M. (1998). Coming back to life: Practices to reconnect our lives our world. Gabriola Island, Canada: New Society Publishers.

Macy, J. & Chris Johnstone, C. (2012). Active Hope: How to face the mess we're in without going crazy. Novato, CA: New World Library.

Macy, J. (2012) The Work that Reconnects. In T. Patten. Beyond awakening: The future of spiritual practice [Teleseminar series]. Retrieved from http://beyondawakeningseries.com/blog/archive/

McGushin, E. (2006). Foucault's Askesis: An introduction to the philosophical life. Northwestern University Press.

Patten, T (2004) The Terrible Truth And the Wonderful Secret:

Answering the Call of Our Evolutionary Emergency [unpublished manuscript]

Patten, T. (2010-2013) Audio recordings of previous dialogues. Beyond awakening: The future of spiritual practice [Teleseminar series]. Retrieved from http://beyondawakeningseries.com/blog/archive/

Patten, T. & Hubbard, B. (2010). The integral implications of conscious. Integral Theory Conference 2010. Retrieved from: http://www.integraltheoryconference.org/talks

Patten, T. & Morelli, M. (2012). Occupy Integral! Beams and Struts online magazine. Retrieved from http://beamsandstruts.com/articles/item/814-occupy-integral

Patten, T. (2013) Enacting an integral revolution: how can we have truly radical conversations in a time of global crisis. Integral Theory Conference 2013.

Patten, T., Wilber, K. (2013) The Evolution of the integral we-space: A conversation with Ken Wilber. Integral Living Room, The Conversation So Far, July 27th, 2013. Retrieved from http://bit.ly/1cKWBiw

Patten, T. (2015) Integral Soul Work: The Integral Marriage of Spirit, Soul, and Social Activism. Integral Theory Conference 2015

Scharmer, C. (2000). The Three Gestures of Becoming Aware: An interview with Francisco Varela. Dialogues on Leadership. Retrieved from: http://

www.iwp.jku.at/born/mpwfst/02/www.dialogonleadership.org/Varela. html

Scharmer, O. (2009). Theory U: Leading from the future as it emerges. San Francisco, CA: Barrett-Koehler.

Senge, P., Scharmer, O., Jaworski, J., & Flowers, B. (2008). Presence: Human purpose and the field of the future. New York, NY: Doubleday Publishing.

Tart, C. (n.d.). Consensus Trance: The sleep of everyday life. Retrieved from http://www.smccd.edu/accounts/larson/psyc390/Docs/Consensus%20 Trance.pdf

Union of Concerned Scientists (1992) World Scientists' Warning to Humanity. Retrieved from http://www.ucsusa.org/about/1992-world-scientists.html#.VXSS1UJcND0

Wilber, K. (2000). Integral psychology: Consciousness, spirit, psychology, therapy. Boston, MA: Shambhala.

Wilber, K. (2001). Eye of spirit. An integral vision for a world gone slightly mad. Boston, MA: Shambhala.

Wilber, K. (2007). Integral spirituality: A startling new role for religion in the modern and postmodern world. Boston, MA: Integral Books.

Wilber, K., Patten, T., Leonard, A., & Morelli, M. (2008). Integral life practice: A 21st-century blueprint for   physical health, emotional balance, mental clarity, and spiritual awakening. Boston, MA: Shambhala.

Chapter 12

Awakening Through Conversation and Culture:

An Exploration of Practices From Craig Hamilton and the Living Evolution Community[1]

Suzanne E. Shealy, Ph.D., Linda A. White & Lisa Foxley

Introduction

What are the potentialities of an intersubjective consciousness that embraces collective awakening and the evolution of humanity with deepening levels of care and compassion for all of life as its primary purpose? Teachers such as Craig Hamilton are working the emerging edge of human consciousness, embracing this question with the goal of evolving culture and enabling the greater care, commitment and creativity needed to face the staggering demands of our current planetary circumstances. In this chapter, we will describe key principles, practices, and the evolution of Craig Hamilton's work with evolutionary spirituality through his Integral Enlightenment[2] programs. Where relevant, we will identify parallels and contrasts

---

1. We would like to acknowledge the contributions of Liz Allmark, Richard Bissonette, Clare Conway, Manon Desjardins, Marcia Davies, Linda Lubin, Clare Rosenfield, Lali Sher, Ruth Smith, and Living Evolution Program Director Wendy Van Horn who shared their observations and experiences related to the practices described in this chapter, as well as, Mark J. Simo who offered feedback and comments on the manuscript. We would also like to express great appreciation to Craig Hamilton for his teaching, innovative spirit, and love for the evolving We.

2. www.integralenlightenment.com

with other evolutionary teachings and practices and our experience as Integrally-informed psychotherapists in the addiction recovery field.

The work of Craig Hamilton has its roots in the EnlightenNext spiritual community that grew up around the teaching of Andrew Cohen on what came to be known as "evolutionary enlightenment" (Cohen, 2011, p. 65). Hamilton explains that after years of dedication to individual practices, such as meditation, it became natural for him and other community members to share insights in their conversations together.[3] At some point, breakthroughs in consciousness occurred in which experiences of self-transcendence and unity became shared intersubjectivity within their conversation. In a recent interview, Craig Hamilton offered this description:

> Spiritual experience and awakening became something that was alive in the conversation between us. ...The group would enter into a single higher mind together if you will. ...We would become one being that had many voices, many faces, but there was one consciousness that was alive between us and that seemed to have a will and agenda of its own that we were all participating in and partaking in. ... It didn't delete or do away with our individuality. To the contrary, it amplified the better parts of our selves. In other words, each individual was still very much an individual and perhaps more of an individual because they weren't lost in a stream of conditioned responses from their past. They were being liberated and freed by this group awakening. (Hamilton, Shealy & Por, 2014, p. 120)

Eventually, he and others from their community began to identify ways of creating a practice container for inviting this quality of presence in conversation, and they began to introduce the resulting form of collective dialogue practice to others outside of their community. They observed that individuals who did not have all of their years of intensive spiritual practice together within community were often able to join in and experience a taste of the self-transcending states of consciousness that emerged. Craig Hamilton eventually left the community and began teaching on his own via on-line events and courses. Over the past six years, he has attracted and supported the development of an international practice community, the present iteration known as Living Evolution,[4] that continues to engage, experiment with, and

---

3. This history is recounted in an interview with Craig Hamilton that was published in *Spanda Journal* (Hamilton, Shealy & Por, 2014).

4. Craig Hamilton's courses include a seven-week Awakening the Impulse to Evolve

reflect upon collective practices that support awakening to and living from a larger sense of self, from Source or soul, "for the sake of the whole" (Cohen, 2011, p. 159).

Contextual Container for Collective Awakening Practice

In setting context regarding the relevance and potential impact of evolutionary we-practices, Craig Hamilton offers a vision of the potential for the conscious evolution of culture:

The emergent we-space is giving rise to a new kind of co-creative conscious evolution of the shared culture. Individuals are awakening to the We-space and at the same time the We-space is becoming conscious of itself, thus giving rise to greater capacity for self-reflection. This mutual awakening has unknown implications for the evolution of human beings in groups, giving rise to a new emergent potential... The current basic assumptions and shared context of culture can evolve into a more caring and healthy expression that allows for different points of view and functions beyond ego. The group is aligned with something higher than the individual self with a mutual intention to serve the process of manifesting heaven on earth, living as our highest potential. The we-space experience gives us a taste of what is possible in the future evolution of human consciousness. (C. Hamilton, personal communication, February 3, 2012)

Consistent with this vision, collective awakening practices in the Living Evolution community guide and support entry into a sense of self as a conscious participant in the evolution of humanity, transcending egoic motivations, and manifesting the highest potential of the creative imperative of eros. Principles of Evolutionary Culture (Hamilton, 2015b) invite a "whole-hearted intention to transform" (para 2) and describe practices that support opening to and relating from creative emergence and a larger sense of shared purpose.[5] A foundational exercise from Hamilton's introductory course offers a direct experience via pointing-out instructions of three distinct states of consciousness: the relatively contracted and limiting state referred to as *ego*, the open, spacious *ground of being*, and the creative spark and

---

course, the Evolutionary Life Transformation Program (ELTP), Living on the Edge of Evolution Program (LEEP), the Journey into Freedom meditation course, and the current ongoing Living Evolution (LE) practice community.

5. Principles of Evolutionary Culture can be accessed at http://integralenlighten-ment.com/academy/culture/

drive of the *evolutionary impulse* (Shealy, White, Dueck & Geidt, 2012). A process akin to the voice dialogue practice of Big Mind[6] (Merzel, 2007) invites participants to speak or journal from each of these three distinct states. Awareness of the distinctions between these aspects of human experience offers a glimpse of the potential to choose where we place our attention. Awareness of this "choosing faculty" (Cohen, 2011, p. 71) and the experience of these higher state invites a choice to transcend ego and live from a place of greater freedom, care, and a larger sense of purpose. Exploration of motivating perspectives such as interdependence, divine love, the drive of the evolutionary impulse, and the view from one's deathbed promote reflection on larger context and purpose (Shealy et al., 2012).[7] Ultimately, the intention is for participants to integrate and embody these perspectives and open to and align with emergent wisdom, so that all of life becomes the context for practice.

Awakening Through Conversation

Guidelines for Awakening through Conversation (ATC)[8] invite participants to engage in an interactive "experiment in the evolution of consciousness" within specified dialogue practice parameters (Hamilton, 2015a, para. 2). The guidelines encourage participants to refrain from the sharing of problems that might occur in a support or therapy group and, instead, to access and speak from "the part of ourself that was never wounded or traumatized" (Hamilton, 2015a, para. 6). The list of instructions that follows invites everyone to participate, to let go of preconceived ideas, and to put attention on the shared intersubjective space. Participants are advised to "suspend personal story and intellectual abstraction" and instead to "listen for the deeper currents" (Hamilton, 2015a, para. 12) or threads in the conversation and to be willing to express what emerges on the edge of awareness. Typically, a beginning group would read the guidelines

---

6. The experience of egoic self-contraction is evoked and generally identified as a limiting perspective to be surrendered, seen through, or subordinated, in contrast to Big Mind where there is an attempt to elicit the cooperation of protective aspects of the self.

7. Practices for reflecting on various motivating perspectives can be accessed at http://integralenlightenment.com/academy/practices/transform/

8 .Guidelines for Awakening through Conversation can be found at http://integralenlightenment.com/academy/awakening/

aloud together and then engage questions related to a topic of exploration.

The following is a list of themes extracted from the Principles of Evolutionary Culture (Hamilton, 2015b; Hamilton & Zammit, 2008)[9] and Guidelines for Awakening through Conversation (Hamilton, 2015a) that support the practice of awakening through conversation:

> Whole-hearted engagement – Willingness to fully participate and take responsibility for the outcome of the group's practice. Beginner's Mind – Suspending the "already-knowing" mind and bringing a sense of openness and curiosity to the practice. Placing attention on the shared intersubjective space, and listening for the deeper resonances within the conversation. Speaking authentically, responding to the deeper chords and building upon the contributions of others.
>
> All of these require willingness to risk stepping into new territory of the self or soul,[10] manifesting and realizing new potentials.

The invited evolutionary we space is intended to be post-personal as attention to personal story, self-referencing, and self-consciousness is suspended. Suspension of prior knowledge and problem-solving agendas may open space for awareness to become increasingly subtle and open to glimmers on the edge of consciousness. As participants take the risk of speaking from the deepest, most authentic place within their present moment awareness, they stretch into new insights and potentials glimpsed, manifesting and exercising these potentials within the collective space.

Entry into the evolutionary we-space may be experienced like a birth process, as participants open to the unknown and speak from a place beyond what is personal, conditioned, and habitual. As one surrenders into the experience, there is a sense of entering into a flow of emergence that may be characterized by softened boundaries and a sense of space, openness, and curiosity. There is potential for the distinction between "inner" and "outer" experience to dissolve

---

9. Hamilton and Zammit (2008) describe a version of the Principles of Evolutionary Culture that supports collective intelligence and evolution within an organizational context.

10. In his writing on soul realization, Almaas (2004, p. 4) observes that, through phenomenological study: ...we have discovered the nature of the human being to be a dynamic, living organism of consciousness, an ever-changing, open, multidimensional field whose experience can come to know and actualize all dimensions of being.

as attention is placed on the collective field. One Living Evolution participant writes:

> My own experience of putting attention on the space between us is that of a forward movement of energy into what I can only describe as the actual relationship. ... My individual identity seems to merge into an expanded space; but far from *loss* of identity, there's a sense of reality in relationship to my true identity being more than my individual self. It's like being magnetically drawn into an empty space which, from the outside, feels fearful...but when inside the space, there's an awareness of fullness and wholeness. (personal communication, April 28, 2015)

There may be an experience of great care, enthusiasm, or even a sense of urgency; aspects of energies or state experiences evoked by the theme of inquiry and the shared intention of the group. Participants may experience themselves *as* consciousness and as able to feel into and reflect upon the potential of consciousness becoming aware of itself and evolving. Qualities of an evolutionary we-space appear to transcend time and space, as by listening to a recording of a practice group call and feeling into the inquiry, it may become alive in a listener's experience in the moment.

It can be noted that all of the qualities described above can be viewed as individual interior (UL) experience that participates in and contributes to collective (LL) inter-subjectivity. In ATC, interior experience may include visual images, kinesthetic sensation, or verbal description that has a poetic quality. The process can be viewed as multi-sensory, with each participant serving as a sense organ and unique expression of the whole. There is a sense in which expressed interior perceptions are inter-subjectively verified via shared resonance, and deepening may occur through successive responses that build upon them in the on-going perceiving and sharing process.[11] These varied

---

11. At times, a voice may be discordant, which is a call to discernment. On one hand, it may reflect an instrument that is "out of tune" with the depth of the collective space. On the other hand, this could be an invitation to a new insight, a deeper dive, or a different facet of the emergent experience. While there is not an easy answer regarding how to make this type of discernment, one can take the risk to verbalize their perceptions of what is happening in the group, with humility, recognizing we might be the one who is missing something (and have an opportunity to deepen our own understanding and awareness). It is sometimes helpful to ask someone to say more about what they have shared or to directly point out and encourage the group to explore a sense of discord within the group field. Addressing feelings of discord within the group helps to keep the inter-subjective field clear.

expressions have the potential to flow into one voice very much like the music of individual instruments blend into the shared expression of an orchestra. A retreat participant writes of a visceral experience of resonance with depth that some of us have experienced as "goose bumps":

> I remain curious about the physical sensations that accompanied the deepening of WE space....whenever a participant spoke from genuine depth, I experienced that same stimulating vibrational hum. I keep wondering, "What is that?" ... It is most definitely NOT an intellectual response. Many conversations elicited no such reaction – only those that, both in the moment and in retrospect, conveyed some sort of deeply genuine universal truth – even if that "truth" was seemingly trivial. (personal communication, January 26, 2012)

Craig Hamilton observed that engagement in this type of collective awakening practice seemed to accelerate spiritual development for practitioners in his community as it was engaged regularly within a committed group (Hamilton, et al., 2014). While this may be a speculative observation, a number of aspects of these practices could support increased capacity for more open and awakened consciousness in the lives of practitioners. The intersubjectivity within a group relating from a more open and self-transcending awareness may exert an upward gravitational pull that exceeds an individual's normal ceiling of consciousness, making this quality of awareness at least temporarily available to them. Ongoing collective practice may help to support more stable access to post-personal consciousness and open receptivity to creative emergence by providing a supportive container as well as the motivational power of shared commitment, intention, and fruitful practice. In addition to spiritual and self-sense development of individuals, DiPerna (2014, p. 168) has proposed that a line of "we-intelligence" may be cultivated via engagement in group dialogue practices. This may include skills for participation and a kind of depth-sensing capacity that develops through ongoing group practice (Hamilton, Shealy & Por, 2014).

Co-Meditation

In 2012 during a live retreat, Craig Hamilton introduced the interactive practice of co-meditation, which serves as a companion practice to Awakening through Conversation. Small breakout groups were given the instruction to verbalize their experience in the moment, allowing it to become part of the group's experience, and shifting the focus from I to We (Desjardins & Bissonnette, 2015, p. 8). Since that time, the practice has been embraced by the Living Evolution community within practice circle meetings and in co-meditation groups.

Participants generally practice a meditation instruction that would be followed in solo (or silent) meditation, such as to "let everything be as it is" (Desjardins & Bissonnette, 2015, p.11). According to participants who practice regularly, co-meditation, like solo meditation, is designed to disrupt or decondition attachment to the mind and its contents and facilitate opening to the part of our Self that never entered the stream of time and space and is undisturbed by the movement of experiences within consciousness: the formless ground of being. It is speaking aloud that differentiates co-meditation from solo meditation, and this dimension may facilitate a certain immediacy of experience, a capacity of trust in letting go, which may potentially have a powerful application to daily life. Craig Hamilton has offered the following instruction:

> When you feel moved to speak, allow yourself to speak without filtering. In other words, when you have a thought or experience that moves you to share, go ahead and speak, but first, let that initial thought go rather than try to capture it in words. Instead, allow the thought or experience only to serve to move you into speech. Then, when you actually speak, allow yourself to express your direct experience of this present moment. ...This takes a supreme surrender and trust in not knowing what to say and allowing something to come through. In this surrender and trust we let go of what we already know and allow our self to expand into a new emerging fullness of the moment and allow something to speak through us. It is the practice of freedom out loud. (Desjardins & Bissonnette, 2015, p. 9)

Similar to ATC, in co-meditation one is invited to allow the boundaries of one's personal self to soften and become permeable, opening to the inter-subjectivity of the group (Desjardins & Bissonnette, 2015, p.9). Unlike ATC, there is no need to build on what is shared by others or to keep a constant flow of conversation going, only speaking what feels called to be spoken and in doing so allowing the direct experience of the present moment to be voiced. The practice is allowed to unfold naturally with no preference for any particular feeling or experience and no effort exerted to change anything about what is occurring in the moment. Regarding the experience of co-meditation, participants have observed that the interactive context allows a sense of separation between self and other to dissolve in a way that is quite vivid and specific:

> In solo meditation the sense of "them" doesn't arise so much it seems. So in co-med[itation] there's an initial focus on something else "out there" that I begin to realize is not out there at all......that there is no such thing as "out there." There is only "what is," what is right here, right now that includes "out there" and "me." And this is not something fixed and solid, but a movement or process that is simply Me. I am all this. (Desjardins & Bissonnette, 2015, p. 10)

Practitioners also report that with regular practice, a deep stillness and infinite space starts to become available (Desjardins & Bissonnette, 2015, p. 9). Ultimately, the space is the container. The vast open space of awareness is the container for all that arises as life expressing itself through the group.

Evolution of the Practices and Community

Awakening Through Conversation continues to serve as a core practice in the Living Evolution community along with the newer practice of co-meditation. Program Director Wendy Van Horn offers her observations about how these can work together:

> I've noticed a synergistic relationship between the practice of co-meditation and ATC inquiry. [Co-meditation]...supports an increased capacity to engage in ATC practice where participants are encouraged to let go of individual agendas and self-referencing and give primacy of attention to the shared inquiry. It is one thing to understand this instruction cognitively, quite another to really "get" it and put it into practice. Co-meditation practice seems to provide a helpful entry point to understanding experientially what it means to place attention on what's emerging between us and suspend self-reference when contributing to the conversation. In groups with novice participants, I've found that engaging these two practices in sequence seems to catalyze explicit understanding of and sensitivity to the "we" space in a very helpful way. (personal communication, May 4, 2015)

Over time, these basic principles and practices come to be engaged more naturally, with less need for specific instruction, and practitioners develop skill in inviting engagement and supporting movement into greater depth. Participants begin to embody these practices within daily life, particularly beginner's mind, whole-heartedness, and the wider, more spacious self-sense experienced during these collective practices. This may enable them to more fully inhabit their daily lives; to flex and flow with life, remaining present, attuned, and open to what is emerging.

In further reflection on the practices and their potential impact, we observe that co-meditation can serve as a bridge to wider awareness and inclusion of all aspects of one's being. By opening to all experience, nothing is excluded, and all can be witnessed, embraced, and permitted to liberate within the vast space of awareness. Ultimately, this may include experience that has been outside of conscious awareness (shadow), conditioned patterns of reactivity, and what may have been formerly excluded as *egoic*. While the instruction in ATC has been to avoid the "personal," some practice groups report engaging emotional content, such as grief, allowing it to be expressed authentically and to move through the collective field as immediate emergent experience.

Related to this expanded openness of expression, practice group participant Clare Conway writes:

> It seems to me the we-space can hold all states. It can contain the joy and the pain. What I sometimes feel is that (we) do not want to bring our pain because it might disrupt the meeting. But from experience, the radical truth coming forth from any individual can resurrect great care and compassion from all present...As we develop in this work it seems clear that our ability to hold much more of life – and what we do and feel within it – is able/allowed to be present, to be seen, and to show up.[12] (personal communication, April 12, 2015)

We observe that deep listening increases the capacity to listen through story to hear the glimmers of truth and depth of expression which are making their way into collective consciousness within the field.

Over the past two years, there has been considerable leadership development within the Living Evolution community. While there was initially (and necessarily) a strong sense of distinction between teacher and student in Craig Hamilton's programs, over time students

---

12. It can be noted that the expressed pain of an individual participant may touch unhealed or unconscious individual or collective trauma.

have matured and are stepping into a greater degree of co-creative participation. On community calls, it is increasingly common for community members to flesh out topics of engagement, noticeably enhancing the depth and fullness of the large group conversation. Community members in the coaching profession offer a monthly coaching call, and senior students facilitate community-wide interactive/integration sessions, organize regional retreats, publish a newsletter, and engage participants in exploration of the monthly inquiry topic. There is a generative sense of abundance as participants challenge themselves to grow into new levels of competence and contribution that enhances the emerging evolutionary community.

Over the past three years, increasing numbers of Living Evolution participants have been concurrently studying with other teachers, such as Thomas Hübl, and more recently Jeff Carreira, Patricia Albere, and Stephen Busby. Hübl's practice of *transparent communication*, in its focus on subtle attunement to the full range of what is present, and ability to identify areas of reduced energy that may be a source of limitation, can be viewed as complimentary to ATC. These capacities expand the meaning of deeper listening and the quality of feedback that can be offered, thus enhancing the transformative potential of evolutionary relationship.[13] The experience of being met with presence and being clearly seen in relationship can serve a natural healing function in which energies are released and integrated. Practices of co-meditation and transparent communication, through their emphasis on being present with what is, may help to support a more fluid and embodied sense of presence among practitioners, as well as sensitivity to increasingly subtle nuances of experience.

Some Psychological Considerations

Development might be characterized broadly as moving from pre-personal to personal and potentially to post-personal or "supra-personal" levels of self-development (Marquis, 2008, p. 82). In general, a healthy psychological ego or self-sense provides a stable foundation for practices such as meditation and dialogue practices such as ATC. As integrally-informed psychotherapists, we are aware that seeking to catalyze direct experience of post-personal states of consciousness through collective awakening practices could precipitate

---

13. Feedback within practice circles or evolutionary partnership relationships is engaged to raise awareness of what may be blind spots that then support transformation.

de-stabilization of individuals with more fragile self-structures, and/or histories of significant trauma or addiction[14] (Shealy & White, 2013). For these individuals, there is potential of entering into dissociative states rather than transcendence in the face of the uncertainty and depth of ego surrender inherent in the higher stages of consciousness. While this issue is not unique to these particular practices and may arise in a range of spiritual and personal development contexts, risk may be heightened in programs that offer a more direct path to self-transcendence and/or a high intensity of practice. Those in leadership roles need to be alert to this type of risk and prepared to offer assistance and support. In some cases, an individual may derive more benefit from individual psychotherapy where interventions and growth opportunities can be more carefully tailored to his or her needs. For some, there may be greater value in supporting a more integrated and coherent self-story[15] and/or engagement in trauma-processing work.

In addition to concerns regarding self-development and unprocessed trauma, all individuals have areas of unconsciousness that may interfere with clear expression and embodiment of otherwise high levels of development. This has led to recognition of the value of shadow work that supports awareness and reintegration of unconscious material and energies into the "stream of wholeness" (Hübl, 2010, p. 8), "cleaning up" in order to be a clearer vessel for service in the world (DiPerna, 2013, Chapter 3, Section 4, para. 1). Related to this, Brabant (2013) asserts that:

> ...the cleaning up process is inextricably linked to waking up and therefore through our humility and integral approach to awakening, we must remain open to continually clean our vehicles so the clear light of awareness can shine brighter and with more integrity, moment by moment. (Chapter 6, Section 6, para. 5)

---

14. An area of inquiry for those in long term recovery from addictive tendencies was the surrendering to the urgency of the evolutionary impulse as it brought up body memory of the compulsive energy associated with past addictive tendencies. They found the movement from the serenity of the ground of being into surrender to the evolutionary impulse required a deeper level of trust in "a power greater than self" than the first surrender from ego to ground of being. With this second surrender was a deepening into the evolutionary potential embedded within the 12 steps of recovery programs and the discernment between the destructive compulsive drive of addiction and the loving forward creative movement of eros.

15. From a mental health recovery standpoint, all individuals can be supported in connecting to a sense of meaning, purpose and engagement that enhances their life and enables them to make a positive contribution within their community.

Thomas Hübl's work addresses some of these psychological considerations by emphasizing the importance of having a solid base of grounding within the body and encourages the embrace of shadow aspects both individually and collectively. The shadow work may extend to addressing the residue of trans-generational trauma by working with collective trauma as it emerges within the group field.

Comparison With Other Integral We Practices

We-space practices are being engaged by a number of different groups within the integral community, the majority of whom are represented in this anthology. Study, comparison, and sharing of experience and practices from different groups can help advance shared understanding and enable the identification of core themes and best practices. In identifying common threads, we observe many similarities between ATC and Kramer's instructions for insight dialogue[16] (Kramer, 2007). There appears to be a common recognition of the value of opening, suspending the known, listening deeply, and speaking from a place of depth. In both ATC and insight dialogue (which is practiced in dyads), participants refrain from habitual story and engage a specific theme of inquiry (Kramer, 2007). Similarities are also observed in the gestures of "surrendering into witnessing" (Gunnlaugson & Moze, 2012), and it would seem that the quality and depth of awareness invited would be similar to that engaged by the newer conversational leadership practice of "deep presencing" (Gunnlaugson, 2015). There also appears to be a similar valuing and goal of presence and opening to the flow of emergence throughout daily life in a manner that is appropriate to shifting interpersonal contexts.

Regarding the centrality of community and engagement in on-going practice groups, there is kinship with the work of Patricia Albere and Jeff Carreira that centers on "mutual awakening," a shift into evolutionary relationship that supports the realization of the highest potentials of both partners (Albere & Carreira, 2013, p. 72). Additionally, Thomas Steininger and Elizabeth Debold from Enlightennext are working to support others in developing understanding and skill in the process of "evolutionary dialogue" and its application in a range of work and wider community contexts

---

16. Gregory Kramer and Teri O'Fallon completed a joint doctoral dissertation on insight dialogue and insight dialogic inquiry in 1997, which laid the groundwork for this practice related to Buddhist insight meditation.

(Debold & Steininger, 2015). Cultivating an evolutionary relationship to life is reflected in Scharmer's U Theory in which he presences the capacities of "open mind, open heart, open will" and a concern for co-creative impact in the world (Scharmer, 2009, p. 41). Related to this common concern, many in the Living Evolution community have a passion for supporting the manifestation of new culture in LR structures.

Through its emphasis on both motivation and practice, Craig Hamilton's integral enlightenment teaching seems to have affinity with Dustin DiPerna's work to articulate a trans-lineage, integral understanding of religion and his identification of the need for a "dual-conveyor belt" that supports both structure-stage and state-stage development (DiPerna, 2014, p. 174). Reflection on motivating perspectives drawn from both theistic and non-theistic spiritual traditions may support higher structure-stage understanding, updating, or translation of these perspectives. Meditation and collective awakening practices may promote state-stage development.

In comparison with other programs and practices such as Thomas Hübl's transparent communication (2011), there is less emphasis on personal shadow, body awareness, and resolution of psychological issues. Awareness work and coaching are more likely to focus on identifying and moving through limiting beliefs and other conditioned patterns that may be viewed as "faces" of ego. While shadow is not engaged directly, there is emphasis on giving and receiving feedback, which has the potential to bring unconscious aspects of a practitioner's energy dynamics and their manifestation in behavior to light. While participants explore motivating perspectives[17] and seek to manifest higher human potentials, they are also cautioned that "there is no value in trying to be somewhere [you]'re not" and great value in acknowledging confusion and uncertainty, which may open the door for new insights and understanding (Hamilton, 2015b, para 8). Both of these evolutionary teachers agree on the value of feedback and therapeutic work occurring in the context of an overarching commitment to awakening (Shealy & White, 2013).

It is ultimately a high aspiration and glimpsed potential that is at the heart of this evolutionary spiritual work. There is a strong intention to support development of consciousness within individuals and collectives that enables positive, creative, evolutionary transformation

---

17. Parallel to Craig Hamilton's emphasis on motivation, Stephen Busby speaks of "the felt manifestation of strong inner vertical alignment: a frequency of consciousness that synthesizes high-energy, new resources and potentials. We can listen and feel the vibrancy of this: its quality is different from the place where we usually 'make choices." (Busby, 2014).

of humanity. At the same time, it seems important to note that the practices described in this chapter invite experience that is deeply valued in its own right. There's something *passionate* about the we-space, something about experiencing the life force in its raw essence and a quality of intimacy that is not typical of every day relationships. There is an inherent longing for depth and connection, a higher expression of eros, a longing of the greater We that is satisfied and potentially deepened through these evolutionary we practices.

Best Practices, Needs and Evolutionary Potential

Regarding best practices, we observe a common thread of suspending attention to habitual thought and opening the mind. This may be experienced as opening to what is, opening to Source, perhaps even opening to a sense of *being* the space, the container, or the stillness through which life flows, and through which the new can emerge. This receptive capacity of presence may be awakened and supported by meditation and collective practices such as co-meditation, ATC, Big Mind, and other dialogue practices that engage post-personal awareness. Practices that help cultivate inner space can lay a foundation for creative emergence and may create a container for witnessing a range of energies. Related to this, Thomas Hubl's practice of *attunement* invites development of subtle awareness capacity that expands the territory of what can be witnessed, enabling healing integration.

A range of practices supports engaging and enacting higher soul potential and creative emergence. These would include ATC's evoking and speaking *from* higher perspectives or, more generally, the practice of "letting come" (Sharmer, 2009, p. 241): allowing new insights to be presenced. Opening to Source enables emergence of the new. Practices that engage and invite expression of higher perspectives may help to realize and transmit them within the collective. Related to higher perspectives, the energy of *evolutionary urgency* comes to the forefront of awareness: we truly need to wake up as a species and evolve our culture, systems and structures! There is great need in so many areas of our world. As we awaken to a larger sense of purpose, we can open to creative possibility regarding the best deployment of our attention and energy to contribute the gifts that we uniquely have to offer.

In considering the relationship between integral we-practices and the evolution of culture, it is important to consider the depth dimension of individual and cultural stage development (Graves, 1970; Kegan, 2009; Wilber, 2000). We believe that it is no accident that evolutionary we-practices are emerging as values development begins to extend into second tier (Beck & Cowan, 2006) consciousness, transcending and including earlier first tier memes and enabling capacity for holding multiple perspectives and post-personal consciousness. This development seems crucial as we face an increasing array of global crises. Could it be that evolutionary we-spaces will support culturally and values meme-sensitive responses to current world challenges (Maalouf, 2014)? Can these practices enable leaps in human capacity to envision and enact solutions to problems from a higher, wider and more open vantage point, such as when humans first became able to stand on their legs? Is it possible that containers of collective awakening may carry the second tier cultural competence, subtle attunement capacity, and transmission of higher potential to permeate and impact wider culture *as* elevating, healing and creative energy and momentum within the whole? It is a tall order to emerge from the mire of current circumstances, yet we are convinced that evolutionary we-space work has the promise to provide the necessary support, traction, and perspective for working with and evolving the existing systems and structures in which we are embedded.

Summary Integration

In exploring various approaches to engaging and understanding the integral/evolutionary soul, we observe the identification of a triad or trinity of higher We experiences across communities of study and practice. First is that of the formless, unmanifest ever-present ground of being, stillness, or Source which may involve opening of the mind via suspension or relinquishing of attachment to or identification with thought. Second is experience of *dynamic presence* (Almaas, 2004, p. 359) or *evolutionary impulse* that is vigorous and alive, the energy of Eros, bringing a sense of power, inspiring creativity and moving us to action as a manifestation of open will. Finally, as we return to an agapic embrace, bringing consciousness down through all variations of movement, levels, valences, and particularities of experience, the possibility for opening to aspects of soul that manifest as great care for the whole or *divine love* (Almaas, 2004, p. 291) emerges, a healing gesture of the open heart. Craig Hamilton asserts that "the inner reality (of these aspects of our true nature) becoming manifest in the world is *"evolutionary non-duality"* (personal communication, August 1, 2015). As we open and awaken to these higher dimensions, we access wisdom, empowered creativity, compassion and capacity for deeper intimacy with self, other and world. As we do this *together*, we are empowered to participate in evolution of both (LL) culture and (LR) structures. May we bring our highest human potential to face the innumerable challenges of our times with whole-hearted compassion, creativity, commitment, and reverence for all of life.

Author Bios

Suzanne E. Shealy, Ph.D. is a clinical psychologist who received her Ph.D. from the University of South Florida in 1990. For the past 19 years, she has facilitated outpatient addiction recovery and domestic violence intervention groups for military veterans. Her work related to recovery has been published in the Journal of Integral Theory and Practice (most recently with co-author Linda White). An ongoing member of evolutionary practice groups, she began studying with Craig Hamilton in 2010 and has participated in courses offered by Thomas Hübl.

Linda A. White is a Licensed Clinical Professional Counselor, New Zealand Registered Psychologist and long-term practitioner of integral psychology & evolutionary spirituality. With over 30 years of experience as a clinician and mentor, she is currently in private practice in Camden, ME. She specializes in the integration of somatic and spiritual technologies which are deeply grounded in evidence-based psychological practices and recovery as a spiritual path.

Lisa Foxley is a humanistic therapist, environmental activist and group facilitator, currently retired and living in Devon, UK. She has been a member of Craig Hamilton's Integral Enlightenment community since 2011 and has served as a practice circle leader and Course Assistant.

References

Albere, P., & Carreira, J. (2013). Mutual Awakening: Opening into a new paradigm for human relatedness. Santa Fe, NM: Evolutionary Collective.

Almaas, A. H. (2004). The inner journey home: Soul's realization of the unity of reality. Boston, MA: Shambala.

Beck, D. E., & Cowan, C. C. (2006). Spiral dynamics: Mastering values, leadership, and change. Malden, MA: Blackwell.

Brabant, M. (2013). Cleaning up: The reciprocal dance of psyche and spirit. In D. Diperna (Ed.) The coming waves [Kindle Paperwhite Version]. Retrieved from Amazon.com

Busby, S. (2014). Higher consciousness. Online call on the practice of Higher Consciousness. August 23, 2014. SoundCloud.com

Cohen, A. (2011). Evolutionary Enlightenment. New York, NY: Select Books, Inc.

Desjardins, M. & Bissonnette, R. (2015). What is collective meditation? Evolving Voice, Issue 6, 8-11.

DiPerna, D. (2013). Wake up, grow up, clean up, show up. In D.

Diperna (Ed.) The coming waves [Kindle Paperwhite Version]. Retrieved from Amazon.com

DiPerna, D. (2014). Streams of Wisdom: An advanced guide integral spiritual development. Integral Publishing.

Graves, C.W. (1970). The levels of human existence and their relation to welfare problems. Retrieved from http://www.clarewgraves.com/articles_content/1970/welfare.html

Gunnlaugson, O. (2015). Deep presencing: Illuminating new territory at the bottom of the U. Integral Leadership Review. Retrieved from http://integralleadershipreview.com/author/olen-gunnlaugson/

Gunnlaugson, O., & Moze, M. G. (2012). Surrendering into witnessing: A foundational practice for building collective capacity in groups. Journal of Integral Theory and Practice, 7(3), 105-115.

Hamilton, C. (2015a). Awakening through conversation. Retrieved from http://integralenlightenment.com/academy/awakening/

Hamilton, C. (2015b). Principles of evolutionary culture. Retrieved from http://integralenlightenment.com/academy/culture/

Hamilton, C. & Zammit, C. (2008). Thinking together without ego: Collective intelligence as an evolutionary catalyst. In M. Tovey (Ed.) Collective Intelligence: Creating a prosperous world at peace. Oakton, VA: Earth Intelligence Network. Retrieved from http://www.oss.net/dynamaster/file_archive/080227/8580f18843bf5c10f17c38f7ad9fdf71/Complete_022508-C%20FINAL%201420.pdf

Hamilton, C., Shealy, S. E., & Por, G. (2014). Collective intelligence and the evolution of self and culture. Spanda Journal, 2, 119-126. Retrieved from http://www.spanda.org/SpandaJournal_V,2.pdf

Hübl, T. (2011). Transparence: Practice groups – an adventure in seeing yourself and others more clearly. Germany: Sharing the Presence.

Kegan, R. (1994). In over our Heads: The mental demands of modern life. Cambridge, MA: Harvard University Press.

Kramer, G. (2007). Insight Dialogue: The interpersonal path to freedom. Boston, MA: Shambhala Publications.

Maalouf, E.S. (2014). Emerge: The rise of functional democracy and the future of the Middle East. New York, NY: Select Books.

Marquis, A. (2008). The Integral Intake: A guide to comprehensive ideographic assessment in integral psychotherapy. New York, NY: Routledge.

Merzel, D. G. (2007). Big Mind – Big Heart: Finding your way. Salt Lake City, UT: Big Mind Publishing.

Shealy, S. E., & White, L. A. (2013). Integral evolutionary recovery: Re-visioning the 12 Steps through a kosmo-centric lens. Journal of

Integral Theory and Practice, 8(3-4), 66-81.

Shealy, S. E., White, L. A., Dueck, R., & Geidt, E. (2012). Evolutionary Life Transformation Program: Evolving culture through collective practice. Unpublished working paper.

Wilber, K. (2000). Integral Psychology: Consciousness, spirit, psychology, therapy. Boston, MA: Shambhala Publications.

CHAPTER 13

Emerge Dialogue Process:
The Intersection of the Higher We and Dialogue Practice

Thomas Steininger, Ph.D. & Elizabeth Debold, Ed.D.

"*COGITO, ERGO SUM*" wrote René Descartes in *Discourse on the Method,* published in 1637 (p. 159). That simple statement, quoted in every introductory philosophy class, represents the culmination of a process in human development that began around 800 B.C.E., which some historians call the "Axial Age" (Jaspers, 1953, p. 1). This period marked a new axis in human and cultural development across the globe, from China to India to Greece. What began to emerge then is something that we take so for granted today, a "sense of individual identity, as distinct from the tribe and from nature..." (Cousins, 1997, section 2, para. 6). Nearly a thousand years later, Descartes's "I think, therefore I am," represents the culmination of this development in the West. The achievement of the self-reflective, self-contained, separate, rational "I" eventually made the scientific revolution, the Kantian Enlightenment, and liberal democracy possible.

Today, argues theologian Ewert Cousins (1997), we are at the beginning of another, equally significant time of transition that he calls the Second Axial Period. Noting that consciousness evolution proceeds by recapitulation, Cousins argues that this next great current in cultural evolution will incorporate the ground of unity that pre-Axial tribal cultures had access to, but on a deeper and larger scale. As he notes, "having developed self-reflective, analytic, critical consciousness in the First Axial Period, we must now, while retaining these values, reappropriate and integrate into that consciousness the collective and cosmic dimensions of . . . consciousness" (ibid.). Cousins recognized the urgency for such an integration to happen in order to respond to the crises we are facing as a globalized human community.

We agree with Cousins that the emergence of a new capacity for collective consciousness would have implications as profound as the emergence of individuated consciousness. If the "I think, therefore I am" consciousness brought about the scientific revolution, what revolution, or evolution, could such an integrated, collective awareness bring about? As this volume demonstrates, through serendipity and intention, higher orders of intersubjective awareness are beginning to emerge in collectives. These new forms of collective awareness are often called "We Spaces" amongst those engaged in integral philosophy and practice. The two of us writing this chapter were engaged for over twenty years within the EnlightenNext spiritual community, led by Andrew Cohen, in an experiment in the conscious development of a particular variant and manifestation of We Space that we call the "Higher We." Since 2001, we have been exploring, developing, and refining Higher We practice, most recently and notably through the Emerge Dialogue Process.[1] Just as the "I" of Descartes's *cogito, ergo sum* made new realms of human innovation possible, our belief is that the "we" in the Higher We will bring about new capacities of creativity that can better address the complexity and conflicts we face in a highly networked, globalized world. Our hope is that Emerge Dialogue Process is and can be a small contribution toward pragmatic application of the emergent capacities of the Higher We.

In this chapter, we briefly trace the trajectory of our work from the beginning at EnlightenNext through the present. After defining our key terms, we then discuss the development of and weaknesses in these earlier phases of the Higher We at EnlightenNext. Then we provide a description of the fundamentals of the Emerge Dialogue Process and make distinctions between our approach and others'. We also discuss the capacities that facilitators need to have or develop in order to guide

---

1. Emerge Dialogue Process developed in EnlightenNext-Deutschland over the past nine years under the name "Evolutionary Dialogue." The impetus for the dialogue work was twofold: to create a "lower bar" of entry into the collective spiritual practice that EnlightenNext was engaged in and to discover a new way to work across differences in perspective, most notably at the Herbstakademie, a partnership between Die Integrale Akademie, info3 (a progressive anthroposophic magazine), and EnlightenNext-DE. We would like to express our thanks to our partners in the Herbstakademie, Sonja Student and Jens Heisterkamp, and our colleagues at EnlightenNext-DE. We particularly want to thank and acknowledge Katrin Karneth, whose heart, sensitivity, and intelligence have been essential to the development of Evolutionary Dialogue. Without Katrin, this work would not have been able to develop and reveal the potential that it has.

such a dialogue. Finally, we conclude with some of our ideas for using our dialogue process as a catalyst for creative emergence.

Emerge Dialogue Process and the Higher We

Before one can understand the Emerge Dialogue Process, one needs to understand what we mean by the "Higher We." While it may sound almost self-explanatory, it's actually somewhat counterintuitive. Imagine a group of individuals sitting in a circle, engaging in dialogue. The Higher We is not the group, nor about individuals in a group, nor is it about an experience that they are having together. While the starting point is a specific "we" in a conversation setting, what we mean by the Higher We is not constrained by any kind of limited "we space" that is defined by the people present. Its meaning and reality are not reduced to any particular individuals. The group is a gateway for an awareness of consciousness as process within the shared internal or intersubjective space. The Higher We opens up when a sufficient number of individuals within a group are awake to this intersubjective dimension as a living, creative reality. The Higher We is an awakened intersubjective field that is consciousness aware, process aware, and content conscious. The human heart experiences the Higher We as something sacred that one feels humbled by, and compelled to protect and nourish. At the same time, it is simply and most profoundly who we are.

The Higher We emergence depends on a deep, ongoing experiential awareness of the reality and living presence of consciousness between human beings in a committed conversation. While many contemporary spiritual practitioners have had meditation experiences of consciousness as the timeless formless Absolute, the experience of consciousness *in* time and space is both dependent on awareness of that ground of IS-ness and is different. Just as sitting on a meditation cushion is a limited setting in which one can realize the infinite Ground of Being, a group conversation setting is also a very limited setting in which one can become aware of an unlimited potential unfolding that is part of a much bigger process. They are, needless to say, related. Deep, sustained realization of that One-without-a-second in meditation leads to an ongoing, sensed recognition of a "prior unity" in the present moment, a sense of non-separation within a field of undivided interrelatedness (Adi Da, 2015). The human experience of depth in both meditation and Higher We practice is freedom or ecstasy—which literally means "unfixed," referring in this case to a release from the bounded sense of self. As the sense of limitation drops, it gives rise to a living current between individuals that then "un-fixes" our creative capacities, making it possible to realize, understand, and make connections that weren't available before. In fact, being aware of consciousness in motion in time and space, together within the circle of individuals engaged in dialogue, always has a slight upward pull, a lift, toward the horizon of potential. Inherent to it is an alertness, curiosity, and interest about the Not-yet. Placing attention on the shared field within the dialogue circle, the possibility and potential of the next moment, unknown, pulls. "This unknown New gets born in the dialogue between us and through us out of a creative Nothingness and the 'Not Yet Thought' that happens as the unspeakable We starts to shine as an intuition in our experience," Maria Zacherl, an Emerge Dialogue Process facilitator, says. "As we surrender to this it becomes alive in our expression." So, the more each participant gives to the whole and leans in to the field with genuine curiosity, the more the whole awakens to itself and a shared intelligence begins to be expressed through the group. In this, the Higher We emerges.

The Higher We is a decisive shift from individual consciousness; it creates a new identity of self-as-process within a larger, cosmic process. Something completely undivided opens up between the collective in the intersubjective that is self in a much deeper sense than one's usual identity. Unlike individuated, personal subjectivity, the inner space of the intersubjective has no limits: the inner is the outer, the outer is the inner. In other words, when the individuals in the group have the repeated, almost uncanny experience of having their own thoughts and insights expressed by others in the group, the recognition of a shared interior experience develops. Each participant experiences being a focal point of the whole field in which Life is unfolding at the level of consciousness between human beings, rather than simply being part of a circle or a point on the circle. One begins to identify more with the process, relaxing into a deeper sense of self as limitless, non-separate, undivided unfolding. Simultaneously, because the Higher We concerns collectives of human beings, the process is always dialogical: it is an unfolding of human culture and, ultimately, of the cosmos that has no end because there is always more to include and integrate. Through us and as us, in the emergence of the Higher We, the Whole wakes up to the Whole.

While the Higher We is a profound spiritual practice and experience, the Emerge Dialogue Process is a form of dialogue practice that is much more pragmatic. We have used this practice as a process facilitation method for conferences, as a means to think better together in business or Board meetings, as a way to deepen community and support individual realization and transformation, and as a practice to engage in complex problem solving in business. The Emerge Dialogue Process doesn't demand that participants, or a critical mass of them, shift their identity. It isn't primarily about consciousness or awakening/enlightenment. In fact, this process has been used successfully in business contexts where participants had no understanding of meditation, consciousness, or spirituality. Emerge Dialogue Process facilitators, who have deeply experienced that they are not separate from this larger process, can hold an awareness and space that liberates the creativity between a group of human beings. It's not identity changing but when there is enough gravity, or weight, given to the field to open up space for the creative process as such, something new is possible.

The Emerge Dialogue Process, thus, is a practical application of the Higher We that can be used in any context where real dialogue is called for. By "dialogue," we mean a group conversation in which perspectives are shared with the aim of coming to a deeper understanding or resolution. This process catalyzes creative momentum within a group by asking participants to follow certain guidelines under the direction of a facilitator who is skilled in holding a Higher We context. The guidelines (which we will explain later in this chapter) ask participants to behave in ways similar to the ways that individuals who are awake to the Higher We consciousness would respond. Thus, they begin to function as a whole, and through the facilitator's awareness of the field of alive non-separate intersubjectivity, they can catalyze creative emergence. As Mike Kauschke, an Emerge Dialogue Process facilitator, clarifies, "we often experience how a field of higher consciousness is not simply pre-existing between us. It gets born in its own aliveness to the degree that we start to be open for it." Truly emergent dialogue requires participation, and participation in such a dialogue often leads to the recognition that we can work deeply and creatively together with our differences, and that the creative flow is more important than one's self-importance. If a significant number of the individuals in the group have the interest and capacity to care about the project that the group is engaging with, beyond their own sense of what "should be" or their status in the group, it is possible to facilitate emergence in a dialogue. Thus, it can be productively used and understood by people with a more secular understanding of consciousness. Particularly given the fact that the awareness is growing that we, on this planet, are in a process together and have to find ways to really interact that does not start from the presumption of primary differences and our individuated self-sense but on being together in a living society on a living globe—or even just in a living organization. We see the Emerge Dialogue Process as a potentially key cultural practice for developing a post-individualistic (i.e., post-personal) culture. Since one of the unintended consequences of our "I" (or "me") focused culture has been an unsustainable consumerism that now threatens the biosphere, a more holistic and collective intelligence would value our relatedness and interdependence with each other and with the rest of life on Earth. Moreover, the complexity of the "wicked" problems that we now face as a human species call for more than individual genius and thereby calls that we bring together a wide range of human knowledge and experience in order to begin to find new solutions. Perhaps Emerge Dialogue Process could be one method to assist in our transition from the First Axial Period where the individual was the focal point into a Second Axial Period in which the "collective and cosmic" dimensions of consciousness become incorporated into our ongoing, daily awareness (Cousins, 1997, section 4, para. 6). However, given our current planetary crises, we may not have another thousand or so years to make this new consciousness a living reality for a small but significant proportion of us. Such a transition will undoubtedly take hundreds of years to bring into being and our current planetary crises call us to do everything we possibly can to hasten the process.

The I, the We, and the It of Potentiality

To bring a Wilberian Integral frame (1995) to the Emerge Dialogue Process, working in this way brings into awareness three different perspectives of "potentiality space;" the I, the We, and the It.[2] This potentiality space refers to the previously unknown capacities and awareness that arise in a collective context, both in its pragmatic form in Emerge Dialogue Process and in an intentional Higher We practice. First, there is the potentiality space for the individual to discover that there is room to grow both horizontally and vertically. Horizontally, the individual expands her or his understanding related to the topic under discussion. Vertically, the individual can realize that there is a depth of Being and capacity for shared creative consciousness that lead to a more inclusive, transpersonal experience of self. Participants often experience aspects of self within the dialogue that loosen the grip of a fixed belief in the limitations of the psychological self while at the same time deepening one's individuated autonomy. One caveat, however, is that these vertical I-shifts are initially dependent on the Higher We context: when one leaves the context, the habitual patterns of self reassert themselves. This can be confusing. Also, one can become consistently able to lean in, as it were, and *respond to* the collective field of a Higher We yet not be *responsible for* holding this

---

2. Thank you to Sonja Student for giving us this integral perspective on the "Möglichkeitsraum" in the context of our dialogue work.

consciousness.[3] However, by becoming increasingly sensitive and responsive to the Higher We context through practice, one gradually develops the capacity to be responsible for it. To develop the sensitivity and awareness to maintain contact with these more transpersonal dimensions, outside of a context in which the Higher We is evoked, takes a great deal of spiritual effort and capacity.

From the We, there is a similar horizontal and vertical potentiality space. In a more "functional" or pragmatic emergent dialogue, the horizontal We creates a greater sense of interpersonal connection and possibility to work well as individuals together. Yet in a dialogue that evokes the Higher We, a sacred dimension opens as a collective awareness of unity beyond the apparent diversity of the individuals present. In fact, this unity goes beyond the group in dialogue to embrace the Whole that everything is part of. There is a realization that there is someplace new to go *together*, and that only we can do this—there is no other higher power that will intervene to take the next steps forward. This vertical recognition of the potentiality space of the We can be seen as a fourth face of God, that extends into the collective or lower left quadrant. Wilber (2007) has recognized the different faces of Spirit (p. 159) as the I, the Divinity in each human being, the You, the ultimate Other, and the Its, the cosmic process itself.[4] This fourth face of God is the enlightened intersubjective space that comes alive between us as us.

The potentiality space of the It within an Emerge Dialogue Process relates to the content or subject matter of the conversation itself. Because this dialogue work is expressly concerned with content through generating solutions or developing new ideas, the It has more significance here than in Higher We practice. The It in Emerge Dialogue Process also has a horizontal and vertical dimension. Horizontally, this dialogue process can organize existing information and bring the various participants and their perspectives into a more unified understanding of the issues at hand. Vertically, a really alive and synergistic dialogue can produce breakthrough ideas that often come from "left field," which the participants often experience as an emergence. The sense in the group is that "everything falls into place"

---

3. The distinction between being "responsive to" and "responsible for" the Higher We was made by Andrew Cohen in a meeting with his core students.

4. Thomas Steininger observes that there are seven Faces of God: the I, the Divine within the individual self; the You, the Absolute Other to which one bows down; the It, the Divinity expressed in a particular thing; the We, the enlightened intersubjective the plural You, the many faces of the Divine in the diverse Deities humans worship; the Its, the panentheistic Divine Cosmic Unfolding, and the aperspectival Absolute that reveals itself in deep meditation.

and a new creative coherence with a whole new potential comes to life. From the point of view of this new perspective, the problems or concerns at the beginning of the dialogue seem almost to disappear, as the solution or right response simply becomes evident. Developing the It as content in this way is the key purpose of the Emerge Dialogue Process.

Lessons From the Higher We Emergence at EnlightenNext

Between 1999 and 2002, after years of individual and collective spiritual practice, a series of powerful Higher We emergences burst forth amongst Andrew Cohen's committed students in his organization/community. While much has been written about a particularly powerful cluster of Higher We experiences centering on July 30, 2001, the development of both competence in and stability of this consciousness began many years before and took at least five years afterwards through an ongoing ordeal of trial and error (e.g., Cohen & Wilber, 2007; Debold, 2002; Patten, 2013; Phipps, 2001). In Andrew Venezia's (2013) study of We-space practices, he commented that "EnlightenNext...[has] what seems to be the most effective and efficient method for bringing people into an Awakened We" (p. 93). In this section, we will discuss the emergence of the Higher We at EnlightenNext, key insights about engaging in the Higher We, and learnings from this experience that led to the development of the Emerge Dialogue Process.[5]

Beginning in 1999 and culminating on July 30, 2001, four powerful collective state experiences of a Higher We emerged within different

---

5. More specific questions about Cohen and his method of teaching, which has been controversial and even abusive, we will leave aside here. A great deal of controversy surrounds Cohen's teaching methods, which included profound insight and creativity as well as coercion, humiliation, and other abusive or questionable practices, but that is beyond the scope of this chapter. His stepping down as a teacher and the dissolution of EnlightenNext has considerably to do with these errors of heart and judgment. From our perspective, we trusted the source of Cohen's spiritual vision and his compulsion to bring something into existence between human beings that had not existed before: this was why we were with him. For more on our experience and perspective on these issues, we refer readers to Steininger's public conversations on October 5 and 15, 2014 with Terry Patten on his Beyond Awakening teleseries, which can be found in his archive (beyondawakeningseries.com/blog/archive/) and Debold's blog post (http://www.artemisforum.com/open_letter_to_my_former_teacher/).

groups of Cohen's committed students. The first occurrence, in 1999, was among a group of fourteen women "novices" who were on a public retreat with Cohen. This emergence, which Debold was part of, was the first time that Cohen saw in manifestation the collective awakening that he had been driving for. The experience was of being fully at ease as oneself and simultaneously united in consciousness with all the others in the group. After this, also in the context of different public retreats, two additional groups of Cohen's women students ignited into a shared, ecstatic communion and passionate inquiry almost by accident. Then, in the Summer of 2001, Cohen had a substantial number of his committed male students on a prolonged silent meditation retreat. The majority of the men would meditate all day, and then meet together at night. On July 30, 2001, when Cohen was absent, the men broke through and catalyzed the first of the Higher We emergences in which there was a self-aware recognition of the nature of what was happening. Not only did the men intend to catalyze a leap beyond the separate self sense, according to Steininger who was present, within the fire of the experience they were able to speak about the emergence from the perspective of one consciousness.

Despite the power of these emergences, particularly the last one, this did not mean that everything flipped into some ongoing Higher We state nor did it mean that the Higher We was easily accessible. From 2002 through about 2008 was a time of stabilization and experimentation. Christopher Parish, one of Andrew Cohen's senior students, developed a dialogue process called Enlightened Communication, which was a first form of open dialogue that invited interested people to attempt to have the state experience of the Higher We. Within the community, the Higher We was no longer simply an explosive, emotionally ecstatic experience but became a more consistent reference point for Cohen's closest group of students as a deeply interested and liberated perspective that came alive in an intentional intersubjective context. In fact, over time we have come to believe that the fireworks of breakthrough only happen when a new capacity is released into human consciousness, but is not inherent in that new capacity itself. With far less effort, by 2005, persons who were new to EnlightenNext and the Higher We work were able to join groups and participate in the collective field. In conversations with Cohen, integral philosopher Ken Wilber referred to this stabilization as the creation of a "plateau state experience" that "could be extended pretty much indefinitely and that [individuals] have more or less permanent access to" (Cohen & Wilber, 2007, p. 57, 50). During and since this time, some of those in the EnlightenNext context have worked to develop greater clarity about the demands of engaging within the Higher We.

The Higher We needs highly individuated autonomous individuals who freely choose to surrender to a process larger than themselves. It is a trans-individual We-space that transcends and includes individuality and responsibility, rather than a pre-individual tribal We based on custom and conformity. For the Higher We to flower, individuals willingly surrender to non-separation out of free choice and the freedom of recognition of the significance of this larger, unfolding process. Individuals involved cannot be forced to submit nor be lacking in individuation but need to be fully responsible as a separate self in order to choose to *not* be separate. The fully conscious surrender of the individual to this larger process requires an *active*, not passive, letting go of individual motives toward separation. While surrender and will are usually opposite to each other, here the two literally merge. It is not will as one typically understands it; it is will in the form of surrender. Through this willing surrender, the Higher We can emerge as a co-creative unfolding that has its own motivation toward integration. In other words, the autonomous agency of the individual is expressed through the deep letting go of surrender. Paradoxically, surrender and agency become one.

Through this willing, agentic surrender, the individual awakens to a new identity as and in the larger cosmic process of consciousness development that has a new and different motivation. The preoccupations and motivations of the personal self, or ego, are transcended through a deep ease and wholehearted intention to give oneself to this process. The capacities of the personal ego, most notably self-reflection and self-awareness, are necessary for the Higher We and the Higher We depends on transcending the self-focus of these ego capacities. The ego, as we are speaking about it here, is the capacity to separate—to see thoughts, feelings, motivations, and behaviors as one's own—in order to take responsibility. Such responsibility is necessary for the willing surrender to the larger process that the Higher We requires.

This development of the personal ego was an evolutionary breakthrough that Jaspers (1953) recognized by naming the Axial Period as a fundamental shift in history and it is foundational to Higher We emergence. With the development of the "I" or ego, human consciousness became individuated and could stand against what one could call the "Lower We," an undifferentiated, tribal, collective consciousness. Individuated moral agency thus became possible. In the two thousand years since the Axial Period, human consciousness has developed so that now, as postmodern individuals, our attention is habitually focused on the self-absorbing and mesmerizing stream of thoughts, feelings, and sense impressions occurring within us. *And* this structure of individuated experience, and the sensitivity and awareness that it has given rise to, are necessary to cognize and hold depth and an understanding of the cosmic process that is critical to the Higher We emergence.

For the individual participant, the Higher We entails a shift of identification from the personal ego to the emerging, intersubjective process itself as self, accessed through the Higher We. "Identification" is a tricky concept in psychology that is related to "shadow," or the elements of our experience that have been deliberately placed outside of our conscious awareness. However, while shadow is something we consider to be negative, identification is not. At least not until and unless one wants to shift it! We tend to expect, or assume, that we each have an identity that relates to our gender, race, class, religion, and cultural backgrounds. In addition, our identity is related to our special gifts, habitual fears, and coping strategies developed through our personal history. Identity, then, is how we construct ourselves as different and separate from others. For many of us, our adult identities have been hard won and are fiercely defended even though much of what we are identified with is not conscious. What we identify with as self is truly the skin we are in, the eyes we see with. It is "me." Our identifications are not our ideas or feelings, but the actual values that structure what we think, feel, and do. While our unique identities are the gifts we bring to the intersubjective space, we have to loosen our grip on our separate identity to make room in ourselves for deeper dimensions of who we are. To become a portal for the Higher We, one works to shift one's identity so that, before thought, one's reference point is on the ever-changing process that is unfolding within and around us within the larger process of cosmic evolution. It's a tall order. Such a shift brings one in touch with a depth of non-separation that penetrates and holds all of life—this is the ground of consciousness that holds everything. Simultaneously, one awakens to an evolutionary impulse motivated toward higher integration. One then experiences a new kind of whole that is not a homogenizing, undifferentiated whole, but a differentiated unity in which unique voices and experiences arise without creating fragmentation. One experiences one's sense of self as a focal point of this whole, in which inner and outer are distinct but not separate, and one's particular knowledge and life experience aligns in service to the particular conversation that one is in, which one realizes is an expression of humanity's striving for increasing wholeness.

The Higher We emerges once such a shift is made by enough participants to tip the weight of intention and attention away from just the individual and toward this integrated whole. How many people or what proportion this is, we don't know (this could obviously be consciously explored). Returning to the distinction between being responsive to the Higher We context and responsible for it, many, if not most, participants could make themselves available to engage but were not actively creating and upholding the perspective and depth of consciousness that would enable them to initiate the emergence of the Higher We. The shift of identity was thus situational—a willing suspension of self-focus. It's important to realize, however, that even the willingness to make this shift temporarily is significant.

There are several simultaneous paradoxes that curtailed the ongoing development work with the Higher We at EnlightenNext and led to some of the innovations with Emerge Dialogue Process. Initially, the pyramid hierarchy of a guru-disciple relationship was useful in catalyzing a shift away from a focus on one's individual identity, yet over time this became problematic. So, the first paradox is that the highly individuated human has to give up self-preoccupation to even see the deeper dimensions of self, but to achieve the goal of catalyzing a Higher We, and to create a spirituality for our time, that individuality also has to be preserved, upheld, and also developed (see Stein, 2011). The second paradox has to do with the context of obedience within the older social form of the guru-led pyramid in which individuation didn't exist. In such a context, obedient surrender can be enormously useful to go beyond one's perceived limits, but for ongoing engagement with the Higher We, unindividuated obedience isn't enough, and in fact it can, and did, lead to groupthink. The goal is surrender without regression. The moral authority and autonomy of the individual is essential to sustained Higher We work. While it may have been essential to have very strong direction, if not emotional and moral suasion, coming from a spiritual authority to hold human beings together long enough to pierce this possibility, fundamentally and paradoxically, a pyramid hierarchy conflicts with the ethos and function of the Higher We. The pyramid is pre-individual, with one individual ruling the rest who are not individuated; the Higher We is trans-individual, demanding a fundamental equality of responsibility from participants at their varying levels of capacity.

Emerge Dialogue Process provides a way that the power of the Higher We work can be brought to the service of human creativity without demanding so much of the individuals participating. Only the facilitator needs to have a deep connection to and understanding of the Higher We space, lessening the demand on individuals as well as creating less of a hierarchical structure within the group. Participants can be complete novices or have little experience with the practice themselves. They do not need to shift their identity but only need to shift their attitude, from self-interest to concern for and interest in what is emerging in the group. In fact, the pragmatic intent behind the dialogue—that human beings are coming together to engage in a real concern or issue—supports making this shift in attitude beyond self-importance to the question at hand that is held in the group. The Higher We work reaches one of its evolutionary potentials when it is opened to creative pragmatic use in this process of emergent dialogue. This pragmatism cuts against groupthink, because creativity needs the friction of different perspectives. Egoic conflict thus can become transformed into creative emergence, as we will discuss below.

The Emerge Dialogue Process

The focus on the Higher We within a dialogue context where individuals meet to create solutions or explore some particular pragmatic or intellectual terrain is Emerge Dialogue Process. It catalyzes a freedom from old, stuck patterns of response to release a creative momentum in a group. The intelligence of the whole becomes far more than the sum of its parts. The focus on what is happening between dialogue participants, rather than on individual contributions, allows for more synergistic engagement in the process. Yet, the additional importance of the dialogue's content adds new difficulties: it is easy to become hypnotized by the content, particularly when feelings run high in any direction, whether positive or negative, and lose touch with the potentiality of the intersubjective space. While there are guidelines for engaging in the practice, in order for this type of dialogue to be most successful, the skill of a facilitator who has had a significant awakening to the Higher We context is most often necessary. Below we will speak about the guidelines, important aspects of the facilitator's role, and briefly compare Emerge Dialogue Process with other dialogue practices.

The guidelines for the Emerge Dialogue Process are just that— guidelines. They aren't rules or instructions to be handed out, but potential talking points for the facilitator to use in setting the context for the dialogue. The guidelines that we have developed came from observing how group participants in a Higher We context actually behave when their attention and intention is focused on the living intersubjective process unfolding between them. This creates a context that looks, from the outside, "as if" the members of the collective have made a shift of identity and are consciously awake to the Higher We—which can happen spontaneously—but they only need to shift their attitude. In other words, while a full shift of identification isn't necessary, participants need to set aside their self-importance, sense that "I'm right," superiority/inferiority and other ways of insisting on being separate for the sake of the dialogue process. The less any one person acts out of the habit that one's individual perspective is more important than the intersubjective engagement, the more successful, joyous, and surprising the dialogue will be.

These five guidelines are not injunctions addressed to the individuals who are part of the conversation, but grounding statements that express certain truths about engaging in a Higher We together. Intentionally, the statements primarily reflect the "we," not the separate "I's" who are participating.

1. *Real dialogue arises when we are more interested in what we do not yet know rather than in what we already know.* The position of not knowing and wanting to know creates a space that helps undercut the fixed positions that individuals hold, particularly when the dialogue is about matters that are emotionally significant or have critical implications for the participants. Moreover, listening for what isn't known places the attention of the group on the living moment and the creative potential within it.

2. *It is easy to be too intellectual or too personal. Dialogue comes alive through our shared interest in what emerges, between us, in our developing understanding and in the field of consciousness.* Being too intellectual means speaking in a way that is disconnected from one's own human experience. We can engage in highly philosophical matters when each statement arises from a reckoning with what is real or true. Being too personal means being caught in one's story, which pulls the attention of the group away from creating a shared "we" space. Authenticity in this context means that a broader truth shines through the specificity of individual experience. Engaging from such an authenticity creates a currency of aliveness from which develops deeper comprehension and an increasingly palpable field.

3. *Really listening to each other enables us to develop a conversation that builds on each others' contributions. Really listening allows us to come together in an ever-opening comprehension.* "Really listening" means attending to the field from which the contribution is coming while suspending one's usual habits of reaction and judgment. Really listening means not slotting another's contributions into one's own preconceived ideas or frameworks. From really listening, responses come into shared consciousness that are unexpected and alive. As Daniela Bomatter, an Emerge Dialogue Process facilitator, explains, "This process can catalyze a Higher We when enough people in the group are willing to completely let

282

go of their conditioned minds and listen deeply into the field of consciousness between them."

4. *Every conversation lives through our active participation. Even when you are not speaking at the moment, stay with the others and be with the conversation. Bring yourself fully in.* This is the most directive of the foundations: dialogue demands engagement. This doesn't mean that every participant must speak, however, each needs to pay attention and give oneself energetically to the whole. Otherwise, the circle can have "dark" spots that affect the creative momentum itself and prevent valuable information and perspectives from entering the dialogue.

5. *Each dialogue finds its true meaning in recognizing itself as part of a larger dialogue.* When a group begins to access the Higher We consciousness field reliably, there is often an exhilaration that can very quickly turn into a group narcissism—the hubris of specialness. The desire to engage in dialogue, the movement toward integration, is an evolutionary movement that is happening across the globe. Searching for new possibilities in the face of the increasingly complex problems we face is simply the work we have to do.

Depending on the context, these guidelines can be adapted or revised to meet the needs or level of the participants. The facilitator can use much simpler, directive language in situations where Emerge Dialogue Process is being used in a business/work context for the purpose of facilitating collective work, rather than really seeking creative breakthrough or emergence (e.g., "be more interested in what you don't know rather than the ideas and beliefs that you have brought to the meeting"). For example, in Caritas, a large nonprofit organization, Marlene Pothoff used the process in a hundred-person all-day planning meeting. She trained some of the members of her staff at Caritas to be "facilitators" so that they could understand and work with several aspects of the guidelines (being interested in what you don't know, listening, and building on prior contributions) so that they could lead the process at a table of eight to ten people. She introduced the dialogue process to the whole group, giving them confidence in her competence while maintaining her own awareness of the whole consciousness field, thus "holding the space" for the group. Afterwards, Pothoff noticed that there was a qualitative difference in the consciousness field compared to previous planning meetings: there was greater focus at the tables and a greater intention held by the whole group. However, none of the participants were aware of the difference. Within the context, they responded in new ways, but as individuals, they did not notice that their behavior had changed. More importantly, and pragmatically, many of the teams at the tables came up with creative ideas that had not been considered before. They also worked with much greater cooperation. At the end of the meetings, when a representative of each group was asked to present, the representatives spoke with a simplicity, directness, and clarity that was unusual. Even more interesting was the composure that they expressed when, toward the end of the presentations, the Director decided unexpectedly to shorten the meeting to give himself a longer time to speak. In a situation that usually would have created anxiety and chaos, the group as a whole and the representatives making the final presentations kept their cool and clarity.

Facilitating an Emerge Dialogue Process

While the guidelines provide a strong foundation for engaging in creative dialogue, we find that a facilitator is necessary to provide a portal to the Higher We space so that the dialogue is liberated from the usual grind of meetings or problem-solving. Yet facilitation is an art, and the art of facilitation in an Emerge Dialogue Process is quite demanding because it requires more than mastering a skill set or technique. The facilitator needs to have the subtlety and capacity to awaken the participants to the potentiality space in the collective—often without using terms like "consciousness" or anything that seems esoteric. There isn't a one, two, three process that works every time. The facilitator holds the complexity and tension between perspectives in the group, intervening and guiding the dialogue through a subtle sensing process of building resonance and seeking opening. Often the facilitator catches the very edge of what is new and alive in the dialogue, and risks speaking before knowing, allowing the words to come from the Higher We consciousness rather than from preconceived ideas. It is a form of "presencing," to use Otto Scharmer's (2000) term: the facilitator senses into the potentiality space of the field in which the dialogue is happening and brings into presence the intelligence that becomes apparent through such transrational sensing. Ultimately, the facilitator focuses the consciousness for the group, tunes into the Higher We, which is not simply a passive stance but an active, sensitive engagement.

We've found that facilitators need a solid base in meditation in order to trust enough to let go of the mind's reactions and to stay present in the face of confusion and complexity. The point of the meditation practice is to realize the fullness and nothing-missingness of Emptiness. The consistent practice of meditation enables a letting go of attachment to everything so that, in dialogue, something can arise and come into awareness beyond what we hold in our minds. We break the habit of grasping onto our thoughts and feelings. Through this deep letting go in meditation, one also discovers an impenetrable solidity and strength, an Is-ness that sources everything. When one has confidence in That, which is pure consciousness, then one finds it easier to stay open in the face of conflict or chaos and not lose one's balance. Meditation also creates a sensitivity to consciousness itself—from the powerful silence of Absolute No Thingness to subtle movements and shifts in awareness to the ultimately meaningless raging of the mind and emotions—that consistent sitting practice develops.

We also find the facilitators need to have some experience with the Higher We. This is for several reasons. First, most obviously, without experiencing the Higher We, the facilitator will not be clear about the intersubjective potentiality space and cannot facilitate from it. Yet, equally importantly, explicit Higher We practice helps to purify one's motivation. In a sensitive Higher We field, increasingly subtle self-oriented motives—rather than giving to the whole—become apparent. One can see and feel the places that inhibit us from being able to engage in the potentialities of the intersubjective space. One becomes familiar with one's blind spots and reactive tendencies that make it difficult to be a conduit for a different intelligence. Within the Higher We context, as a collective, these different habits of separation are seen, not as the exclusive problem of the individual, but as a reflection of where we are as human beings. They represent the evolutionary conundrums that we all face. This impersonal view on the most personal human defenses and habits that subtly divide us from each other provides a larger and more liberating perspective on one's self. Both meditation and Higher We practice, taken together, give the facilitator a basis for sensing the alive edge of consciousness in motion within a dialogue.

The facilitator establishes the context for an Emerge Dialogue Process through his or her own confidence in consciousness itself—awake to the living presence, nonseparation, and utter Now-ness of Life. After the facilitator introduces him- or herself, s/he explains the purpose for the conversation and introduces whichever guidelines are appropriate for the context. The details of the introduction (Do the participants know each other? What are their expectations?) are typically arranged in advance. After these basics, the facilitator can invite the group to sit for a few minutes quietly in order to ground the group and open the participants to a wider sense of being present. In this way, the facilitator's depth begins to bring a subliminal coherence to the group as a whole. If this isn't possible because the participants would find it too uncomfortable, reading an inspiring quote about collective dialogue or emergence can also cohere the group in a larger perspective.

With this grounding, the facilitator then opens the dialogue by focusing attention on the potentiality space that exists in intersubjective engagement—the interpersonal We of the group held within the facilitator's deeper awareness of the Higher We that goes beyond those present. The focus of attention is twofold: first, the facilitator invites the participants to sense the potential of the group, and second, s/he holds an awareness of the prior unity underlying and interpenetrating the diversity in the group. Maintaining this deeper awareness is crucial. Particularly as conflicting perspectives come to light and the tensions in the group become apparent, holding an awareness of this whole enables the facilitator to stay alert to opportunities to make unifying distinctions and clarifying integrations within the conversation. Rather than getting trapped in a problem-oriented mindset in which one is trying to come up with solutions, by holding the whole in awareness the facilitator stays with "possibility consciousness"—an attitude in which one realizes that there is always the potential for a surprising resolution or creative emergence that no one can foresee. To hold this attitude means that the facilitator has to be *in* the conversation that s/he is *actually in*. In other words, holding "possibility consciousness" doesn't mean having an idea about the way the process should go or the outcome should be. If one has these ideas, they will destroy the potential of the dialogue because the facilitator will be responding to something that is not the reality in front of him or her. The potential and possibilities for the dialogue cannot come from what one thinks should happen but only from what is actually happening. This is so obviously true that it seems strange to mention it, but time and again, as a facilitator, one feels a creeping dissatisfaction or frustration and interprets this to mean that the "right" things aren't happening. But it is the conclusion—that the dialogue is somehow going wrong—that means that one has stopped engaging "in" the dialogue. Frustration, impatience, irritation have to be born by the facilitator without drawing conclusions about what this means about the dialogue or the participants. Only when one is tuned into the dialogue happening in the intersubjective can one intervene in ways that can catalyze new understanding in the collective.

Emerge Dialogue Process, as we have said, is consciousness aware, process aware, and content conscious. Consciousness awareness refers to the space, or dimension, in which *everything* is occurring. To be process aware means to be attentive to the dynamic unfolding happening in time and space. Content conscious refers to the topic of the dialogue. In a dialogue, the facilitator holds this three-fold focus. Throughout the conversation, the facilitator keeps his or her focus on the Whole and on the living edge of the dialogue rather than becoming engrossed in the content. This takes practice and skill. The facilitator has to respond in the language of the content, but needs to anchor his or her attention in consciousness and unfolding process. In many ways, it's like simultaneously listening to and conducting music, except the "notes" of the music relate to the different shades of space in between. When does it feel shut down, heavy? Where does the heaviness seem to be located? What has weight and gravitas in the conversation? What leaves a hole, a sense that no sense was made? Where are the sharp edges? When is an opening made? What is the rhythm? Following this music, the facilitator supports the dialogue by inviting individuals to continue when an opening happens or by pointing out resonances between speakers or by allowing silences just to be there. Often, but only depending on the capacity of the group, the facilitator can make conscious to the group these different musical strains, which heightens and deepens the awareness in the group itself: did you sense the shift that just happened? Can you feel that there's a heaviness in the room—is there something that needs to be said but hasn't been said? And so on.

Since the facilitator holds the consciousness field for, and hopefully with, the collective, he or she can be particularly challenged to maintain this focus when there is conflict in the group. One has to develop a sense of how much tension the group can hold and stay together. When it becomes too much, the group will almost instantly fragment. Staying calm and not personalizing the tension is really important in order to look for ways to intervene by calling the group's attention to some authentic means of integration, and thus model how the participants can respond to these tensions themselves. Not personalizing the conflict also can be freeing for the participants who are experiencing the contrary perspective. This often means making room for emotions—anger, fear, or tears—but not making them the focus of the conversation. In postmodern interpersonal contexts, we tend to focus on the pain or hurt, giving the individual time and space to process their feelings in ways that, while they may create an empathic connection, also tend to reinforce separation. In an Emerge Dialogue Process, we don't stop or stigmatize the feelings, but we focus on the meaning and intention of the feelings that the individual is bringing into the dialogue and room. When the facilitator responds in this way, by pulling out key points and ensuring that they are part of the mix, the individual integrates into the group and the group, then, as a whole can consider the contributions, work with them, and find a creative way forward. Sometimes, it may be useful and necessary to bring dialogue groups into dialogue with each other—such as across divisions of gender, culture, or race—so that the collective blind spots in one group can be made visible by the other and vice versa.

While sometimes even the best facilitator can be stymied by a participant who does not want to engage in collective inquiry, when these dialogues do catalyze emergence, they are often illuminating and surprising to everyone involved—including the facilitator. The collective feels uplifted, connected in a fresh and light way that they experience as compelling and unusual. Often participants note that they "saw" each other differently, in a new light, as it were. Solutions to stuck points in the organization, between people, and relating to work arise throughout the dialogue process in ways that seem almost too simple. Afterwards, many participants speak of a sense of liberation. And, once a creative momentum develops within the dialogue, the sense that one person "owns" an insight or solution drops away because new ideas seem to emerge from the whole, through individuals certainly, but different participants often say with astonishment that they were thinking the same thing. The solutions are sourced by the field, which is the potentiality space of the We.

Differences with Other Dialogue Practices

While this may already be evident, the Emerge Dialogue Process differs from other contemporary dialogue practices in significant ways. First, it is *transpersonal*. The term "transpersonal" has a specific meaning in psychology, which generally refers to individual development into higher states and stages of conscious awareness (see, e.g., Walsh & Vaughan 1993). Yet we are using "transpersonal" to mean which includes and goes beyond individuality. Perhaps, in fact, a better term is *transindividual*—in which our individuality is both maintained and transcended. Regardless, the focus, anchored by the facilitator, is on the intersubjective, both as a field of consciousness and as an unfolding creative process—the We potentiality space. In other words, attention is *not* on the disparate individuals who make up the group and their subjective experiences. While individual experiences make up the whole, it is the whole and what is happening in the whole that is the priority.

In other words, Emerge Dialogue Process starts from a "We" space not with an "I-You" space. Many important practices for personal development create a sense of "We" through a focus on the feelings and emotional responses of an individual "I" in relation to another, the "You." These practices generate an intimacy and catalyze a sense of togetherness that breaks the isolation of the postmodern separate self (see, for example, Patricia Albere's Evolutionary Collective).

These methods look into the feelings and emotional responses of the participants as a primary driver of insight and dialogue. Some also focus on achieving an interpersonal transparency between the participants—through doing pairing exercises or small groups where individuals speak about their thoughts and feelings as they arise, such as Thomas Hübl's Transparent Communication. Others, in the collective intelligence field, look to gather ideas and insights from as many individuals as possible to see the themes and "shared wisdom" held in the group (see Brown & Isaacs, 2005). In distinction, Emerge Dialogue Process regards individual experience within the context of the whole that is working to integrate and create something new, and so, it tries to amplify the shared field of consciousness that the collective abides within. The attention of the facilitator is on the potentiality space of the We, which is about being conscious of the prior unity that we share and the movement of consciousness in manifestation. In this way, such a dialogue becomes *consciousness aware.*

Second, Emerge Dialogue Process holds *diversity within unity.* This is something different from unity or Oneness. Some dialogue or creative group methods call on the spiritual insight of nonseparation that is experienced in meditation as the foundation for their work. One particularly notable example of such a practice comes from the Adi Da community (see, e.g., Lee, 2009). We have great resonance with their practice of discussion from a position of prior unity. The shared realization, or even assumption, of prior unity enables groups to engage with the creative friction of diversity without falling into factions around identity, thus it is an essential starting point. In our work, though, we have come to realize that diversity is the source of creative potential. Unity without diversity often creates homogenization or groupthink. Diversity without unity creates relativism and division that keeps fragmenting into nihilism. Emerge Dialogue Process allows for multiple perspectives—and in fact, needs them—within a depth field of unity in order to create meaningful integration as a whole.

This leads to the third point: an Emerge Dialogue Process is *process conscious.* The process that we are referring to is the process of the evolution of consciousness itself. While many dialogues or group process methods explore the dynamics arising between individuals (such as Tavistock or the work of the A.K. Rice Institute), this isn't our focus. We are not referring to an interpersonal process, as important as that can be. The process that the facilitator attends to is based on the movement in consciousness toward integration through differentiation. When one is awake to the unfolding process in the whole at the level of consciousness, the dynamics of integration and differentiation become more transparent—visible as a creative momentum. Awareness of process provides both directionality and multiplicity of perspectives because, just as there is only One at the deepest level of Being, the process itself is and can only ever be one entire evolving cosmic whole. Emerge Dialogue Process is an invitation to consciously engage in this cosmic process for pragmatic purposes. The result, for many participants, is a glimpse at a new possibility of being human together. "In the praxis of catalyzing emergent dialogue," notes Emerge Dialogue Process facilitator Nadja Rosmann, "we transcend the division between the spiritual and the profane. There is only ONE life and we try to find out how to express the ONE, and how to live it."

Conclusion

Our hope for our Higher We and Emerge Dialogue Process work is that it can become an instrument for integrating the diverse perspectives on this globe that are now so fragmented and causing such harm. It is needed at every level of our society. The everyday difficulties that we have with getting along in our workplaces and organizations keep good ideas and ethical concerns from guiding us. Beyond these all-too-ordinary difficulties that we humans have in working together, there are far bigger divisions that we have yet to figure out how to work with holistically and creatively. The historical rifts and ruptures between peoples on this planet need to be faced, on all sides, and repaired. To return to Ewert Cousins (1997) again, we need to develop a "complexified global consciousness" that would "not [be] a mere universal, undifferentiated, abstract consciousness. It will be global through the global convergence of cultures and religions and complexified by the dynamics of dialogic dialogue" (section 4, para. 5). The new human capacities that we have seen emerge in the intersubjective potentiality space give us great inspiration and hope that humanity can develop such a global consciousness and find a way forward together, even as so much seems to be falling apart. Our survival depends on realizing that we share one human project on this planet, and our humanness depends on the deeply knowing that we are One and that our differences are essential to the full expression of that One. As the West begins to realize the limitations of Modernist instrumental reasoning and exploitation and Postmodern individualism and consumerism, there are stirrings of a need for a post-personal culture that honors the individual yet holds a larger unifying depth and context. The often desperate search among postmodern Westerners for meaning and purpose is an almost instinctive recognition that we need deeper rooting, real connection, and a higher aspiration than can be found in a materialistic, self-focused life.

Even as hundreds of thousands of people are risking their lives to reach the West, we who have had the privileges that the West affords are, more and more, intuitively reacting against the juggernaut of Modernity because it threatens to turn every aspect of human life and all of nature into a commodity for sale. The Higher We emergence has the potential to deepen our humanity, tighten the web of relationship, and ignite a complex creativity that meets our existential challenges. We consider ourselves, along with the other contributors to this book, to be extremely fortunate to be part of that movement that is awakening We, us, to the urgency and potential of such a transformation. The achievement of individuated identity has been so significant and, as we have come to realize, dangerous for the world we live in together. The emergence of collective thinking, sensing, caring, creating, and knowing offers, as Cousins says, a Second Axial shift in the direction of human life on this planet that couldn't come too soon. Our work and wish is that this Emerge Dialogue Process can be used to further develop our collective capacity for creation and open the door to the Higher We through which we can discover this new potential for being human together.

Author Bios

Thomas Steininger, Ph.D. and **Elizabeth Debold**, Ed.D. respectively a philosopher and a developmental psychologist by training, have each committed over twenty years toward the emergence of higher collective potentials in human consciousness. Both were deeply engaged in the seminal Higher We work at EnlightenNext, which is where they first discovered the potential of the awakened intersubjective for greater creativity between people in a committed group. Steininger had been developing the Emerge Dialogue Process (formerly "Evolutionary Dialouge"), which is a less demanding collective practice than the Higher We work. Steininger and Debold conduct training programs on the Higher We, on facilitation of the Emerge Dialogue Process, and on global dialogue.

References

Brown, J. and Isaacs, D. (2005). The world café: Shaping the world through conversations that matter. San Francisco, CA: Berrett-Koehler.

Cohen, A. & Wilber, K. (2007). The Guru & the Pandit: Dialogue XIV – a living experiment in conscious evolution. What Is Enlightenment? Magazine, 35,46-58.

Cousins, E. (1997). The world religions: Facing modernity together. Retrieved from: http://globalethic.org/Center/ewert_an.htm

Adi Da, (2015). Prior Unity: The basis for a new human civilization. Bethesda, MD: Is Peace 723.

Debold, E. (2002). Epistemology, fourth order consciousness, and the subject-object relationship...or how the self evolves with Robert Kegan. What Is Enlightenment? Magazine, 22, 143-154.

Descartes, R. (1637). Discourse on the method of rightly conducting the reason, and seeking truth in the sciences. Retrieved from: Gutenberg Project E-Text 59: http://www.gutenberg.org/etext/59, release date July 1, 2008

Jaspers, K. (1953). *The origin and goal of history.* (M. Bullock, trans.) New Haven, CT: Yale University Press.

Patten, T. (2013). Enacting an integral revolution: How can we have truly radical conversations in a time of global crisis?" Paper presented at the 2013 Integral Theory Conference, San Francisco, CA.

Phipps, C. (2001). A matter of integrity. What Is Enlightenment? Magazine, 20, 2001, 24-27.

Scharmer, O. (2000, May). Presencing: Learning from the future as it emerges; On the tacit dimension of leading revolutionary change. Retrieved from: http://www.welchco.com/02/14/01/60/00/05/2501.HTM

Stein, Z. (2011). On spiritual teachers and teachings. Journal of Integral Theory and Practice. 6(1), 57-77. Retreived from: http://www.zakstein.org/wpcontent/uploads/2014/10/Stein_SpiritTeachersFINAL-copy.pdf

Venezia, A. (2013, June). I, we, all: Intersubjectivity and We Space, post-metaphysics, and human becoming: An integral research project. (Unpublished master's thesis). John F. Kennedy University, Pleasant Hill, CA.

Walsh, R. & Vaughan, F. (1993). Paths beyond ego: The transpersonal vision. New York, NY: Tarcher.

Wilber, K. (1995). Sex, ecology, spirituality. Boston, MA: Shambhala Publications.

Wilber, K. (2007). Integral spirituality. Boston, MA: Shambhala Publications.

CHAPTER 14

The Miracle of "We"

Ken Wilber

An aspect of Integral Theory that is starting to get a fair amount of attention is what are generally referred to as "We practices"—that is, serious group practices of groups *as* groups, of groups taking up practices acting as a whole group, meant to evolve or transform or otherwise engage the entire group as an entity. This is not just a group of individuals each doing an individual practice together, but a group practicing collectively. There is a common saying: "The next Buddha will be the Sangha (the group of Buddhist practitioners as a whole)." In some cases, this is little more than a green, pluralistic-stage platitude (inasmuch as, for some varieties of green, "individuality" itself is close to a sin, and only group, team, and collective activities are enthusiastically endorsed and actively engaged in). However in other cases, it is something much more significant—the felt recognition that since there is already *an entirely new and higher type of "I" emerging at 2nd tier* (namely, inclusive, embracing, and integral—and actively appreciating all previous stages of development, a historically unprecedented first, a genuine emergent novelty), then there will also be *an entirely new and higher type of "We" emerging as well*, made up of individuals at Integral and higher stages (simply because all phenomena have four quadrants, including an "I" and "We"). What would this higher "We" be like? How can we engage it? What would it feel like? What practices specifically would help us contact this new and higher "We"?

To begin with, it might be noted, for those new to the idea, that according to Integral Theory, every phenomenon in the Kosmos possesses four "quadrants," or four major dimension/perspectives. Every phenomenon in existence can be looked at from the interior and the exterior, and in a singular and plural (or individual and collective) fashion. This gives us four major distinctions—the interior and exterior of an individual and the collective (i.e., a subjective "I" space or Upper-Left quadrant, an intersubjective "We" space or Lower-Left quadrant, an objective "it" space or Upper-Right quadrant, and an interobjective "its" space or Lower-Right quadrant)—that Integral Theory claims are the very distinctions that this manifest universe is built of. And this is true all the way down, all the way up. Even atoms have an interior (which Whitehead called "prehension," or "proto-feeling" or "proto-awareness") and of course an exterior (described as a nucleus with protons and neutrons, with orbiting electrons), and it exists in its typical individual form as well as in various group or collective forms (atoms join other atoms to form molecules, crystals, etc.).

What initially often got people interested in Integral Theory was its developmental component (of "levels and lines") that noted the general agreement among progressive developmental models that, beyond the typical individual self or "I," which places an emphasis on its own separate, individual existence, was what pioneering developmentalist Clare Graves called "a monumental leap of meaning" to an entirely new type of "I," one that emphasized, and felt, a larger, systemic identity with the world at large—and further, unlike any prior stage of development in all of history—believed that every previous stage of development had some sort of importance or significance (unlike those stages themselves, each of which felt the other stages were all childish, goofy, or just plain wrong, while its stage and only its stage had the correct truth and values). This meant this new stage—generally referred to as "2nd tier" to distinguish it from all of the previous or "1st-tier" stages (the same distinction Maslow had referred to as "basic needs" versus "being needs")—was the first stage that was truly comprehensive, genuinely inclusive and embracing, and thus was often given a name like "integrated" (Loevinger) or "integral" (Gebser).

And thus, individuals were hot on the trail of exercises and practices that would help them, if they had not already, make this "monumental leap of meaning" and transform their "I"-space from 1st tier to 2nd tier. Items such as "Integral Transformative Practice" were created to help individuals "integrally transform" to this new and higher "I" space. This particular type of transformation was not available in any of the great Wisdom Traditions or systems of meditation, because the stages of this type of transformation could not be discovered merely by introspecting. Take the stages of moral development, for example: I can sit on my zazen mat for 20 years and never once will I see a thought that says "this is a stage-4 moral thought" or "this is a stage-6 moral thought." The reason is these particular stages are much more like the rules of grammar than like any specific and obvious sentence or string of words—they are the hidden patterns and rules that govern how the words fit together, and these could not be seen by looking within, but only by studying large groups of people and seeing what rules they were all following. Just as if you look within right now, you can't see the rules of grammar that you are otherwise following perfectly, so you can't look within and see the stages of this particular type of development. Now the interesting fact is that, for any individual brought up in a particular language-speaking culture, they will end up speaking that language quite correctly—they will put subjects and verbs together correctly, they will use adjectives and adverbs correctly, and all-in-all they will end up following the rules of grammar quite correctly. But if you ask any of them to write down what those grammar rules are, none of them can do so. In other words, they are following these extensive sets of rules, but not one of them knows that they are doing so, let alone what the specific rules are. The stages of this particular developmental process that had just revealed a 2nd-tier stage are like the grammar rules governing each stage—they can't be seen by looking within, and are generally referred to as stages of Growing Up.

These are unlike the stages of Waking Up, which deal with direct, 1st-person, immediate and obvious experiences such as those had in meditative and contemplative paths of development—if you have an experience of "being one with all things in a state of universal love-bliss," you will definitely know it! Further, the paths of Growing Up—with their hidden rules—and the paths of Waking Up—with their obvious experiences—are relatively independent developmental axes, so that you can be quite highly developed in one of them— say, Waking Up—and poorly developed in the other—in this case, Growing Up. The oddity is that, until Integral Theory pointed out the existence of both of these axes, nowhere in history were these two paths brought together, thus allowing training in both of them to occur simultaneously. Things like Integral Transformative Practice and Integral Life Practice were concerned with ways to increase this Growing Up dimension while also practicing meditative and contemplative exercises to increase the Waking Up dimension—a combined training that was a true historical first.

So individuals began taking up various transformative practices— in addition to their regular meditative or contemplative practices— in order to reach into these higher dimensions of their own Growing Up. And as that progressed, more and more people in the integral community began to notice that this "I" space is *always* connected to some sort of "we" space or spaces, and if there was indeed a higher "I," there had to be a higher "we." And thus integral attention began switching more and more to this intrinsic perspective/dimension of all reality—this rather miraculous "we" space and "we"-space practices.

One of the most astonishing, miraculous, stunning, and mysterious events in the entire Kosmos is that one being—let's say a human in this example—can actually reach a mutual understanding with another human being—that they can look each other in the eye and say, "I understand what you mean." If we take the general conclusion of the great Wisdom Traditions—that there is ultimately one and only one Spirit and Self in the entire Kosmos—then it is as if this one and only Self of the Kosmos has illusorily "split" and "divided" itself into billions of individual selves, and two (or more) of those selves can, playing on the underlying unity between them, mutually resonate with and mutually understand the other. If you want to see evidence of Spirit, look no further than right here, in what I call "the miracle of the We." It's one thing for something to come from nothing; quite another for one of those somethings to look at another something and say, "I know what you mean." The ultimate One Mind showing up as two, and being able to establish that oneness through something like communication: what else is mutual understanding but a hidden reaffirmation of the singleness of Consciousness underlying the communication, a miracle if ever there was one, the miracle of We.[1]

The "We"-space is, of course, the Lower-Left quadrant, the intersubjective domain, which, as noted, I maintain goes all the way down and all the way up. What we find in human cultures is, in the Lower Left, a "layer cake" of holarchical dimensions of structure-Views (or the stages in Growing Up) in any situation where human beings congregate, work together, play together, or otherwise exist together. "Layer cake" (with reference to the developmental stages in this overall axis of Growing Up) means this: since every human is born at square one (the first major stage of this developmental process, however conceived) and begins its growth and development from there, stage by stage by stage, each group or collective of humans consists of individuals at various stages of this growth, forming an overall "layer cake" of developmental strata (much like any geological formation, to switch metaphors, with the older layers at the bottom and the newer, higher levels at the top, and all sorts of developed levels in between, laid out in the chronological order they emerged). In most groups—to use Gebser's version of this Growing Up in worldviews as a simple

---

1. Erwin Schroedinger, the cofounder of modern quantum mechanics, said that "Consciousness is a singular, the plural of which is unknown"—and yet communication and "we" spaces depend upon that plurality—as if one Spirit pretended to divide itself into two parties so as to have a relationship, and that indeed is a something of a "miracle."

example of many—there will therefore be a percentage of those at Magic, a percentage at Mythic, and then, depending on the group and its aims (and thus whom it attracts), possibly a percentage at Rational, a percentage at Pluralistic, and a percentage at 2nd-tier Integral (in addition to a possible group at any higher levels that might exist— several models suggest at least a few higher stages in Growing Up).

In organizations, these layer cakes will often be predisposed and weighted to a particular stage (and thus possess a disproportionately thick layer at that level), depending on the job or the department or the area in which the individual works: so with on-the-floor or assembly line work, a greater percentage at conformist Mythic (who excel at rote repetitive tasks); in middle management and sales, at modern Rational (who thrive on achievement, accomplishment, and success); in human resources and public relations, at postmodern Pluralistic (whose "sensitive self" flourishes in helping and supporting customers); in upper management, at least a cognitive line at Holistic or Integral (or overall 2nd tier—the best of these often fit the descriptions of Jim Collins' "5th Level Leaders" or Spiral Dynamics' "Spiral Wizards"). Jacque Eliot's work has documented this "layer cake" nature of most organizations, certainly when it comes to cognitive development and associated job or task, where his research indicated clearly that the level of individual cognitive development naturally gravitates toward the complexity of the particular task required—with the greater the complexity of the task, the higher the level of cognitive development one tends to actually find in individuals doing well (and thus succeeding) at that job. This is the "layer cake" in real action.

Often, the success of a company's culture depends upon (accidentally or intentionally) matching the individual (with a particular level of development) with the job or office or task that especially draws on that specific level of development, so that the human skill set/aptitude and the vertical job-task complexity fit together nicely, matching *altitude* and *aptitude* (as in the above examples).

Many business consultants focus merely on "aptitude" and "skill" training to help business individuals become more successful—thus focusing only on the "horizontal" skill set of the individual, and teaching him or her new skills or ways to refurbish their old skills to become more effective, more efficient, and more successful. But a newer class of business consultants also realizes the profound importance of not just horizontal "aptitude" but also vertical "altitude"—or the degree or level of consciousness possessed by the individual and thus the degree of complexity that individual can handle. And hence they focus not just on teaching new skill sets, but on practices that help individuals grow and evolve their altitude of consciousness (the level of their basic structures and Views—the vertical stage of their

Growing Up). From Robert Kegan to Dave Logan to Dean Andersen to Stagen Associates to the Air Force Academy to—well, to many (rapidly increasing) numbers of others, who have taken due notice of the steadily increasing number of studies that show that *degree or altitude of development* is a crucial, and in many cases singularly indicative, determinant in the degree of success in leadership.

The inclusion of the We-dimension as an inherent component of Reality in Integral Theory has meant that, virtually from the start, the We-dimension has been given special attention. And, as we earlier noted, one of the more recent movements has been the particular focusing on the development of intensive practices and groups oriented especially toward common We-experiences and, to a certain degree, a common We-consciousness—although treading lightly is required here, since social holons do not possess an "I," or what Whitehead called a "dominant monad"; they possess instead a dominant mode of discourse or a dominant mode of resonance. For example, when my dog gets up and moves across the room, 100% of its organs, cells, molecules, and atoms get right up and move with it. But no group or society or organization has anywhere near that type of totalistic control, such that the governing mechanism of the group governs 100% of everything its members do. That's simply impossible. Rather, the governing "nexus"—or "nexus-agency"—of the group provides certain rules, values, guidelines, ethics, and semantics that influence, to one degree or another, its members. But there is no "super-I" that fully controls every member of the group. In other words, the relation of a member to a group is not the same as the relation of a cell to an organism, or a part to a machine—there is no "super-organism" or "Leviathan" to which all members of the "We" are welded (and no social group, society, nation, etc. is a "big organism"). Rather, members are partners in a network of intersubjective and interactive capacities, said network governing some, not all, of the members' actions. We have to be careful here because there is a tendency to treat, for example, Gaia as a super-organism or super-I, whereas it is more of a song harmonizing its various members' notes, not a machine controlling all of its parts with perfect totalitarian control.

So what we find in the real world—and in real groups and collectives and "We's"—is a "layer cake" of different structures (and states)—that is, different stages—of development, with each layer containing a nexus-agency that exerts a significant influence on the members also at that layer—and then overall, a main central cultural layer or nexus-agency, which particularly defines the group's overall characteristics—and how the group specifically and officially defines itself (Mythic, Rational, Pluralistic, Integral, etc.)—and this exerts a particularly strong influence on its members whose center of gravity is at the same basic level as the group's central level (and this cluster of individuals would, in most cases, be the cluster that would be expected to be the largest, since it is attracted to this particular group precisely because of the group's particular value system that the member shares and wishes to participate in and to advance).

Thus, to give an extremely simple example, take a fundamentalist Christian church group. Given its Mythic-level View and characteristics, its "layer cake" will have a few individuals at Magic (who interpret the religion in Magic terms); a slightly higher percentage of individuals at Magic-Mythic (who interpret the religion in "PowerGods" terms); and the bulk of percentage of individuals—probably close to 70%, 80%, even 90%—will have their structure center of gravity at Mythic-literal (the same as the group's central nexus), and thus that layer of the "layer cake" will be particularly thick and influential; and finally, a smaller percentage at higher levels—a few at Rational, fewer still at Pluralistic. Each of those layers will have (implicitly or explicitly) a nexus-agency that the members at that level tend to follow; and the overall social holon itself will have a basic central organizing level (in this case, Mythic-literal), which is the origin of a "dogma" nexus-agency, meant to govern all individuals who are members of that church's particular orthodox View of its religion. This "dogma" nexus-agency consists of the beliefs, values, ethics, worldviews, and semiotic meanings that are "kosher" for that church, and are meant to be embraced by all those who identify themselves as members of that church (you are "in" the church when your religious thoughts are "internal" to the church's dogma nexus). The bulk of this "dogma" nexus-agency (in the Lower Left) will come from the deep structures of the Mythic-literal View; and of course will be strongly influenced by factors from the Upper Right (the actual behaviors that are allowed and that are banned or disallowed); the Lower Right (the actual physical forms and patterns of the church organization itself, including even things like the simple layout of the physical spaces used in worship); and the Upper Left (particularly the psychograph and character type of the "leader" of this particular congregation; and in general the "acceptable psychograph" that all members are expected to reflect). Then, as for the particular features or surface structures of the dogmatic beliefs, this church's actual version of all of the specific beliefs, stories, concepts, narratives, and notions of the particular religion itself at that level (the Mythic-literal level) of spiritual development, as interpreted through the idiosyncrasies (in all four quadrants) of this particular church and its leaders.

As individuals enter the topographical space in the AQAL Matrix[2] that defines a particular religious service (e.g., going to a Sunday church service), they will have their entire psychographic being-in-the-world temporarily merged or conjoined, to one degree or another, with the church's sociograph (containing the ideal member psychograph); and the nexus-agency of the resultant sociocultural holon will, for as long as the individual is in that topographical space, exert a strongly (but not totalistically) governing influence on each individual's thoughts, feelings, ideas, awareness, and behavior.

What's interesting is that the members of this church, whose psychographs can shift significantly to fit with the overall dogmatic sociograph of the church itself when and while they are in its topographical space, will often find a significantly different psychograph is activated when they are in different circumstances with different sociographs and different "layer cakes." Many scientists, for example, manage to segregate their religious and scientific views, and thus, while at their scientific work or job, will likely be in a social holon with a sociograph and "layer cake" that has the thickest layer of the cake at Rational (or higher), and thus they will, in that particular topographical space of the AQAL Matrix, be resonating, not with their Mythic beliefs, but with their Rational scientific beliefs. The "layer cake" of the "We" at work is significantly different from the "layer cake" of the "We" when they are at church, and they manage to simply separate these different and contradictory beliefs, compartmentalizing their lives and handing each over to a different "layer cake," sociograph, and conjoined psychograph. Sometimes they will work at ways to "hold together" their differing beliefs—imagining, for instance, that when the Bible says the Lord created the world in 6 days, a "day" for the Lord might be a million or billion of years, and thus their science and their religion can indeed fit together (other contradictions between the two are brought together in similar, not always convincing, ways).

The point is that all individuals exist in a wildly large number of different "We's," each with its own "fingerprint" or "layer cake" composed of different percentages of layers and Views at considerably different levels of development, and the predominant defining nexus-agency of any social holon will have to be at an altitude—that a particular structure-level of the individual can resonate with—in order to become a functioning member of that particular group or collective.

---

2. "AQAL" is short for "all quadrants, all levels, all lines, all states, all types," which is the general name of the Integral Theory I have presented. All individuals are maintained to have all 5 of these basic dimensions, and their "Kosmic address" is their overall location in the AQAL Matrix space that they are located.

If a specific group's dominant nexus-agency (or cultural center of gravity) is at, for example, Rational, then that group will especially attract individuals at the Rational level-stage of development.

In order to be a genuinely functioning member of a group, the individual must possess a structure-level and its View that is at least as developed as the central nexus-agency of the particular group. Thus, an individual whose structure center of gravity is Magic may be physically "in" a group whose nexus-agency is Pluralistic, but that individual's communication will not be "internal" to the group—or an actual functioning member—because there are two or three levels of being and consciousness in the group that are "over his head," and whose communications will simply not make full sense to him. He'll never quite "get" what the group is about—its central values, aims, goals, or ethics. Physically he might be "in" the group, but mentally he is not, and thus he actually stands as an outsider to the group's main activities, even though he is physically fully present.[3]

A Higher "We"

One of the experiences of individuals practicing together, particularly when most of them are at 2nd tier or higher, is that of being in a "group mind" or something that *seems* like an individual organism—it's not actually that, as we have seen (it's physically impossible), but phenomenologically it feels almost as if it is; and the point is simply that, particularly with higher levels of development, those higher levels of consciousness involved can start to feel their intersubjective connections in a very strong, palpable way. Some groups have begun mapping the common stages that groups seem

---

3. This is the problem, for example, of creating "teams" at work, when the only criteria for being a team member are exterior—e.g., a set of behavioral skills, physical proximity to the group, and so on—and not taking into account their interior realities—such as the team member's actual center of gravity in vertical altitude. A team that is predominantly oriented around a Pluralistic nexus-agency may have several team members working in the same physical area, but whose centers of gravity are Magic and Mythic, and those individuals will never be actual members of that team, no matter how closely together they are located. A member's "fitting" into a team is a matter of fitting into all four quadrants of the team's characteristics— including, of course, levels—and if that doesn't happen, the individual will never be a true member of the team, no matter how close in physical proximity the person is. This person will consistently fail to grasp the team's priorities and goals, and constantly be the source of the team continuing to perform poorly. This will confuse managers who don't take vertical dimensions into account, because this person's skill set might be exceptional.

to go through, from things like pre-conventional to conventional to post-conventional to integral and unified. What is happening, I believe, is that in these cases, higher and higher *state-realms* are being simultaneously experienced by the members, and as that heads toward the ultimate Nondual ("One Mind") condition, then that Unity condition is increasingly reflected through each and every individual, with a correlative feeling of each person being "part" of a "single" Consciousness (which is true in a certain sense, just not in a literal "single Leviathan" or "single organism" sense).[4]

The I-We-It dimensions of the AQAL Framework (the "Big 3" or the four quadrants) show up in Buddhism, we have noted, as Buddha-Sangha-Dharma, with Buddha being the ultimate "I-I" or consciousness domain, Sangha being the ultimate "We" or group/collective domain, and Dharma being the ultimate "It" or Thusness domain. The point is that the "We practices" outlined here are exploring the leading-edge of the Sangha domain. This is an important, evolutionarily cutting-edge realm of recent research and practice, and any current Integral Theory and Practice might want especially to keep an eye on this Lower-Left quadrant.

There are, at this time, several individuals who are actively exploring and experimenting with various "We practices." What follows is a very narrow and somewhat arbitrary selection of several of them to discuss, just to show what is involved. I certainly mean

---

4. The stages of Growing Up consist basically of *structures* of consciousness, whereas the stages of Waking Up consist basically of *states* of consciousness. Structures are 3rd-person, subconscious, rules and patterns governing thought and behavior (governing interpretation and experience); they are like the hidden rules of grammar we discussed; they cannot be seen by introspecting, only by studying large numbers of people and determining what they all have in common. Individuals at a particular structure-stage of development (in Growing Up) have no idea that they are following its rules and patterns (e.g., Magic, Mythic, Rational, Pluralistic, Integral), and yet, like the rules of grammar, they follow them faithfully without knowing it. States of consciousness, on the other hand, are 1st-person, direct, immediate experience that are fully conscious when they occur, and can be tracked easily by the individual him- or herself. The paths of meditation and contemplation consist of various "nonordinary" states of consciousness as they unfold from the narrow, partial, fragmented ego states to ultimate states of "supreme identity" of the individual with the groundless Ground of Being, a nondual "unity consciousness" known as Enlightenment, Awakening, moksha, satori, the Great Liberation. Virtually all Western models of development deal only with structures (so they have no items such as Enlightenment or Awakening); and all meditation paths deal with states, so they have no understanding of the hidden rules or patterns of Growing Up that even their meditation experiences are being interpreted by. Again, it is only recently that both of these developmental axes have been recognized together and thus have been able to be practiced together.

no judgment on the many approaches that space prevents me from discussing—virtually all of them have very important contributions.

Perhaps one of the earliest influences on the we-space was David Bohm, who maintained, in his book *On Dialogue*, that the world is in a dire state largely because of self-centered, fragmented thinking. What Bohm proposed was a new process of thinking—driven by his particular approach to dialogue, where group's suspend assumptions and judgments through a deeper process of being aware of our thought process and its limiting nature. For Bohm, this we-process would open the door to deeper insight and creative thinking capable of dealing with the world crisis. Varela (in work that Sharmer developed later on for his purposes), recommended a process of becoming aware that is based on (1) the *suspension* of past associations and knowledge; (2) *redirection* of awareness to the timeless present source and away from the object, co-enacting a group field; and (3) *letting go* (and *"letting come"*), and away from "looking for." Scharmer adapted this into his U process, which also deals with the three major states of consciousness (namely, gross, subtle, and causal). The U process involves getting a detailed overall awareness of the gross problem; shifting into subtle awareness and viewing the issue from that richer and fuller vantage point; then drawing on the causal source, will, and creativity to allow for new solutions; moving those back down into their subtle dimensions for fleshing out; and then finally materializing the solution in the gross realm (hence, gross to subtle to causal back to subtle back to gross). Andrew Cohen recommended a type of "intersubjective yoga" (Lower-Left quadrant) where the individual lets go of self-identity and instead identifies with awareness itself (and "the ground of being") and especially identifies with the evolutionary impulse per se and its urgency, and then letting this evolutionary intelligence speak through every group member. When done correctly, this is often reported as feeling like a "group enlightenment."

Gunnlaugson has done considerably important work on establishing second-person we-space approaches to higher education, examining intersubjectivity from numerous perspectives. For example, with M. Moze in an important work on the we-space "Surrendering into Witnessing: A Foundational Practice for Building Collective Intelligence Capacity in Groups." Thomas Hübl has done some profound work on, for example, taking gross shadow material manifesting behaviorally and reading "behind" or "beneath" it into subtle and causal factors, and working with a field of an "us without a them." Decker Cunov and his colleagues at Boulder Integral Center have adapted and advanced practices such as "circling," where members of the group are taught to focus on others and to openly, honestly report all feelings and reactions moment to moment. This can lead to moments of extraordinary intimacy in the group as a whole. Dustin DiPerna and colleagues have been working with what they call "we-practice" that seems to involve the "we" itself evolving through several level/stages of Growing Up ("conventional, personal, impersonal, interpersonal, transformational, awakened, evolutionary, and Kosmic"). While I am in general and strong agreement with this work, it should at least be mentioned that this is a delicate and complicated issue, because the "we" itself does not possess a dominant monad but a dominant mode of resonance or discourse. What that means, as we earlier put it, is that when an individual holon, such as my dog, gets up and walks across the room, 100% of its cells, molecules, and atoms get right up and move across the room as well— because of its dominant monad (and governing agency). But no group or collective has anywhere near that sort of control over its members, who rather "resonate" with each other (in the "layer cake") depending upon their own Kosmic address or psychograph. Thus, the levels that DiPerna discovered might very well be connected to a specific set of individuals with specific psychographs—all members were at (green) Pluralistic or (teal) Integral or higher; all had access to higher states; all had done shadow work, and so on. It's not clear that a (red) Magic group would—or even could—move through those same levels in that same order. But this is important exploratory research that I fully support.

Terry Patten has made important theoretical research and living experimentation with "we practices," including many of those mentioned above, and his "Integral Trans-Rhetorical Praxis." His first step is to describe, in 3rd-person terms, the general Integral Theory involved; then he switches to a type of 1st-person confessional mode and talks about exactly how he is feeling in the moment as he tries to convey ideas that some people will find silly, threatening, unnecessary, and so on. This is an open, naked—and, as we noted, *confessional*— mode. This shifts the stage from abstract philosophical terms to deeply personal and intimate terms. He then addresses the group in a "ragged truth telling" and invites them to adopt a similar type of dialogue. If this actually connects—sometimes it does, sometimes it doesn't—the whole process leaps into a type of hyper-space of collective intelligence, where the "We" itself seems to be learning how to process and function in this new atmosphere. At this point, every perspective (1st-, 2nd-, and 3rd-person), every type of discourse (framing, advocating, illustrating, inquiring), every mode of exploration (trans-rhetorical, trans-rational, transpersonal) can all come into play, each under the aegis of this group intelligence. When it works, it generates—as do many of these practices—feelings of joy, inspiration, spiritual sacredness, creativity.

Excitement has been generated by these practices that Tom Murray, in an understandable and helpful response (called "Meta-Sangha, Infra-Sangha: Or, Who Is This 'We,' Kimo Sabe?" in *Beams and Struts*), notes that much of the discussion in this area is diffuse, poorly defined, and nebulous. These various practices can, he points out, actually be involved in (1) feelings, (2) shared meaning, (3) state experiences, (4) an emergent collective entity, or (5) collective action. And, of course, he's right. And, in my opinion, that's not a problem, that's exactly as it should be.

The real problem confronting the "we practices" is simply the problem of evolution itself. Evolution has just barely poked its head into 2nd tier in individuals; of course, any number of individual "I's" at 2nd tier will of necessity generate a number of corresponding "We's" at the same altitude (teal or turquoise—"Holistic" or "Integral"—in this case; occasionally higher). But, as a community, we don't yet know how to reliably transform individuals into 2nd tier. Transformation isn't understood well in psychology on the whole. It's not clear exactly what factors consistently produce transformation, and which one's don't. Kegan correctly points out that developmental transformation involves the right combination of "challenge and support"—but exactly what is challenged, and exactly what is supported in our experience?

People are almost always drawn to "integral" approaches because they first read an account of development and its higher Integral stages, and they got a profound "Aha!" experience—"this exactly describes me!"—and in most of their cases, that is not an arrogant over-estimation, but a profoundly relieving realization that they are not crazy, that their way of looking at the world—holistic, systemic, integrated, whole—is not off the wall, as almost everybody around them seems to think, but is in fact a genuine stage of real human development that has more depth and more height and more width than any previous stage in history, and they have finally found something that makes sense of this to them.

But the point is that *exactly* how they came to be at an Integral stage, no psychologist really and fully understands. Everybody has some sort of theory—as noted, for psychoanalysis, it's a consistently applied "selective frustration," giving the present level enough satisfaction to keep it healthy, but not enough to keep it fixated or embedded; and for Robert Kegan, it's the right combination of "challenge and support"—challenging the present level, and supporting higher-level responses. Precisely how any of those actually applies to every action, nobody really fully understands.

When it comes to "We" practices, all that is certain is that with regard to the same "Aha!" experience that the individual had when he or she first discovered Integral, they absolutely know it must be possible to discover its correlate in the "We" dimension (every Upper-Left quadrant has a correlate in the Lower-Left quadrant—since all four quadrants tetra-enact). *This "higher I" that they have discovered must have a "higher We" as a correlate*, and they are hot on the trail of that. They also realize that the discovery and elaboration of this "Integral We" is something of a prerequisite for implementing Integral institutions in the Lower-Right quadrant.[5] The urgency of finding Integral "We's" thus couldn't be greater given the general series of world crises we are now facing.

For the first time in history, virtually all of our truly serious and wicked problems are global in nature. Even fifty years ago, if a nation was facing serious problems, it could take actions itself to ameliorate them. Now, today, most serious problems are such that actions taken by any single nation are largely worthless—virtually all nations have to participate: the problem is global, the solution must be global. America, for example, could completely cut its carbon emissions, and that wouldn't affect global warming in any significant fashion at all. Virtually every nation—and every person—on the planet has to participate. The same is true of the world's financial crisis, environmental degradation in general, starvation, the water crisis, global terrorism, over-population, species extinction, warfare, planetary health crisis and runaway global viral infections, geopolitical conflicts, and world governance to name a few. It is likely no accident that as humankind's problems, for the first time in history, have become global—requiring global solutions—humankind is also developing levels of consciousness that are, also for the first time in history, genuinely and deeply global, Kosmocentric, Integral. Global problems, global solutions, global consciousness—all of a piece. Integral is not just an armchair philosophy, but a clear-cut road to any inhabitable future at all.

But evolution moves as it does. Mike Murphy reminds us that evolution "meanders more than it progresses," and the same is true of the general Integral stages of evolution themselves—and in every quadrant (I, We, It, and Its). Again, not much more than 5% of the population is at Integral levels, and that population has not yet learned to self-identify (i.e., most of the people at Integral stages don't know

---

5. People keep forgetting that Integral solutions to problems require individuals actually at Integral levels of development. This is not just learning a new theory or learning a new skill or implementing a new tool—it is an actual overall multi-dimensional *vertical stage in development* that must be lived, that must be actually grown and developed, and without that, all we have are Integral opinions, not Integral realities. Integral actions—in the Lower Right—require Integral individuals in the Upper Left and Integral "We's" in the Lower Left manifesting as real behavior in the Upper Right—as actual developmental realities, not just theories.

they are at those stages). So the fact that "We practices" can wander all over the areas pointed out by Tom Murray is not only understandable, it's desirable. We are learning how to address all of those areas—from feelings to shared meanings to state experiences to collective action—from Integral perspectives, and there are as yet no guide books here at all. All we can be assured of is that Eros will continue its unrelenting pressure to transform in all four quadrants, and human beings will respond to that drive, come what may. Evolution, like so many learning processes, operates through trial and error—and so, across the Integral board—we are seeing many trials, many errors—and a slow, inexorable growth to greater Truth, Goodness, and Beauty.

One last thing about "We's" in general and "We practices" in particular. The psychograph of *each individual* in a particular group will be a determining factor in the depth or height that the group itself can achieve. With 5% of population at Integral, a group with only 5% of its members at Integral will never be able to form an Integral "We"—the mutual resonance (and overall governing nexus-agency) will be at considerably lower levels in the "layer cake" (hence, "We practices" are mostly taken up today by explicitly Integral organizations, where a good majority of individuals involved are already at Integral levels or higher). Integral is sometimes described as "an elitism"—and that's absolutely true, but it's an elitism to which all are invited. It is simply unavoidable that individuals who will find "Integral" ideas anywhere near attractive are largely those who are themselves at Integral levels of development in the first place, and at this time, that is relatively rare (as we said, perhaps 5%). The same is true of "Integral We" practices, and these prerequisites simply must be acknowledged, delicate as the topic is. Although one of the points of an Integral approach to any problem is to language that issue in as large a number of levels as possible (Magic, Mythic, Rational, Pluralistic, Integral, and Super-Integral—as with the "conveyor belt" of spirituality), this doesn't mean to cavalierly overlook Integral itself.[6] The Integral level in individuals is

---

6. The "conveyor belt" is a term in AQAL Integral Theory referring to the role that religion can play in the modern and postmodern world. There are, today, individuals at every major level of development (e.g., Magic, Mythic, Rational, Pluralistic, and Integral) who subscribe to a particular great Religion (whether Christian, Muslim, Jewish, Buddhist, Hindu, Taoist, etc.). An ideal situation would thus be to have religions, after recognizing that their members span the entire developmental spectrum, create level-specific versions of their main teachings—moving from egocentric to ethnocentric to worldcentric to Kosmocentric levels of Growing Up—thus acting as paces of transformation for humanity at large. No other discipline can do this, because no other discipline has adherents at all levels—science is a largely Rational endeavor; but there are Magic Christians, Mythic Christians, Rational Christians, Pluralistic Christians, and Integral Christians. If religions realized this,

a prerequisite for "Integral We" practices (although anybody can be invited to those practices; but realize that an "Integral" depth of the "We" will not be achieved in any group where the majority of those individuals are not themselves at Integral).

What is particularly important for an Integral Spirituality is the realization that, just as there is an entirely new and historically unprecedented "I" space emerging (with a radically new capacity for higher inclusiveness and caring—and a deeper Enlightenment process reflecting this higher "I"), so there is a new and higher "We" space, or Sangha, that is also emerging, and it, too, is historically unprecedented in many of its characteristics (including access to fundamental forms of intersubjective intelligence never before seen or experienced by humans). There's not only a new and higher "I" or Buddha (at higher structure-rungs of existence) and a new and higher "It" or Dharma (or Truth that includes not only that disclosed by states but also structures), there is also a new and higher "We" or Sangha (with a substantially more inclusive nature and vibrant group intelligence).

But what is central for an Integral Spirituality is not that it focus merely on the collective "We," but that it integrate all four quadrants in each and every moment—the "I," the "We," and the "It"—self, culture, and nature—all brought together in the fresh aliveness and radiant Presence of the Present. The new Buddha is not going to be the Sangha, but the unification of the Buddha, Sangha, and Dharma in a single ongoing nondual Awareness and Awakening.

---

they could become a genuine force of vertical transformation for the world at large, instead of being—as most of them are—in a case of arrested development at the Mythic level (what Fowler called "Mythic-literal"—the 3rd in his 6-7 stages of the Growing Up of faith or spiritual intelligence).

Author Bio

Ken Wilber is best known for his contribution to Integral Theory. He is among the most widely translated philosophers in America, with 25 books translated into some 30 foreign languages. He currently lives in Denver, Colorado, where he continues to write and publish on the subject of Integral thought.

CHAPTER 15

We-Space Practice, the Future, Circling and All There Is

Sean Wilkinson & John Thompson

Introduction

WE practice is a spearhead in the evolution of psychological/ spiritual development. It has the potential to enhance and also go beyond the fulfilling of a personal awakening or embodiment, pointing to a new and powerful frontier in developing collective consciousness. The unfolding set of practices brings more depth, love, wisdom and integrity to the individual while simultaneously fulfilling a fundamental yearning for communion and mastery in relating with others. This work has the promise of inspiring and evolving human relations in the twenty first century in the same way that therapy, coaching and meditation[1] have done in the last century.

As Integral practitioners, we have been captivated and compelled by a group practice called Circling. Circling is guided by simple principles into a deep inquiry and cultivation of presence, connection and aliveness. The practice, as we are developing it, is guided by ongoing surrender to what is revealed in connection. This surrender to the essential nature of connection has led us to an increasingly simplified form that makes the practice easy to learn and immediately effective. At the same time, this simple method creates continual self

---

1. Though mediation has been around for thousands of years, the comment refers to how much it has impacted the last century, especially in Western Culture where it has really become a more widespread and more understood practice. This development has felt essential for the emergence of Circling that has utilized learning from the meditative traditions applied to relationship.

transformation that we believe is unique. Although other practices include authenticity as a key part of their form, Circling has an emphasis on a radical honesty that we personally have not seen elsewhere. Although it catalyzes deeper therapeutic and transpersonal insights and experiences, it is still about developing real, in the moment connection in all relationships. In this way it does not require participants to have any kind of training or developed awareness to enjoy the practice and still be part of a deep transmission.

We want to demonstrate here the simplicity, authenticity and depth of Circling. For this we will outline the deeper principles of the practice, tell our own story to bring color to what is possible individually and with the larger community growing around this practice and how this has led to the development of a deeper group practice that we are calling "All There Is."

What Is Circling?

Circling combines the meditative wisdom of being with what is arising, as it is, while cultivating the intimacy of being with others. Instead of focusing our attention on breath, body or a mantra, the point of focus includes what the felt sense of connection is like in the We and sharing this together. However, authentic sharing is not just bold and blunt honesty; it is connecting in an artful way that takes the deepest responsibility for the full range of our experience in each moment. Thus, Circling becomes both a radical truth *and* nourishing relationship. It is about embracing a greater acceptance and awareness, as is primary to meditation, into the real, living connections between people. This could mean sharing the raw forms of our disgust, awkwardness, or judgment of others while being open to their vulnerability in receiving these expressions. It can also be about sharing our in-the-moment wisdom, empathy and love for others in a way that feels true and grounded rather than sentimentalizing, which can create less trust in the connection.

In Circling, the subjective sense of connection in relationship becomes an object in awareness. With practice, this subtle sense of connection becomes palpable and opens us to a new world within the invisible forces that connect us. It is much like how a microscope reveals a whole world of complexity in a drop of water. In this way, being in conscious connection enhances attention and, usually, the capacity to access subtle and causal states[2] within the individual that are often

---

2. Although unique to each individual, subtle and causal states can be recognized

harder to access in a personal meditation practice. This self-awareness is being fostered while simultaneously developing higher capacities to connect with others. Examples of these capacities include: the ability to speak from our personal truth, the capacity to listen deeply beyond words to what the other is communicating, feeling a deeper empathy and literacy of the emotions of self and other, seeing and accepting ways of being that are normally shamed and hidden, an increasing ability to see and speak unconscious personal and relational patterns as they occur, and the ability to recognize when abstract or impersonal expression is deepening or limiting intimacy.

Circling is different from therapeutic approaches (and many meditative We practices) in its emphasis on authenticity. Authenticity in our understanding is a discovery of what is true in the moment and goes a stage further than honesty. One can be honest and inauthentic due to unknowingly not paying close enough attention to what is present at a deeper level; authenticity has to be discovered in each moment and often requires inquiry and support from others. Authenticity to us also means that no one is receiving or acting specifically for the sake of someone else's well-being or awakening. Although in doing this we believe it to be in a deeper service of other's well being and awakening. The deeper intention is therefore about developing presence and connection regardless of whether that is deemed therapeutic or spiritually awakening. It is about revealing as much truth as possible into the room and being in connection around that, in meeting it, being open to and holding all the perspectives that are present. In this way there is a trust in the intelligence of presence and connection combined rather than a rational knowing of what is best in the moment. This might seem obvious, but in our experience it can be subtle. For instance, someone could be experiencing a feeling of anger and 'stuckness,' simultaneously. In this connection, it is very easy to start to want to help the other become unstuck and facilitate the expression of the anger. In Circling we hold a different intention— to check deeply into the experience as it is. We are as interested in exploring the 'stuckness' as much, if not more, than the anger which would typically be the focus of a therapist or coach. It could be that in feeling and exploring the 'stuckness' it dissolves and reveals deeper emotion, or that a whole other insight into what's happening relationally could be discovered. Frequently, by radically being with

---

by general patterns. Subtle states are often characterized as inner movements of emotion and sensation becoming conscious, seeing images and thought palpably in experience, erotic sensations and/or energy moving up and into the body. Causal states refer to a deep witnessing of what is unfolding in experience, the dissolving of separation, and the feeling the interconnectedness of experience in the moment.

what is present, people feel met in places they never have previously and the intimacy and insight are viscerally deepened. It could be in this case that the anger and 'stuckness' actually have little internal impact on our being. We then inquire into the sensations of the feelings to discover a deeper authenticity, sharing our own truth at the embodied level. An embodied truth might be a feeling, sensation or gesture that is happening viscerally in the body in the moment of connection.

Further, something that is even more challenging to see for experienced therapists and meditators is the subtle ways they 'work' in connection from a place of experience or knowledge. This way of connecting can feel insightful and in tune with the other but often does not include authentic revealing of their own embodied truth. This is very easy to see in a Circling environment and stands out, especially to those who are more experienced. Therefore, what is asked of them is to share how they are impacted personally and within their own embodiment to clarify their intentions and intuitions, which result in expressions and interventions. Otherwise, it is not clear whether the therapist/meditator is taking more responsibility for the truth of the connection based on experience or theory than in-the-moment embodied knowing[3]. A recent example is where an experienced therapist was challenged in his seemingly compassionate way of holding another participant, especially with his supportive words of encouragement. Through this challenge he discovered that he did not actually want to engage with the other at a deeper level and felt tired and held back. With further exploration, he found that he was actually longing for meetings with others that were not full of 'drama' and insecurity. This led him to express to the whole group in a way that felt to most present as a transpersonal transmission into seeing a deeper light in experience. Therefore, subtle intimacies co-arise in connection rather than any sense of having to facilitate each other therapeutically, or having an attachment to reaching a particular experience.

Practice Formats

Circling is both a one-to-one and group practice. The group practice typically takes two different forms; the most classic form is an individual having the attention of the group and is called a 'Birthday

---

3. This is a difficult distinction to make because a lot of therapists would argue that they work within an authentic relating context built on embodied knowing and embodied presence. However, our experience is that when they come into a Circling context, many are by default using subtle therapeutic boundaries when there are deeper states and emotions in the space.

Circle.' There can be any number of people in the circle, though it tends to be between three and ten. It typically lasts between thirty and ninety minutes. During this time, the aim is to maintain attention on the Circlee's world and to offer authentic, in the moment feedback to explore the moment and what is present together. The Circle is a meditation to explore deeper layers of presence and connection, with a fixed point of focus on one individual. It is often a unique experience for the Circlee to receive a group's exclusive attention and is usually a powerful journey. It is also a co-discovery of what wants to happen; each connection is important and the meditation involves everyone.

The other most common form is an 'Organic Circle', where the attention is not purposely put on any one individual. Instead, participants are invited to follow their natural flow of attention in a group experience of what is present. This form allows more room to explore and follow the moment by moment arising in the group, often bringing the tensions and group dynamics forward. All Circles have a leader who has the significant role of maintaining the meditation by encouraging the principles of Circling (detailed below). Leadership is a kind of art form that requires substantial practice and training to guide but not control the Circle, to be deeply with the participants, while showing up with what is present and authentic.

Leadership Development Circling

Another form that we are exploring is a 'Leadership Development Circle.' This practice is more advanced and is more deeply guided by surrender to the flow of the group. There is an emphasis on self leadership in the discovering of presence and connection. This includes the 'leaders' of the Circle who actually become full participants. While it may seem that there is less of a role for the leader, the surrender required in this process takes a greater capacity than in normal Circles, automatically compelling everyone to feel their part in the whole and in what way they are leading themselves and the group. Furthermore, leaders have blind spots and this points to a greater opportunity for everyone to fully participate in the arising presence. In this kind of Circling, there is more emphasis on participants taking responsibility for what is happening. In this case, there is a corresponding opportunity for a greater empowerment and leadership from each participant. In Leadership Development Circling we consistently experience deeper themes coming up, greater challenges with people taking their own responsibility for their experience, and a more profound sense of mutuality when the uncertainty is accepted and felt.

What we experience in these Circles feels most aligned to Terri O' Fallon's Pacific Integral's work on Causal Leadership (2013). Although Circling seems to enter this space more from the personal into the transpersonal and Pacific Integral vice versa, it appears that the two practices create a similar space. Without experiencing their approach directly, it seems their emphasis is more on maintaining a meditative presence and practice during connection, while Circling is more guided by authenticity in presence. This quotation could be used to described our own group experiences with Leadership Development Circling:

> This collective experience arises as the individuals let go together into a shared field of at-one-ness. Ironically, each individual becomes a clear channel or sense for the whole in all of its definitions and dimensions. Each person as a clear voice of the One in service to the many, while not losing the authenticity of their individual voice of relevant experience. As a result each person is simultaneously both more fully and clearly who they are. (Ramirez, Fitch, O'Fallon. 2013)

This sums up succinctly how individuals begin to show up more fully in their essence and how this serves the group as a whole. The group becomes a collective intelligence that creates a space where presence and connection become more deeply witnessed and, thus, enhanced. When an individual is able to show the vulnerability and embodied response to being with the whole, the collective is nourished and inspired by this unique revealing of what is present. Conversely, if someone tries to speak for the whole, or deny their own presence in the collective, there is usually a counter reaction against this.

Five Principles of Circling

In our exploration of larger group practices and the integration of a high level of presence in relationship both within and outside of a Circling context, we have developed five principles or guidelines that underpin Circling:

1) Commitment to connection

This principle is an invitation for practitioners to increase their level of commitment to stay in connection with whatever is arising—especially between each other. This often means remaining in connection while feeling resistance or impulses to break it. This is not to be mistaken for a commitment to not separate. The key is to distinguish between an authentic desire to move away (which could be communicated and then done) and an avoidance or habitual impulse to break the connection because it feels difficult or uncomfortable. This principle encourages practitioners to stay with the connection in the same way they would stay with difficult sensations during a sitting meditation. When embodied and not misunderstood as a fusing of boundaries, this principle radically changes what is possible in relationship.

Connection becomes a place of discovery, and the commitment to stay present and authentic allows more risks to be taken in finding a true expression because there is a sense of staying in it together. This has consistently inspired stronger emotions, both light and dark, to be expressed and received. For example, when deep in practice, it is common for emotions like anger, attraction, disgust, love, shame, spiritual significance, darker primitive impulses and sexuality to be revealed. This often creates powerful opportunities to build a deeper connection and self acceptance within a wider range of emotional experiences. Everyone has their own level of commitment to stay in connection and this principle invites people to be more aware of where they move away and to broaden what they are willing to meet in connection.

2) Owning experience

This principle is about individuals communicating their personal experience in the here and now. It involves taking responsibility for what is most personally true for them rather than making assessments or assertions about others. It is clear when a feeling is owned, as it is something that is being directly felt by the person expressing themselves. Assessments, projections and assertions are always arguable; the truth of one's own experience in the moment is more visceral, does not give any responsibility to others, and is easier to relate to. It is this level of truth that creates a rich space in Circling. The distinction between taking responsibility for one's experience and implying responsibility on others can be subtle, but it can make all the difference in the power and intimacy of connection.

Part of owning experience is a willingness to be vulnerable. It means being open to face difficult emotions within oneself and to potentially encounter something unconscious being revealed. Owning unconscious feelings is a challenge because it is likely to show ambiguities, inconsistencies and uncomfortable revelations of former behavior. This is also where insight occurs. The polar opposite of owning experience is aggression, which is making someone else responsible for what you are feeling (Masters, 2010). Some simple examples will illustrate this: 'You're being aggressive' compared to 'I'm feeling fear'; 'I hate how the room feels' compared to 'I feel tension sitting here.'

Inversely, it is important that Circling does not become overly focused on language separate from the in-the-moment feeling behind the words. Connection can be limited by an excessive attempts to turn every expression into an 'I' statement, and can actually also turn into a way to hide the truth of one's feelings. We have witnessed people who have learned to own the language of their expression from approaches like Nonviolent Communication and still underneath a passive aggressive tone can be felt by others. In addition, sometimes the actual feelings the words are expressing become hard to sense under elaborate language constructions. Likewise, a statement that is not fully owned in words can have such a clear sense of embodied expression of feeling that connection is deepened without finding the exact way to word/own it. However, this is not to be mistaken for a privileging of big emotional expressions that are clearly aggressive. Owning our experience is a principle that guides us to take responsibility and ownership of our experience, to encourage the expression of the true energy of emotions and not become a way to control language to not cause offense.

3) Trust in experience

This principle points to having a fundamental trust in the experience of ourselves and others. It is a willingness to stay with experiences that may not make rational sense or would normally not be shared. Importantly, it includes keeping an openness to one's experience so one is not attached to anything being right or wrong. It can be vulnerable to trust when it seems others are in a state of care and we are in a more fiery or frustrated feeling, or someone is expressing gratitude for us and we feel empty from this seemingly loving expression. From these examples it shows how easy it is to assess how we should be feeling based on how we perceive others. In Circling, we trust our embodied response and share that. This does not mean we make our experience right, but we reveal the truth even if it seems at odds with what we are perceiving. Therefore, if we do not feel an embodied response from another's expression of gratitude we would share this discrepancy to explore any assumptions that the other was definitely expressing gratitude under their words, or that we might have problems receiving. Instead sharing the truth opens the opportunity to connect in the moment at a deeper level to see what is happening in both with the expression of gratitude.

By trusting what is present at an embodied level and owning it, unexpected levels of understanding and connection can emerge between people. This means all previous conceptions of what is not good in relationship become challenged as a much greater range of emotions are accepted and included in intimacy. For instance, someone being distracted, confused, in a subtle trance, sleepy, jealous or distant can all be explored within the connection. It is common for a feeling or state to arise that one sees as not appropriate to the situation rationally and so it is not brought into presence. By bringing it into presence it is more possible to see the deeper truth of what is emerging and can often lead to learning for everyone.

For example, in one Circle the group was restless and getting 'distracted' by another group. The way the attention moved away from the Circle was trusted until finally someone in the group shouted from a deeper anger that he was upset with everyone looking to the other group. He later revealed this was a frustration and vulnerability that he had wanted to own in his life for a long time. From here the Circle became more inspired, empathetic and connected to him for his courage and a group field of presence filled the space. This gives a clear example of a transcending and including of 'distraction,' because we are trusting attention beyond any sense that we can know what is meant to unfold.

4) Staying with the level of sensation

For those with a strong meditation practice, staying with the level of sensation will be familiar, but this is also about ensuring that speaking is in resonance with what is being felt. It means having the intention to bring attention to and stay in the sensations and subtle feelings in the body while being in connection with others. This does not mean that conversation has to be limited to feelings in any way, just that connection at the level of sensation in the body is not lost like it can be through descriptive telling of the 'story' of experience. A recent example in a group was a man who was desperate to express himself and kept saying he was fed up of holding back his truth. He even got close to wrestling some of the other men as a way to 'release his power.' Despite his best efforts, the group was largely irritated and not very engaged. With an encouragement to feel more at the embodied level, the man started to share that he felt empty and disconnected and this was what was motivating him to find an expression. He found it difficult to understand how to stay with feeling empty but eventually wanted to stay with this sensation. While the man started to access a part of himself that was unfamiliar, the group seemed to be in a deeper space of presence and engagement, which for some present felt more like a spiritual emptiness.

This principle leads to powerful connection and can be taken further by sharing what is happening at the level of awareness;

this could be an expansion of emptiness, stillness and/or Eros that previously the person has not been able to own. Like with meditation, the more this is practiced, the more opens up and is revealed—what lives and breathes within the WE space is brought to awareness.

5) Being with the other in their world

Walking in someone else's shoes is taken to the next level in Circling. It involves a radical curiosity, which assumes nothing and has complex distinctions available for understanding. These distinctions stem from the five principles as we navigate what is present in connection. For example, we ask ourselves: 'is the expression an embodied knowing?'; 'is it owned?'; 'is there a trust in what is happening?' etc. It is being curious about the individual's in-the-moment experience at increasingly subtle levels while challenging assumptions of knowing what it is actually like. For example, if someone says they are sad, one can enquire: 'how do you know you are sad?' This results in a deeper exploration of the actual sensations and subtle experience of sadness, and an openness to our perception of the experience changing. This capacity of being with another has seemingly infinite possibilities for refinement. The more one pays attention, surrenders with another, and reveals what is being experienced, the more feelings, thoughts, states, actual perceptions that mimic/align with, that of the other and body gestures start to become possible to sense in the connection field. This creates a powerful transmission[4] when skillfully shared and opens the possibility of seeing, feeling and ultimately being with the other in their world to increasing levels of depth.

For Circling practitioners, this principle opens a world of possibility to gain more insight and embodiment around connection. It becomes a way of being with another as if you are the awareness in their meditation. This means the way we inquire into the other is similar to how we would ourselves during meditation. It gives the person we are being with a deep experience of being witnessed, which requires us to be in an acceptance of what is revealed. A radical acceptance is needed and further created in this principle that, if embraced, will aid

---

4. We use the term transmission to refer to when the state experience of one person is transmitted to another person through connection. It has been borrowed from the spiritual traditions, especially Satsang, where a teacher can give a pupil an experience of a higher realization of Reality through connection. In Circling, we have discovered that we become more and more open to give and receive transmission. It can be an emotional or perceptual state of the moment, but mostly refers to an energetic or spiritual state being given or received with another. This is happening more powerfully in Circling as we deepen in our practice of connection. It is becoming possible to receive a unique transmission from each person.

the other in a continual journey into the unknown in themselves. This opportunity to discover new parts of themselves is often liberating and also an invitation to go into deeper connection. This is often deeply satisfying in and of itself, however, if we are willing to open in a way that we may be changed by connection, we can often receive the unique perspective from the other. Finally, it is important that this principle includes authentic feedback of what it is like to be with the other. This creates a deeper meeting and stops the connection being just a meditative experience and includes the real relationship dynamics that then can be witnessed and felt at a deeper level.

What Becomes Possible with Circling?

What stands out in Circling is the way it becomes a kind of spiritual/psychological/embodiment cross training. It is common for the practice to create regular personal insight and breakthroughs, deep interpersonal experiences and varied spiritual awakenings. This is all happening while practitioners are developing present moment awareness in themselves while simultaneously being in an arena that is cultivating excellence in relating with others. Part of this is the demand to be able to weave in and out of multiple perspectives. Groups can be up to fifty people all potentially sharing their unique way of experiencing the moment and potentially giving transmissions of experiences that would be hard to access otherwise. It is also common to experience the realization of a way of being that was previously unconscious by being witnessed in intense interactions and being given multiple levels of feedback on how this is seen and received at an embodied level by others. This all has the effect of stretching us into new somatic and emotional experiences that then inform our intra- and interpersonal intelligence. Therefore, many lines of intelligence are being worked with and integrated[5].

The group field of presence and connection, supported by authentically speaking in the moment, facilitates a surrender into state experiences. Individuals that are open to experience spiritual states, and those not even aware of the concept, consistently tap into subtle, causal, and non-dual experiences. We are receiving more experienced

---

5. Lines of development/intelligence are mostly taken from Wilber in *Sex, Ecology and Spirituality* (2000). Wilber pulls together an understanding of many developmental maps that accurately describe what we are seeing in groups. This view is that multiple intelligences can be discerned and participants in a group all have different lines that are less or more developed. This gives those practicing an opportunity to be exposed to these intelligences simultaneously.

practitioners from such schools as the Diamond Approach, Zen, Shamanism, and others that are verifying the depth possible in the practice. One example was when an experienced Core Energetics teacher (over 25 years), was called to go into deeper meditation to access higher wisdom from what she described as the lineage holders of her psychological/spiritual work. For us it felt like a descending energetic experience that brought a profoundly calm and non-dual perception of the moment. She ended up crying, face down with arms spread, shocked that she had accessed something that had not been present with her for some years; she explained life challenges had overpowered her connection to this part of herself. Part of Circling's potency comes from the intention of radical acceptance of the other in the moment, which strongly reduces the egoic boundaries between people, allowing for powerful WE spaces and 'aha' moments.

There is something about bringing attention to the WE space that acknowledges the universe for one of its wonders—the power of relatedness between conscious beings. Circling has shown us how to recognize and bow to the divinity of human connection, making spiritual pursuits not only more potent and accelerated, but also profoundly rewarding in integrating into everyday life. This meeting of diverse individuals leads to the mutual discovery of expansions in awareness, dissolution between 'I' and 'thou,' and even shamanistic-like visions and feelings. In a mutual, awakened space, opportunities arise to draw out deeper territories; to see complexity within and between people, and to create an in-the-moment, broader context of human development and spirituality.

Circling reveals that a great potential is being lost when we hold onto developmental maps too tightly, and the practice opens the possibility for deeper connectedness with others regardless of diverse worldviews. The space does not require that people are all operating from higher, more complex cognitive levels to form a powerful collective. This means non-integral mainstream can—and has been—successfully included and inspired by Circling. If we are willing to be open and vulnerable, meeting another human being in an authentic connection is always unique and possible. This realization also highlights how an over reliance on developmental levels perspective can actually diminish connection and be a way of avoiding presence with others due to them being interpreted as less—or even more—developed.

The space created by Circling becomes a great arena for perspective taking and practicing the discerning inclusion of multiple perspectives in-the-moment within one's own experience. In a Circle, it is surprising how lower and higher complexity perspectives can suddenly become very real in our experience. One of the authors was leading a group and was called into connection with a woman who was experienced in Circling and becoming a leader herself. She felt left out and empty in the last few hours of the group and had difficulty owning this. She had the feeling one of us was not comfortable in her presence. This turned out to be true, which led to an intensive exchange of eye contact and energy. The leader ended up being extremely impacted by the exchange and allowed this to transform his body, especially his face. He became almost demonic and overcome with a sense of menace in his expression and in a position of predatory anticipation. He seemed to be experiencing a lower, or pre-rational, emotion coming to the surface, while also being aware of a higher feeling of connectedness to the moment and to the woman. It ended with the leader actually feeling he had to defend his lower needs and the women feeling overwhelming love for the vulnerability of this and a deep release of tears and hard coughing.

A Circle also provides a way to prevent spiritual bypassing. If someone goes into a spiritual space but is avoiding a personal connection, the group quickly picks it up. This collective accountability encourages one to own shadowed emotions, feelings and beliefs. Shadow is witnessed and naturally owned as it shows up in real interactions. By trusting what is present to unveil what is important, we have increasingly found that much of what we call shadow can be transmuted within a group into more empowered feelings through an authentic meeting. Experiencing emotional releasing in this kind of group field has significantly increased our understanding of how feelings are held in the body and what can come forth when these are allowed. The fact that we are not role-playing or manufacturing conditions means that the distance between workshop and real life is significantly reduced, thereby enhancing the potential for integrating insights into everyday ways of being.

One innovation we have discovered through Circling is being with what is present beyond the fear of projection. This is a big shift from groups that are focused on trying to work out who is projecting and whose feelings are being felt. While avoiding projection can be useful, too much vigilance can give the subtle impression that feelings can be in some way toxic, or unacceptable to feel from others, making it more vulnerable to be in pain. The injunction to broaden our capacity for presence and connection in the face of suffering, meeting another in their pain with our own present moment embodied experience—whether one of defensiveness or compassion—brings a kind of intimacy that is alchemical. This shows a new path for people feeling they have to hide parts of themselves in connection or overly second guess themselves in terms of projection. In this way, the idea of projection becomes transcended and included; it helps us understand how emotions can move in a space but also how it can viscerally dissipate and lose the potential outlined above. When we follow presence and connection and stay with pain or intensity together consistently, we see deep openings to the transpersonal and healing of these feelings. In addition, strong connections are fostered by the willingness to allow our inner feelings to guide us in the moment instead of overly trying to predetermine where the energy stems from.

There are of course limitations to the practice. Circling as described above is largely reliant on the leadership to be able to embody the principles above in the group, especially when the environment is turbulent and challenging. If this is not the case, it is easy for the practice to become one of discussion, reflecting and processing what is coming up rather than allowing what is present to live and breathe in the space. Circling for us is an embodiment practice, but it does not use exercises or experimentation unless there is an authentic desire in the moment for it to happen. The authenticity of a desire is found in connection: usually someone expresses a desire and if others in the group feel resonate with this feeling and are inspired in the moment, the action is encouraged. It is essential that participants continuously check to see if their inner sense of what is happening is in alignment with their own inner knowing. Therefore, Circling may challenge those who want to be put into their body in an instructive way. Although there are moments of guided meditation, touch, and movement to introduce a practice, we emphasize allowing what is already present to show itself rather than trying to open the space with other practices. It is up to Circling leaders to embody and encourage movement, dance, touch, and creativity from a place of authenticity—which often makes it more powerful.

What is essential to understand in Circling is; we are more likely to explore what the experience of 'not being in your body' is actually like rather than actively trying to move beyond this with other practices. This is where there is a critical point for the practice. To be with this experience of 'not being in your body' is in service of honoring what is present and a belief that the wisdom in the moment will guide us to the next stage of potential embodiment, or even an understanding why trying to get into the body is against something more important. However, the idea of continual acceptance of each layer of experience can also be a potential trap. If our acceptance of what is arising becomes a practiced honoring, or a technique to make people feel comforted in their story of themselves, we can lose authenticity and end up literally going in circles. Sometimes an authentic desire or longing in the moment can penetrate through to a deeper connection, even if it does not appear to honor what is being presented. For example, someone in a circle was sharing a feeling of being detached.

The group was patiently exploring the experience of being detached and the subtle thoughts and feelings around this experience. Then one participant got angry and said in a loud voice: 'I'm fed up of this, I want to scream and stop looking at you.' With encouragement, this person met the circlee in the emotional energy of this expression and it touched something deep that was significant in his life and he felt a relief from the sense of detachment. Being with the other in their world and trusting experience can be a tightrope because it is easy to lose connection to a deeper acceptance and try to change what is happening. Acceptance of what is and the expression of authentic desire have to be navigated in each connection.

Our Journey

Our journey gives us an opportunity to demonstrate a more personal account of Circling, and to the mapping of the overall potential of WE practice. The unique contours of our path have played a part in the growing of Circling.[6] It gives clues as to why this WE practice is so potent and what a difference it can make to individuals, communities, and beyond.

When we first encountered Circling in 2008, we sensed a new emergence of an exciting and much needed paradigm shift in integrating all we had learned in psychology, coaching, philosophy and spirituality more powerfully into our lives. Before Circling, we felt a separation between the depth possible inside the container of practice and outside in everyday life. We were troubled by the distance that seemed to appear between those in spiritual practice communities, and their ability to connect with those outside their inner circles. In meeting Circling leaders Decker Cunov and Guy Sengstock, we witnessed an embodied presence and communication that enacted a higher awareness in everyday relationship. As keen students of Integral Theory, we witnessed a new level of Integral embodiment in relationship.[7] This gave a new potential to spiritual practice.

---

6. We currently have regular events and multi-day immersions happening in 15 countries, with other emerging contacts and a growing number of certified leaders (nearly 30).

7. This quote from Decker sums it up succinctly: "We don't throw around the phrase relationship as spiritual practice anymore. We actually mean it. At least once a day I have an interaction with someone where one of us, if not both of us, have the experience of realization of transcending who I thought I was, while more richly including my embodied experience. Effortlessly, by virtue of an integral quality of relating." (taken from *www.integralcenter.org*)

Decker was especially powerful in applying this way of being to men wanting to have better relationships with women. Sometimes men would come to his programs expecting chat up lines, and would end up seeing how at a deeper level they were not willing to feel their true feelings in the presence of women. This ended up with them starting to feel what was previously hidden and a doorway to them showing up with more authenticity in their lives. This way of bringing spirituality and psychology to life was very important, it had more 'street value' that is both deep and exciting. It also meant that we did not have to share our complex maps and language to go deeper into connection and found an organic way that was even accessible to friends sitting in a bar. Yet at the same time, it was incredibly effective at giving us experiential access to the complex theoretical understandings that we had a great passion for. In fact, it was the strongest practice we had come across by some distance.

We started doing one basic Circling practice: looking with meditative awareness into each other's eyes and waiting for an authentic question to arise. It was simple and not easy. Sitting in the tension of waiting for genuine embodied curiosity and receiving questions that went right to the heart of our unconscious ways of being was vulnerable. One time early on, one of us suddenly saw sadness and tension in the other at a more subtle level. With careful attention the sadness and tension grew into tears and then into a sense of being really young. This was a new occurrence considering our relationship was also built on being business partners and wingmen in nightclubs. What was exciting was that this was not a cognitive remembering; it was an embodied experience. With continued presence, the room started to fill with a surreal sense of foreboding; his state changed into a sense of terror and an electric, thick sensation came out from his chest. He realized for the first time how frightening his very early childhood had been. This was emotionally challenging but also immensely pleasurable on the level of sensation, as well as insightful. The above experience was beyond anything we had experienced before, even though we had been doing a lot of psychotherapy and meditation for some years. Although this kind of experience will be familiar to therapists, this happened between two friends who had the intention of being present together.

At the same time, we continually found barriers and challenges to opening together, with many clever defenses, like one blaming the other for not being good enough at Circling to ask him the right questions to open! Gradually, with intention, we started to try to embody what Circling represented in vital areas of our life. We began to see all the places we were avoiding presence and connection, and how much we needed each other's support and direction to confront our avoidance. Good examples were: telling parents of the athletes we worked with as elite tennis coaches the truth of how we saw them relating to their children, showing our vulnerability when dealing with money and being authentic in sexual encounters with women. It was a hard and humbling undertaking to bring an open awareness that was authentic to our worldview, while honoring those around us. This was especially true in our work environment, sometimes relating with the magical world of five-year-olds, then business managers with sharp instincts for profit and traditional parents that had never considered psycho/spiritual development, all in one afternoon. After a few years of almost daily practice, we started to notice our work, relationships and spiritual life reflecting the depth we experienced in the practice together (Wilkinson, Thompson and Tskaris, 2013). This possibility of integration is why we believe Circling can be so important for those passionate about presence and connection.

There were many important insights along the way that became the principles for our later work. A big part was understanding the resistance to intimacy. We explored where we did and did not trust each other, and took a more honest and innocent look at where we liked and disliked each other. This kind of intimate sharing went to the heart of our personal struggles in almost all of our relationships and ultimately highlighted our own avoidance of connection. We also found that when we owned a new level of vulnerability – like overwhelming anxiety around speaking in public and the underlying sense of not being a real man – and brought that into connection, the energy release would often be accompanied by creative insights on development.

From Practice to Leadership

As we participated further in the Integral community, we felt a growing confidence that Circling was bringing us something unique. We were invited to lead a workshop in a well-established spiritual community Venwoude, in Holland, during the Evolutionary Love festival. Circling was a hit; there was a big impact in trusting connection and especially the shared WE space experience. From this small beginning, we started leading workshops from our home. There were consistently deep group fields happening in the workshops. This led to us expanding our offerings organically while we were still running an Integral Tennis academy in England.[8]

---

8. For more information on how we spent 5 years bringing Integral theory and practice to a Tennis Academy where the center of gravity was traditional to rational, see

The experiences we were having following the five principles in groups were consistently breaking new ground. On one occasion, two people in a workshop were going into what seemed to be a non-dual connection in a break; an hour's silence brought many other people to their first mystical experience, others getting insights around surrendering in their lives, and a direction for the rest of the workshop to increasing mutuality and exploring what we termed the 'star trek' state.[9] Another time the group was witness to and connecting in an extremely tense and uncertain state. When some participants said they wanted to change what was happening, one of the leaders expressed a deep and vulnerable anger. Suddenly three people in the room started crying about feeling powerless in their self-expression in life, touching a collective resonance in the group.

The Forming of a Community

From these initial workshop experiences, we were offered more opportunities to lead groups. Within a year we had led workshops in 7 countries. In each place we would work with a small community that were often built around the practice of Circling and Authentic Relating games inspired by Decker Cunov's Authentic World and The Integral Center in Boulder, Colorado[10]. These communities wanted a deeper experience of the practice with people in their local area. We would come to them to demonstrate the principles the practice had shown us. While this would create special group experiences on a weekend, we would also work deeply with the community members in real time with the issues facing their growth. This was always key to our understanding of the practice: the weekend spaces were magical, but if the principles were not practiced by the leaders and between key people in the community in every moment, especially to organize the events, then the full potential of the practice was being missed. When the practice is being grounded in every moment, it brings insights from

---

Matos, Thompson and Wilkinson (2012).

9. During the workshop people kept sharing that they were feeling big shifts in aware-ness that felt 'drug' like. In these states there was a lot of exploration of our shared experience that become humorously known as the 'Star Trek.' This was a way to capture the unique experience we were having together.

10. There are some significant others to acknowledge for these communities, especially; Guy Sengstock, Bryan Bayer, Alexis Sheppard, Shania James, Robert McNoughton, Michael Porcelli, Kendra Kunov, and others.

more subtle and real areas we struggle with and gives more opportunity for the practice to become part of a new way of being.

An example of this work happened with a leader in Toronto. He started to feel suspicious of one of our assistants in the evening after the first day of the workshop. When we encouraged him to trust this and further his commitment to connection by staying with this assistant, his body moved into a more warrior like position and he raised his chin. It seemed to those present this was a tribal like sign that he was showing his willingness to expose his throat to his enemy. In an Integral view it could be interpreted that he was accessing shadow that allowed him to feel a more tribal part of his being. It is the combination of awareness that comes from connection, with the vulnerability of the human experience of being together in an important event, that helps to stir this level of emotion. The level of presence increased immensely when he acknowledged and thus owned and trusted his experience of the desire to fight very aggressively. Eventually, after accepting his aggression and vulnerably sharing it, a deeper fear and sadness emerged around feeling powerless and uncertain in connection and his life's purpose. This ended with convulsions and trauma releasing that lasted several hours. Then when he shared this later with his community a closer connection was created, especially around its sense of purpose. Many had been feeling this struggle in the leader and had difficulty approaching it; the level of openness and insight he gained was also a good example to them of the potential of the work.

Through this approach, the communities started to flower and grow. We felt a calling to teach the principles in a longer, more sustained format, especially with people returning to multiple workshops and community leaders that wanted a deeper taste of the practice. This inspired the creation of the SAS Leadership program,[11] a way to bring the power of this WE practice in a more robust way that can be taken further out into the world. This went beyond Circling and was also created to develop people's capacity to access and inspire others to the kind of consciousness the principles point to. One of the important ingredients required to enter this kind of consciousness, and the greater potential of this WE practice, is being in a group with a commitment to trusting connection and presence for a sustained period of time.

---

11. SAS has been taken from the British elite military squadron 'Special Air Service'. This started with a sense of humor but the name did capture some of the essence behind the intention of the training. This was to create a group for those that are drawn to a deeper and more focused journey into being present in connection. Part of the vision of this name is also from the experience of how a group that has been prepared to be with each other in a deep authenticity and trust, starts moving into a synergy that seems like a well-trained military team.

Therefore, we structured our leadership training to take place over six months.

'All There Is'

After a year and a half of fast growth, we started to experience a deepening in the collective intelligence of practicing Circlers and our own embodiment. It was in this period we met Alanja Forsberg and discovered a synergy in our collaboration that spawned a new understanding of what is possible in groups. It was here that, 'All There Is' was born.

The 'All There Is' intention in a group is to be witness to the fullness of the moment, that all there is (oneness) is available in opening to the eternal present and its simple perfection. At the same time, it is also an intention to bring down, descend and expand into all there is inside of us; to invoke, to show up in the presence of the collective. In this space, we are playing with the saying 'the world is perfect as it is, including our desire to change it.' This is the perfection of the moment beyond any conception or judgment that could believe in improving on such a vast and complex universe and the mystery of existence. However, part of this embrace is an acceptance of our drive for growth, or the evolutionary impulse that moves through us. Part of 'All There Is' is the play between bringing deeper surrender to what is, while vulnerably daring to bring all that wants to be expressed through us.

From an Integral perspective, the space we created with Alanja seemed to access capacities coming from higher stages of awareness. Barrett Brown's descriptions of later stage developmental capacities offer a clear way to illustrate some of what we are experiencing in groups. Brown's research outlines a perspective that seems to capture what this practice is about:

Hold a unified perspective with the other as One; hold a partnership of beyond us and them; hold and rest in the tension of not knowing and wonder into the moment – without predefined constructs and perspectives – allow what is needed to emerge; each time a solution arises, wonder and inquire into...hold the space for the integrative nature of consciousness to express...hold a mirror up to individuals and groups so that they may see themselves, self-reflect, and wonder...attune to evolving nature of consciousness and wonder "where are we?" "what are we becoming?" and "what is needed and wanted next?" (Brown, 2011, p. 217)

Brown outlines how from a deeper layer of awareness we can feel 'the creative ground that exists before perspectives are generated.' We understand this as staying open to experience in a group from a deeper witness that lets what is unfolding happen without attachment to judgments, mental/emotional framing or perspective taking. This opens up a more embodied sense of 'what is' and invites others to similarly let go into a more direct contact with reality (Brown, 2011: 220). In this space the leaders become guided by a sense of surrender that includes and encourages an active showing up in the wonder of experience. They need to move and stay without predefined structures to hear/allow a deeper intuitive structure to guide them. This can result in silently witnessing, going into deeper states and possibly transmitting this into the group, vulnerably sharing and even wanting to be held, being firm or even fierce in sharing embodied experience. Basic structures are held, for example the start and finish times, but then the group is guided by what is arising, held in adherence to and discovery of all there is. While this is supported by the five principles of Circling, even they are held as continually evolving pointers to the consciousness that is being revealed. This dance of sitting in the truth together has created an ever widening embodied knowledge of human development, encapsulated in the name 'All There Is'.

In 'All There Is' we are distinct individuals and we are held as a part of the group field. This is informed by a belief that, fundamentally, we are simultaneously whole and part.[12] This means that each individual holds a unique perspective and gift that supports the whole, while maintaining a firm adherence to the principles that prevent an individual taking a position of speaking for the whole. This perspective helps reveal deeper layers of what is happening, such as how pathology is created when parts try to be or act for the whole. Therefore, when an individual tries to express a truth for the group, there is most often some form of agitation in response. For example, an individual says the space is 'too chaotic'; this is an assessment of the whole, and an assumption that assumes (even if unconsciously) to speak for the whole. If others' experience is different from the assessment, they are likely to respond with agitation. However, when an individual expresses their individual part fully and owned, it reveals for the group a deeper part of its wholeness. Thus, when an individual reveals their own sadness in the moment, the group gets to share this resonance and see a deeper layer of what is present. It also inspires other parts to come forward to feel their part in the whole, even when their part is quite different. Wilber supports this when he states that the health of a whole always relies on the utilization and embrace of the capacity of the parts (Wilber, 2000).

---

12. This is in line with Wilber's 20 tenets of evolution that outline how we, like everything in the universe, are ontologically holons. See *A Brief History of Everything* (1996)

In the challenge to communicate this work, it feels important to illustrate with examples what has happened in these groups. One participant, who was a therapist, came wanting to experience more emotion in himself and in connection with others. He had a long and dedicated meditation practice and his presence had a strong sense of open and calm emptiness. At the same time he was dissatisfied with this and wanted to feel more of what he felt his clients feel in his therapeutic practice. In past therapeutic oriented practices, he had felt nothing could touch him at an emotional level. This dilemma created a lot of movement in the group: some were experiencing distance from trying to get more feeling, as if something needed fixing, while others were challenging and physically wanting to touch his body. What emerged was a collective feeling of both the acceptance and the tension of being in a challenging dilemma: was touching, or any other intervention, a genuine desire or some attempt to change what was so? This participant came in and out of attention over the weekend as it seemed the collective was mirroring his inner experience. In a moment of high presence, suddenly a man approached him wanting to hold him and five women surrounded him wanting to touch or breathe with him. One woman started breathing heavily and started to scream. He gently started to cry, just a little. Some joy came to his face and a relaxation in the collective. Building in him was a sense of fullness that seemed more personal than the ascending and diffuse experience that had been happening in him previously.

The next example points to the potential spontaneous phenomena that is common in the 'All There Is' space. There can be periods of sitting in uncertainty not knowing what wants to unfold which can create a lot of tension. There are also moments of quiet, silence and a sense of the group being in meditation together. The moments that most stand out are where there is a crescendo where suddenly the collective starts moving into spontaneous smaller groups. In these groups, different things happen for the participants: some move into doing emotional healing work, some begin challenging each other to tell deeper truths or be more embodied; some release trauma; and some enter into a kind of expression such as dance or wrestling. At these times participants are sometimes working deeply with other participants and leaders are continually trusting their intuition of where to go. The collective becomes self-organizing into a powerfully efficient and potent whole to support the growth of individuals in the group that then simultaneously nourish the collective field with their presence.

Lastly, there has also been an increasing occurrence of spontaneous, ritual-like ceremony in 'All There Is.' The group starts to move into a collective experience that appears similar to shamanic or tribal like expressions. For example, a woman was feeling frustrated and challenging towards the leadership and the principles of the space by saying that there was not enough structure. She was met in her challenge and encouraged to own what was happening in her in response to what she was interpreting. This led to a deep silence and obvious vulnerability. Some women in the group started getting up and sitting in a small circle around her. Individuals started describing an atmosphere as somber in a profound sense that was confirmed by large parts of the group. The women started to hum as the rest of the circle sat as witness. In the end the woman started to scream involuntarily. She was held and met in this while more animalistic expressions were coming from her body and voice. For many there was a sense of deep loneliness being released, but also a deeper spiritual presence and heightened aliveness in her eyes and body. There was a lot of collective emotion and gratitude for the experience; there was also some dissonance as one experienced therapist was angry with one of the leaders in her interaction with the women at the center of the 'ceremony.' This allowed for voices that showed either a separation from what was happening or personal struggles. It also led to an intense confrontation of perspectives between the leader and therapist that galvanized the whole group into exploring death, meeting each other, the vulnerability of speaking deeper feelings and finally a reconciliation between the therapist and another participant she was longing to feel close to after a long standing disagreement.

'All There Is' is at an exciting beginning that is starting to build momentum. It is creating stronger collective experiences that are empowering for individuals on their own path of growth. It honors each individual by compelling them to take a deeper responsibility for their own experience and their way of making contact with the group. Ultimately, it calls forth a deep collective intelligence that goes beyond anything that can be preordained and comes from a trust that we believe can make a difference in the world.

Conclusion

As outlined in the beginning, we want to illustrate the power of WE practice, and our belief that one plus one in conscious development equals more than two. However, to fulfill the potential of the WE space requires principles that allow for a deeper unfolding. In Circling, there are clear and powerful pointers to guide us into a profound surrender and truths of connection. By outlining our own path, we show how this WE practice has significantly increased our own awareness while also inspiring action that is growing conscious relationship around the world—a form of relating that is putting a premium on being present and connected in the real and authentic moments in our lives. This is empowering a deeper self-leadership to personal actualization and is simultaneously an elegant way to go beyond into the transpersonal experience. 'All There Is' goes one step further. It is a space where the separation of personal and transpersonal is dissolved by a collective intelligence with more depth and wisdom than can be matched within planned therapeutic/meditative structures.

It is an exciting time as this form of WE space practice is growing across the world. The next stage is developing more powerful online global access to Circling, and further education; building more communities of practitioners; increasing literature, media promotion, deepening the knowledge base and supporting certified leaders in finding ways to earn an income while bringing the important principles of the work into more mainstream environments, especially in business. In terms of the inner potential of the work, we are finding more powerful ways to 'meet'[13] in connection with others that brings clearer insight and depth. From here, the movement is to integrate higher and lower parts of the individual in order to surrender more powerfully to the collective. A by-product of this unfolding is a beautiful paradox: an ever increasing surrender to what is and a letting go of development to a greater immersion in what is present; on the other hand, more potent ways of utilizing the evolutionary impulse to bring more insight, creativity, healing and opening to each moment.

---

13. 'Meeting' is a term that is starting to be increasingly important in our work. It describes how connection is enhanced when two people come together fully with who they are in the moment while staying in a strong connection. It is not a process of one person holding the other that is the most common form of connection we have witnessed. This is a more vulnerable and uncertain way of bringing everything that is present and allowing a full meeting of energy.

Author Bios

Sean Wilkinson and **John Thompson** have shared a 10-year journey into human growth and development, bringing a deep authenticity to their friendship that shines through when they lead together. Integral Theory has been a longstanding passion for them both. They are both certified Integral coaches. With a successful background in elite sports coaching, they have a passion for excellence and bring their attention to detail to the world of personal development. In recent years, they have developed several Integral projects, ranging from a major Integral sports academy to an internationally recognized project for Street Children in India. It is the practice of Circling that they have found to be the most powerful. They see their unique flavor of Circling as a paradigm shifting practice and are deeply committed to its principles as well as showing up authentically in all aspects of their lives. To learn more about their work, you can visit: circlingeurope.com.

References

Brown, B. (2011). Conscious leadership for sustainability: How leaders with a late-stage action logic design and engage in sustainability initiative [dissertation]. Fielding Graduate University.

Cook-Greuter, S. (2002). A detailed description of the development of nine action logics in the leadership development framework: Adapted from ego development theory. Retrieved from http://www.Cook-Greuter.com

Gafni, M. (2012) Your unique self: The radical path to personal enlightenment. Integral Publishers.

Masters, A, R. (2010). Spiritual bypassing: When spirituality disconnects us from what really matters. Berkeley, CA: North Atlantic Books.

Matos, N.F., Thompson, J., & Wilkinson, S. (2012). The birth of integral sports: Insight into coaching   parents in sports, Journal of Integral Theory and Practice, 7(4), 53-67.

Ramirez, V, Fitch, G, O'Fallon, T (2013) Causal leadership: A natural emergence from later stages of awareness, retrieved from Pacific Integral website: paper from integral conference, 2013.

Wilkinson, S. Thompson, T & Tskairis, A. (2013) The conception of integral sports: An application of integral theory and practice in athletics, Journal of Integral Theory and Practice, 8(3&4), 111-125.

Wilber, K. (1996). A brief history of everything (1st ed.). Boston, MA: Shambhala.

Wilber, K. (2000). Sex, ecology, spirituality (2nd ed.). Boston, MA: Shambhala.